LIFT EVERY HEART

LIFT EVERY HEART

Collected Hymns 1961–1983
and some early poems

by
TIMOTHY
DUDLEY-SMITH

Collins

Hope Publishing Company

Collins Liturgical Publications
187 Piccadilly, London W1V 9DA

Collins Liturgical Australia
PO Box 3023, Sydney 2001

Hope Publishing Company
Carol Stream, Illinois 60188, USA

First published 1984

ISBN
Collins 0 00 599797 6
Hope Publishing Company 0 916642 21 6
Code No. 1037
Library of Congress Catalog Card No. 83-083215

Typeset at The Pitman Press, Bath
Printed and bound in Great Britain by
Richard Clay (The Chaucer Press) Ltd,
Bungay, Suffolk

With love and thankfulness
to my wife Arlette
in the twenty-fifth year of our marriage;
and to our children,
Caroline, Sarah and James,
remembering many Seacroft summers

O magnify the Lord with me
and let us exalt his Name together

PSALM 34.3

Contents

1. INTRODUCTORY

Foreword		3
Hymns and poetry—a personal reflection		12
'O changeless Christ'—the making of a hymn text		31

2. THE HYMNS*   43

3. THE EARLY POEMS

Introductory note		173
I	Necessity	174
II	Bethlehem	175
III	Night Sky	175
IV	Visit of the Wise Men	176
V	Faith	177
VI	Encounter	177
VII	Fraud	178
VIII	Worldling	178
IX	A blind man healed by Christ	178
X	One of thy hired servants	179
XI	Hands	179
XII	Cathedral Builders	180
XIII	Remembrance Sunday	180
XIV	The Heart of Man	181
XV	Fiat	181
XVI	Treasures upon Earth	182
XVII	Bitter Harvest	182
XVIII	Despair	183
XIX	Escape	184
XX	Security	185
XXI	Dusk	185
XXII	The Island	186
XXIII	The Light of Reason	186
XXIV	The Way	186
XXV	Content	187
XXVI	Earth	187
XXVII	Reflection	187
XXVIII	Pilgrimage	188

* The hymn texts are not numbered, but are listed in alphabetical order both in the notes and in the body of the book. An index of first lines is provided (page 304) for easy reference.

XXIX	Jerusalem, Jerusalem	188
XXX	Ecce Homo	189
XXXI	Simon	189
XXXII	Trees	190
XXXIII	Gethsemane and Calvary	190
XXXIV	Journey's end	191
XXXV	Easter Sunrise	192
XXXVI	Walk to Emmaus	192
XXXVII	Resurrection	193
XXXVIII	Unprofitable servant	193
XXXIX	Christ at the last	194

4. NOTES ON THE HYMNS 195

5. APPENDICES & INDICES

Appendix 1: Hymnals referred to in the Notes 277
Appendix 2: Sheet music referred to in the Notes 280
Appendix 3: Sound recordings referred to in the Notes 282
Appendix 4: Biblical references and other sources 284
Appendix 5: Inclusive language 286
Appendix 6: Discontinued texts 289

Metrical index 290
Index of tunes 293
Index of subjects 299
Index of first lines 304

Part One

INTRODUCTORY

Foreword

It is tempting to find some lofty sentiment with which to begin this Foreword. Perhaps R. W. Dale's dictum (which I suspect may also be attributed to others): 'Let me write the hymns of a church and I care not who writes the theology'. I offer you instead an unassuming rhyme, told to me many years ago, which all hymn-writers would do well to heed:

> There were two little birds in a wood
> who sang hymns whenever they could;
> what the words were about
> they could never make out,
> but they thought it was doing them good!

It serves to remind us that the popularity of hymns does not imply any great understanding of what the writer is trying to say; and that all our efforts at simplicity, vividness, and the communication of truth may be lost upon the worshipper, who nevertheless enjoys what he or she calls a 'a good sing', and feels the better for it. Perhaps it was of such that Robert Bridges was thinking when he wrote (using his personal and characteristic spelling)

> 'It seems a pity that natur should hav arranged that where the people are musical (as Augustin appears to hav been) they would rather listen, and where they are unmusical they would rather sing . . .'

This present volume, which contains all the hymn-texts written up to the end of 1983 which I wish to preserve, is based on a small publication issued privately, *A Collection of Hymns, 1961–1981*, subtitled 'a source book for editors'. The introduction began as follows:

> 'If the sub-title "a source-book for editors" sounds a little pretentious, it is nevertheless entirely accurate as a description of this small volume. Not many other people will want to read the texts of hymns; and no one would wish to use as a hymn-book a collection which comes from a single hand. But since I have been writing hymns for some twenty years now, this seemed a sensible opportunity to bring together the texts written over this period. My hope is that this book may find its way into the hands of those who are contemplating, or concerned with, the publication of hymnals; so that they can run their eye over these texts, including those so far unpublished, and see if there is anything here they wish to use. Otherwise, in my experience, the contents of a new collection are often finally settled before an approach is made to a hymn-writer—so that it is then too late for new or as yet unpublished texts to be considered for inclusion.'

That *Collection* contained, besides the texts of about 100 hymns, a section giving details of publication, suggested tunes and so on, and a number of Indices, by metre, Biblical references, themes and the like. I have used the same pattern in this book, which is primarily designed for the same purpose, except that following the precedent of similar publications I have added some further brief *notes* to most of the texts, explaining something of the circumstances of their writing, and often a point or two which may be of interest to those who concern themselves with the texts of hymns. Perhaps, for the general reader, I ought to add a word here. I am conscious that some of these *notes* (and indeed the whole book) may easily give the impression that I take myself more seriously in this role than the merits of these texts allow. I can only explain that (particularly in America) there are students of the contemporary hymn-scene who I am assured will want the sort of information I have provided, and feel the book inadequate without it. It is primarily with such students in mind that I have added also the brief essay on the writing of a text. It is of course impossible (at least to me) simultaneously to write a hymn-text and to reflect upon the process by which it is written. The best I could do, with an essay such as this in mind, was to wait until the revisions of a possible text were sufficiently clearly mapped-out by my successive drafts and rough working; and then to jot down at each stage of the work all that I could remember of the process of composition and revision. The choice of text was therefore very limited; and it was a pleasant surprise to find the hymn in question included in *Hymns for Today's Church* when that book was published in 1982.

The other essay in the book explains itself. When I took the decision to include some of my early poems, it seemed to me that this might be the context in which to put on paper my occasional reflections on the relationship of hymns to poetry. I have felt at liberty to draw widely on the thoughts of others better qualified to contribute to this theme; and these extensive quotations form the plums in the pudding. The notes at the end are included in order to refer any reader who is interested to the original sources.

The section of early poems is, as I admit, self-indulgent. But I dare to hope that some readers may find a lyric there that appeals to them, and if so that will be justification enough for their inclusion. One or two seem to me suitable for singing; and if composers having run their eye over the hymn-texts go on to look at these poems, it is possible that they may find something which could be the basis of an anthem or a song.

Since the purpose of these pages is to introduce the book, and then (at my publishers' insistence) to introduce myself as hymn-writer, I postpone the more difficult part of that assignment by including here some general notes on the hymn-collection, drawing freely on the opening pages, often in the same words as I used then, of my earlier *Collection* already mentioned.

Changes in the text

To my mind, hymns become harder to write, rather than easier, as one goes on—though it is not always the most laborious that emerge as the most satisfying. In compiling a collection, which means looking again at work done at different periods, it would be a great advantage to be able to revise; as indeed a poet, preparing a definitive edition, can revise poems, notwithstanding their appearance in earlier collections or in anthologies. But this is only open to the hymn-writer in the case of unpublished texts. Once a text is part of a hymnbook, then (as I see it) there is generally no further possibility of change—or not for a long time. People have a right to expect that if a new hymn is coming into use, it will follow the same form wherever they may meet it. After thought and advice, however, I have broken my rule in the case of two of the texts that follow, *Faithful vigil ended*, and *Lord, who left the highest heaven*. Details, for those who want them, will be found in the *notes* on these individual texts.

Apart from these special cases, however, the only changes that I have allowed myself have been some minor tidying-up, largely of punctuation; and some small revisions in the interest of 'inclusive language' to which I shall refer again. Once a hymn has appeared in a published hymnal, I like to avoid all alterations apart from changes in spelling (which is mainly a matter of the different usage between the UK and the USA—this book follows my native style); and in the use of capital letters. The latter depends upon the style adopted for a particular book, and I am happy for editors to follow whatever seems best to them. For my own part, I have moved away from a free use of capitals (for example, in pronouns referring to the deity); and in this collection I have adopted the contemporary practice of forsaking the capital letter at the start of a new line.

Discontinued texts

Since this is primarily a 'source-book' I have felt it right to give the benefit of the doubt to texts which I no longer find particularly satisfactory, but which are in print in one or more collections; except where I have come to feel that I do not want to encourage their further use. In those few cases, the text does not appear in the pages that follow, but the first line, and details of publication, will be found in Appendix 6. I offer my apologies to those who worked to find or write tunes for these texts. In the case of uncollected texts, I have of course been able to reject more freely, and one or two texts are missing from this book which I included in my earlier *Collection*.

Reference to Scripture

Many of these texts are based, more or less directly, on words or passages of the Bible; and I have not thought it necessary to provide a comprehensive index of references to Scripture—it would be difficult to know where to stop. I have, however, added the words 'based on' to the *notes* on individual hymns where I have been actually working (as with *Psalm Praise*) from the text, or have had specific Scripture passages or verses in mind. In such cases, I have tried to keep close to the text and meaning; but these 'metrical versions' are not of course translations, and sometimes little more than allusions. A list of these major verses and passages appears as Appendix 4.

'Inclusive language'

A year or two ago, in a review of my original private *Collection*, Erik Routley wrote: 'He has either not yet encountered, or has decided to pass by, the current disputes concerning "sexist language" . . .' I think the truth lay somewhere between these two propositions, and in preparing this book for publication in America I have had to look more closely at the issues. Something of my general thinking will be found in the essay on *Hymns and Poetry*; while Appendix 5 gives details of how I have tried to come to terms with it in the texts that follow. This has involved certain minor changes in the definitive form of eight or nine texts, as well as some permitted variations in others. I wish that such changes could be avoided, as I expect to be able to avoid them in what I am writing at present. I hope, however, that they will not prove too obtrusive to any who know these texts in an unemended form; and that what is set out in Appendix 5 will be seen as an attempt to meet the strongly-held views of others, so far as is consistent with integrity.

Something of myself

I have included a number of personal references in the essays that follow, and in the individual *notes*. I was brought up in Derbyshire, the son of a schoolmaster, and attended my father's school until his death when I was eleven years old. He was a lover of poetry, with the teacher's gift of being able to impart his own enthusiasm; and I recall his reading aloud to us much verse calculated to appeal to young minds and ears, a lot of which I still remember. I must have been very young when he introduced me to Stevenson's *A Child's Garden of Verses*; and I still have on my shelves two tiny copies which he bought for me (were they one shilling each?) of A. E. Housman's *A Shropshire Lad* and *Last Poems*. As can be seen from references in the following pages, Housman, for all his rejection of religion, remains a poet I regularly re-read. Allingham, Kipling, Newbolt, Tennyson, Masefield, de la Mare, were among my father's favourites for reading aloud; and also Alec Paterson, the Australian author of *Rio Grande's Last Race* and *The Man from Snowy River*, with a marvellous facility for homespun narrative in fast-moving rhythms.

My father's death was a major factor in my sense of God's call to the ordained ministry, a call which came to me, to the surprise both of myself and family, at about eleven or twelve, and remained with me (re-offered with growing maturity) through school and university. I was lucky too, with my later schoolmasters who encouraged an interest in poetry; but apart from an occasional poem for a school-prize I wrote very little. At Cambridge I found myself writing comic verse (which, though I did not know it, is an invaluable part of learning the trade); and beginning the small spate of poems from which a number are included in this book. Re-reading them, I note the absence of what might be called a traditional 'devotional' content; and this at a time when I had recently discovered, or re-discovered, the experience of salvation as a relationship with Christ in a personal way. I think the reason is that most of the 'devotional poetry' of which I had any knowledge was cast in a form so different from the writing of the poets who meant most to me (based, no doubt on my father's choice; some of his books were by this time on my shelves) that I did not see how to attempt it. But in a number of anthologies I was beginning to enjoy the Christian poetry of George Herbert, Alice Meynell, G. K. Chesterton, Chevenix Trench and others.

As a curate a little beyond the outskirts of London, on the edge of the Thames, I continued to write occasional verse and to earn the odd guinea from the old *British Weekly* to augment my stipend. From there I moved up-river to take charge of a 'Settlement', the Cambridge University Mission in Bermondsey, a mission boys' club with a fine Christian tradition; the hymn 'O Christ the same' was later written at the request of the Mission for a Service of Dedication when opening their new girls' clubhouse. Later, in the mid-1950s, I moved up-river once more to Bloomsbury to start and edit *Crusade*, a popular Christian monthly magazine, founded as part of the follow-up of Dr Billy Graham's Wembley Crusade of 1955. In 1959 I married, and worked for the next thirteen years for the Church Pastoral-Aid Society, a home missionary Society of the Church of England. Soon after this, 'Tell out my soul' was written; and I have said a little more about this in the pages that follow. In the same year a young clergyman called Michael Baughen joined the staff of this Society; and his musical gifts, coupled with his experiences in visiting church youth groups in many parts of the country, gave him the vision of a new Christian songbook; collecting together the best of a mass of material which was then being written and composed in a 'youth' idiom, and often available only in locally-compiled duplicated songsheets. I had recently established a publications department; and we worked together on this book, he as editor and compiler, I as publisher. He reminds me sometimes (now he is Bishop of Chester, and has had further hymnals, including *Psalm Praise* and *Hymns for Today's Church*, published under his editorship) that with what I thought was great courage I agreed to a first print-order of 5,000 copies for our new songbook, which we called *Youth Praise*. As I recall, the 5,000 copies were sold out before publication; and for some months copies were sold faster than our small-time printer could produce them. *Youth Praise* became *Youth Praise 1* shortly afterwards, since a second volume was added; and it was while *Youth Praise 2* was in preparation that I wrote a number of texts expressly for the book. It also included a hymn 'Lord, for the years' which had been written in the interval for the centenary of the Scripture Union. On my desk as I write is a handsomely-bound copy of *Youth Praise 1 & 2 combined* which was presented to those most closely concerned with the books, in May 1973, to mark combined sales of one million copies.

Michael Baughen, meanwhile, never one to rest on his laurels, had conceived the idea of a modern collection of metrical psalms. He called together a team to help edit the book, and between them to contribute also the greater part of both words and music. By this time I had been asked by the General Committee of the Church Pastoral-Aid Society to be Secretary of the Society; and I had therefore to relinquish the day-to-day work of Christian publishing. *Psalm Praise* provided an opportunity to work with a team on a project; and a stimulus to write with immediate publication in view. Quite a number of my texts date from this period; often they are marked as written in Sevenoaks, a country town in Kent within commuting distance of London, where we had our home. *Psalm Praise* was launched one snowy day at the Albert Hall in London. The evening 'launching' was soon fully booked; and an additional session had to be arranged for the afternoon. Ten years later, the book is still selling. About that time I moved from the Church Pastoral-Aid Society to be Archdeacon of Norwich. Meanwhile my wife and I, with a family of three schoolchildren, had acquired a small house in Cornwall, the full width of England away, which we have used every year since for our family holiday. I mention this since *Seacroft* has been a major factor in my continuing year by year to write hymns. It is a very ordinary little house, neither new nor old, in a quiet village called Ruan Minor on the part of Cornwall known as The Lizard. If you think of Cornwall as like a foot, Land's End is the toe, and The Lizard the heel. A typical day at *Seacroft* will see us set off in mid-morning for the beach (one of any number of magnificent beaches within easy reach, but often to a

Cornish cove called 'Poldhu, the black pool'). There we swim, surf, read, sunbathe, and eat a Cornish pasty for a picnic lunch. Another swim, perhaps, and we begin to drift homewards, doing a little shopping in the village of Mullion on the way. Back at *Seacroft*, I alternate between reading, writing and snoozing, with a cup of tea by way of refreshment; and in the early evening we are ready to set off to some favourite haunt for a supper-picnic on the cliffs or a drive to Helford, a walk on the moors by Zennor or some late-night window-shopping among the holiday-makers at St. Ives.

No two days, of course, are quite the same; but within the framework of such a day there are two substantial periods in which I probably turn my mind to hymns: over a breakfast-tray, before the rest of the family are up; and at home in the later afternoon. In addition, if things have reached a point where it is difficult to leave them, my MS book has been known to come with me to the beach, or on a picnic, and sometimes to a late-night session when the household has gone to sleep. Some particularly smudged pages bear witness to where the process of revision has even continued in the bath!

This has been the pattern for the last nine or ten years; years in which I have found it difficult, except on isolated and exceptional occasions, to have a mind sufficiently free of preoccupations to write hymns in the course of my life and work in Norfolk. What I can and do manage, however, is to prepare through the year for the days at *Seacroft*; taking with me a notebook reminding me of ideas, themes, requests, scripture passages, an unusual metre, a beguiling tune, sometimes a single word which can be the starting point for a hymn. I record therefore a debt of gratitude to my wife and family who year by year make room in our holiday programme for me to find the opportunity to write.

People sometimes ask, 'Which comes first, the tune or the words?' I am, alas, quite unmusical myself, so that usually it is the words; and then I must look to others better qualified to find (or in some instances, to write) a suitable tune. This is not always so. Sometimes a particular tune 'speaks to me' in the course of the year; and then I ask a kind pianist to play it into my cassette-recorder so that I can take it with me to Cornwall, and re-play it over and over again, in the search for words.

On my return from our summer holiday, when I have dealt with urgent matters, caught up with the back-log, and replied to the arrears of letters, I type out a final draft (which occasionally includes yet further small revisions) of perhaps six or seven texts I have brought home with me; and send them off to the Reverend Derek Kidner, who has agreed for this purpose to be my critic and adviser. Often each text I send will have attached to it a query, or a list of queries, on which I am asking his opinion. Is this word more suitable than that? Have I caught the original meaning of the

Psalmist? Is such and such an expression properly consistent with Scriptural truth? And if the hymn is to a recognized metre, and not written (as mostly my texts are not) with any particular tune in mind, I ask him to suggest a tune. Derek Kidner is now retired; but continuing with his own writing, mostly in the field of the Old Testament. He is not only a scholar and theologian, but also a musical editor and trained musician, and an able critic whose taste and judgment I find invaluable. I should like to say more, but I think it would offend him were I to do so. When I have incorporated any changes which follow from what Derek Kidner has to say to me, I regard the text as settled, and arrange for copies to be duplicated and the hymn added to my collection.

In January 1981 I was consecrated Bishop of Thetford, a suffragan (that is, assistant) to the Bishop of Norwich. In the course of that Service, beneath the dome of St Paul's Cathedral, the Archbishop of Canterbury held aloft a copy of the New English Bible, and delivered it to me with these words:

> 'Receive this Book; here are the words of eternal life. Take them for your guide and declare them to the world . . .'

In writing hymns, I am aiming to fulfil that commission, as I aim to fulfil it in the regular course of my ministry. I covet for my writing the words of Isaac Watts in his Preface to his *Hymns and Spiritual Songs*:

> 'The second part consists of hymns whose form is of mere human composure; but I hope the sense and materials will always appear divine. I might have brought some text or other, and applied it to the margin of every verse, if this method had been as useful as it was easy.'

Acknowledgements

I cannot issue even this modest collection without taking the chance to record some debts. I shall always be grateful to Canon H. C. Taylor and the editorial committee of the *Anglican Hymn Book*, who first printed texts of mine as hymns; and to Bishop Michael Baughen, the editor and originator of *Youth Praise* and *Psalm Praise*, without whose early encouragement I doubt if I should have persevered at all. To him, and other composers associated with him, whose names appear in the *notes*, and to all who have provided tunes to my words, I offer my thanks. Among those others, the names of David Wilson, Noël Tredinnick and Norman Warren constantly re-occur. More recently, like so many, I enjoyed the help and friendship of Dr Erik Routley, whose interest meant much to me. To John Stott's continual encouragement (dating back almost forty years), and to Derek Kidner's generous and sensitive advice over both text and tunes, I owe more than I can say. And there are other individuals, too numerous to list, with whom I have been brought into touch or correspondence on this subject, whose acquaintance or fellowship in the field of hymnody I greatly appreciate.

For this present book I owe a special debt to Mr George Shorney who originally commissioned it, and to Mrs Suzanne Chapman who suggested a British edition, and saw it through the press. No one could have been more fortunate in his publishers.

I also acknowledge with gratitude the help of Mrs Jean Bygrave and Mrs Gill Martin, who between them typed most of this present book; and of Miss Grace Jackson who read the proofs.

Later in these pages I quote some words from the *Preface* written by John Newton two hundred years ago on the publication of the *Olney Hymns*. At the risk of repetition, and despite the gulf between that work and this, I dare to borrow them and let them speak for me here:

> 'There is a style and manner suited to the composition of hymns, which may be more successfully, or at least more easily attained by a versifier than by a poet . . . If the Lord, whom I serve, has been pleased to favour me with that mediocrity of talent which may qualify me for usefulness to the weak and the poor of his flock, without quite disgusting persons of superior discernment, I have reason to be satisfied.'

Ruan Minor, 1983   T.D.S

Hymns and Poetry—a personal reflection

Most people, I suppose, who combine an interest in words with an interest in the words of hymns, have pondered on the relationship of hymns to poetry. Perhaps my own experience, in which I was sharply *aware* of the difference in writing one or the other, with no insight into what lay behind it, is not uncommon; and since this may well be so, I venture to approach my theme from a personal standpoint, related to my own experience in writing the texts which will be found in the following pages.

A. E. Housman in his Leslie Stephen lecture of 9 May 1933 described how he had received from America a request that he would define poetry:

'I replied that I could no more define poetry than a terrier can define a rat, but that I thought we both recognized the object by the symptoms which it provokes in us.'[1*]

He goes on to describe his own experience of creating poetry and says:

'I think that the production of poetry, in its first stage, is less an active than a passive and involuntary process: and if I were obliged, not to define poetry, but to name the class of things to which it belongs, I should call it a secretion: whether a natural secretion, like turpentine in the fur, or a morbid secretion, like the pearl in the oyster.'[2]

Since I first read these words—I think as a schoolboy—I have known what he was talking about: and (for poetry must have its foothills as well as its heights) there was a time when I was writing and publishing occasional poems. They were almost all on Christian themes: and kindly friends would sometimes urge me to try my hand at hymns. I knew however that what 'came to me' in my verses was very different from what would make a hymn: I only recall one effort at hymn-writing at this time and it falls far short of any standard of technical competence. Before the end of my twenties, while I still valued the fifty or sixty poems in my MS book, I had almost entirely ceased to add to them, though there have been one or two additions since. I did not think of myself, therefore, as having in any way the gifts of a hymn-writer when in May 1961 I jotted down a set of verses, beginning 'Tell out, my soul, the greatness of the Lord'.[3] I was reading a review copy of the New English Bible New Testament, in which that line appears exactly as I have put it above; I saw in it the first line of a poem, and speedily wrote the rest. I cannot now recall how it came to the hands of the

* Notes are at the end of this chapter, pp. 26ff.

editors of the *Anglican Hymn Book*, then in the early stages of compilation: but they told me they would like to use it as a hymn, and asked me to try my hand at a hymn-text on the theme of 'home'. So followed 'Lord, who left the highest heaven'[4] and (unsought by the editors, but on a favourite text of Scripture) 'Christ be my leader'.[5] Since then, I have written few lines intended as poetry rather than as hymns.

Faced with this sharp contrast, this *volte-face*, in my own experience, I have been interested in the analysis of the relationship of hymns to poetry; and while it is one in which the last word will never be written, much *has* been written, by practitioners and others, to illuminate discussion.

John Wesley and Isaac Watts each have something to say on this theme in the Prefaces to their respective collections. Here is Wesley in *A Collection of Hymns for the use of the People called Methodists*; a few sentences later he makes it plain that he has the hymns of his brother Charles as much in mind as his own:

> 'May I be permitted to add a few words with regard to the *poetry*? Then I will speak to those who are judges thereof, with all freedom and unreserve. To these I may say, without offence, 1. In these hymns there is no doggerel; no botches; nothing put in to patch up the rhyme; no feeble expletives. 2. Here is nothing turgid or bombast, on the one hand, or low and creeping, on the other. 3. Here are no *cant* expressions; no words without meaning. Those who impute them to us know not what they say. We talk common sense, both in prose and verse, and use no word but in a fixed and determinative sense. 4. Here are, allow me to say, both the purity, the strength, and the elegance of the English language; and, at the same time, the utmost simplicity and plainness, suited to every capacity. Lastly, I desire men of taste to judge (these are the only competent judges) whether there be not in some of the following hymns the true spirit of poetry, such as cannot be acquired by art and labour, but must be the gift of nature. By labour a man may become a tolerable imitator of Spenser, Shakespeare, or Milton; and may heap together pretty compound epithets, as "pale-eyed", "meek-eyed", and the like; but unless he be *born* a poet, he will never attain the genuine spirit of poetry'.[6]

The Wesleys, as has been amply demonstrated, were readers of the poetry of their own day as well as of the 'Spenser, Shakspeare and Milton' mentioned in the Preface quoted. Henry Bett's brief but seminal *The Hymns of Methodism in their literary relations*[7] makes this clear. Bett shows how Alexander Pope's poem *Eloisa to Abelard*, published in a collection dated 1717 (when John Wesley was thirteen or fourteen and Charles about ten) contains the line:

'The eyes diffused a reconciling ray'

which is transmuted to:

'Thine eye diffused a quickening ray'

in Charles's hymn, 'And can it be', written in May 1738. Or again Matthew Prior's long poem *Solomon on the Vanity of the World*, published in 1718, has the couplet:

'We weave the chaplet and we crown the bowl,
And smiling see the nearer waters roll'

—surely the inspiration of the line in 'Jesu, lover of my soul' (first published in 1740) which runs:

'While the nearer waters roll . . .'.

Even better known is the link between:

'Love divine, all loves excelling'

first published in 1747, and Dryden's *Song of Venus* beginning:

'Fairest Isle, all Isles excelling'.

Dryden died in 1700, before either John or Charles was born, but as a playwright he must have been to them as much 'a modern' as George Bernard Shaw (d. 1950) is to a twenty year old today. When therefore John Wesley speaks of 'the genuine spirit of poetry' he knew what he was talking about. And at the end of the same Preface he indicated his own view of the relationship between the poetic gift and the writer of hymns:

'That which is of infinitely more moment than the spirit of poetry, is the spirit of piety . . . when Poetry thus keeps its place, as the handmaid of Piety, it shall attain, not a poor perishable wreath, but a crown that fadeth not away.'

Isaac Watts, in his Preface to his *Hymns and Spiritual Songs*, published thirty years earlier, gives some indication of the restraint under which he laboured in the writing of what he called his 'compositions'. The second part of this work, he says, in contrast with his metrical psalms:

'. . . consists of Hymns whose form is of mere human composure . . . If there be any poems in the book that are capable of giving delight to persons of a more refined taste and polite education, perhaps they may be found in this part: but except they lay aside the humour of criticism, and enter into a devout frame, every ode here already despairs of pleasing. I confess myself to have been too often tempted away from the more spiritual designs I proposed, by some gay and flowery expressions that gratified the fancy; the bright images too often prevailed above the fire of divine affection; and the light exceeded the heat: yet, I hope, in many of them the reader will find, that devotion dictates the song, and the head and hand were nothing but interpreters and secretaries to the heart . . .'[8]

My early nineteenth-century edition of Watts contains the brief essay by Dr Samuel Johnson from his *Lives of the English Poets*, which gives a critique of his powers by one of the most notable literary figures of the time:

> 'As a poet', writes Dr Johnson, 'had he been only a poet, he would probably have stood high among the authors with whom he is now associated. For his judgment was exact, and he noted beauties and faults with very nice discernment: his imagination . . . was vigorous and active, and the stores of knowledge were large by which his fancy was to be supplied. His ear was well-tuned, and his diction was elegant and copious. But his devotional poetry is, like that of others, unsatisfactory— the 'paucity of its topicks enforces perpetual repetition, and the sanctity of the matter rejects the ornament of figurative diction. It is sufficient for Watts to have done better than others what no man has done well.'[9]

Not only Watts and Wesley, but John Newton also, in the Preface to the *Olney Hymns*, written in 1779, discusses this relationship of hymns to poetry:

> 'There is a style and manner suited to the composition of hymns, which may be more successfully or at least more easily attained by a versifier than by a poet. They should be *Hymns*, not *Odes*, if designed for public worship, and for the use of plain people. Perspicuity, simplicity, and ease should be chiefly attended to: and the imagery and colouring of poetry, if admitted at all, should be indulged very sparingly, and with great judgment. The late Dr Watts, many of whose hymns are admirable patterns in their species of writing, might, as a poet, have a right to say, that it cost him some labour to restrain his fire, and to accommodate himself to the capacities of common readers. But it would not become me to make such a declaration. It behoved me to do my best. But though I would not offend readers of taste by a wilful coarseness and negligence, I do not write professedly for them. If the Lord, whom I serve, has been pleased to favour me with that mediocrity of talent, which may qualify me for usefulness to the weak and the poor of his flock, without quite disgusting persons of superior discernment, I have reason to be satisfied.'[10]

If Newton here gives the impression that a hymn is a poem by a writer of only mediocre talent, that is certainly mistaken, and equally certainly not his meaning. He is concerned to point out—to warn the reader and disarm the critic—that the two are not quite the same.

I myself believe hymns can best be considered as a very particular kind of poetry: what Erik Routley has called 'lyric under a vow of renunciation'.[11] Such renunciation extends to both theme and style. Here it is, this time described by Professor J. R. Watson of Durham in his inaugural lecture. He reminds us that in Dr Johnson's view quoted above:

> 'Narrowness of subject and a limitation of figurative language is a pointer to the difference between a hymn and poem . . .'

and he goes on to add:

'The first demand of a hymn is that it must be singable, and in this are comprised a number of characteristics. It has to be rhythmically stable, understandable in the time it takes to sing the words, and doctrinally sound. Because of this the imagery of a hymn is limited by its needs to refer to orthodox belief, and by its need to avoid ambiguity. Above all, perhaps, a hymn needs to mean something while a poem *is* something, means itself; the greatest hymns attain to this condition of poetry, but they start from a different place, where poetry, as John Wesley wrote in 1779, "keeps its place as the handmaid of Piety". The result is that hymns do not, as a rule, use language to suggest multiple meanings or shifting perspective.'[12]

I quote that at length because in thinking that hymns can be considered as a very particular kind of poetry, I find myself in conflict—most unwilling conflict—with Bernard Lord Manning. He will have none of it. He writes:

'To say of any hymn it is "not poetry" or it is "poor poetry" is to say nothing. A hymn—a good hymn—is not necessarily poetry of any sort, good or bad: just as poetry, good or bad, is not necessarily a hymn . . . Hymns do not form a subdivision of poetry.'[13]

But with the inclusion of that word 'necessarily' above, we may not in fact be very far apart. Perhaps Manning is looking over his shoulder at those poor hymns which he valiantly defends as hymns, while deprecating them by every other canon of taste. C. S. Lewis might say that what he personally desired in church services were fewer, better and shorter hymns, but especially fewer:[14] but Manning boldly defends even the halt and the lame of the hymnbook:

'Reverence is due to hymns as to any other sacred object. The hymn that revolts me, if it has been a means of grace to Christian men, I must respect as I should respect a Communion cup, however scratched its surface, however vulgar its decoration.'[15]

Here surely he is recognizing with a proper humility what to Archbishop Benson, for example, was an irritating mystery. Talking with Edmund Gosse, Benson is quoted as saying:

'A great many of our hymns are nonsense, sheer nonsense, irritating nonsense, if you regard them simply as literature, and yet they undoubtedly awaken the conscience and raise the soul to God. It is a great puzzle, the badness of most really effective and stirring hymns.'[16]

Perhaps his son Arthur contributed to this very real problem a generation later. Asked by Windsor Castle for special hymns for the confirmation of Prince Leopold of Battenberg, he wrote two immediately: 'I wrote them on the train from London to Horsted Keynes.'[17] It is a journey which would have taken well under an hour!

Let Christopher Driver, writing in the *Congregational Quarterly*, help to redress the balance from such an impoverished view of hymn-writing. He recognized hymns as being:

' . . . technical achievements of a high order. They attempt the difficult task of marrying verse to theology and clothing religious sentiment in decent and singable language.'[18]

In the same essay he describes four 'crippling technical limitations' of the hymn-writer's task. First, that they are to be sung in public by all sorts and conditions of men; then, that they must rhyme and scan; thirdly, that they must 'not stray far from Scripture and the familiar imagery of devotion'; and finally that they must be free of obscurities and doubts. There is an echo here of Dr Routley's phrase: 'lyric under a vow of renunciation'; and it was Routley also who identified in hymnody the three functions of codifying doctrine, unifying the body, and glorifying God.[19] Similarly, George Sampson called it 'the poor man's poetry, the poor man's theology' and believed that a hymn must present religious doctrine, religious duty and religious mythology. And he recognized also the function of 'unifying the body' by describing

' . . . the special work a congregational hymn has to do; and that work may be called the creation of a sense of belonging to a continuous fellowship.'[20]

A hymn then, to draw my threads together, accepts a number of very severe limitations, found together in no other class of poetry. First, there is the limitation of theme: and this suggests that not only do hymn-writers in general stand in danger of sacrificing quality to quantity and producing too many hymns, but so do individual authors.[21] This was certainly the view of Robert Bridges:

'When one turns the pages of that most depressing of all books ever compiled by the groaning creature, Julian's hymn-dictionary, and sees the thousands of carefully tabulated English hymns, by far the greater number of them not only pitiable as efforts of human intelligence, but absolutely worthless as vocal material for melodic treatment, one wishes that all this effort had been directed to supply a real want. e.g. the two Wesleys between them wrote thirteen octavo volumes, of some 400 pages each, full of closely printed hymns. One must wish that Charles Wesley at least (who showed in a few instances how well he could do) had, instead of reeling off all this stuff, concentrated his efforts to produce only what should be worthy of his talents and useful to posterity.'[22]

There is much here at which to protest: whether the musician's patronizing definition of a hymn-text (for Bridges, although later poet-laureate, thought far more highly of music than of words) as 'vocal material for melodic treatment'; or the slashing attack upon the Wesleys, heroes of all lovers of hymns. But the fact remains that (leaving the Wesleys aside) 'more', in the case of a single writer, can easily mean 'worse'. To mint fresh phrases for old truths is not an everyday affair: and the old phrases lie always about one's path, clamouring for inclusion. Unconscious plagiarism, whether of onself or of another, is a constant hazard. In the search for 'inevitability', something that 'sounds right', it is all too possible that a phrase or a line will sound right because one has heard or used it before. Perhaps a certain repetition does not greatly matter, since few hymns are sung at any one time: and I am conscious that there are, at the least, near-repetitions in some of the texts that follow.[23]

Indeed, where hymns are informed by Scripture (as I believe they should be) such 'plagiarism' is probably inescapable. Ask a Sunday School where the line:

> High as the heavens above

comes from: and they will quote the children's chorus:

> Wide, wide as the ocean,
> High as the heavens above.[24]

The fact that the line was used almost three centuries earlier by Henry Vaughan in his poem 'They are all gone into the world of light'[25] is not evidence even of unconscious plagiarism: both writers were probably setting out an attribute of God, from a picture employed continually in Scripture, in simple and metrical words which may well owe their common derivation to Psalm 103.11, where the AV reads:

> 'For as the heaven is high above the earth . . .'

Apart from the singular heaven, Vaughan's line is there in its entirety.

Alongside the limitation of theme, if not indeed part of it, is the fact that a hymn is written (or, at least, chosen by an editor for inclusion) with an *aim* in view. It has to serve, as we have seen, a defined purpose (edifying, unifying, glorifying) and in order to do so, it must be in entire consistency with revealed truth. It also needs, in the words of B. L. Manning, to be 'combining personal experience with a presentation of historic events and doctrines'.[26] He cites Wesley as his model:

> 'It is Wesley's glory that he united these three strains—dogma, experience, mysticism—in verse so simple that it could be understood, and so smooth that it could be used, by plain men.'[27]

Manning here takes us from purpose and content to style and presentation. A hymn must not only express sentiments with which the generality of worshippers can identify in their own spiritual experience, but it must do so in words they can understand (even if not necessarily, in my view, exhaust at a first reading) and sing to music. This in turn requires the metrical discipline, foreign to

English verse, of working by strict metre rather than by the stress which gives spring and life to so much of our poetry. This is a large part—that part which Manning describes as 'smooth' in the quotation above—of what makes a hymn singable; though of course much more than metrical regularity is required for 'smoothness'. In particular there must be euphony in the choice of dominant sounds, especially in the consonants, to prevent a polysyllabic phrase, over which the reader of a poem might linger with enjoyment, from becoming a mere mouthful of gabble in the singing of a hymn to strict time.

Along with metre, most hymns seem to me to require rhyme. To be sure, some manage very well without it: as does a large class of poetry. But we would be the poorer without a rhyming hymnbook for at least two reasons. The first brings me back to the concept of 'inevitability', the sense of fulfilment and satisfaction that rhyme helps to convey—the knowledge that what is being said is most fittingly and conclusively said in this particular way. The second reason in my view is to do with craftsmanship—the fusing of sound and meaning until the form of expression most aptly conveys the thing expressed. Certainly a true poet does not need rhyme, as a true painter does not need representational form. But as I am suspicious of the abstracts done by an artist who cannot draw, so I am suspicious of certain over-facile lyric poems (or hymns) which evade the difficulties and the rewards of handling rhyme. Robert Frost, indeed, calls it 'the deadly test':

'One of my ways of looking at a poem right away it's sent to me, right off, is to see if it's rhymed. Then I know just when to look at it. The rhymes come in pairs, don't they? And nine times out of ten with an ordinary writer, one of two of the terms is better than the other. One makeshift will do, and then they get another that's good, and then another makeshift, and then another one that's good. That is in the realm of performance, that's the deadly test with me. I want to be unable to tell which of those he thought of first. If there's any trick about it, putting the better one first so as to deceive me, I can tell pretty soon.'[28]

But the heart of the distinction between hymns and poetry lies, to my mind, not in the presentation or style—rhyme, metre, 'smoothness', regularity, rhythm—vital though these must be. It is nearer to those words of Professor Watson's that a hymn must mean something, where a poem '*is* something', means 'itself'.[29] A poem therefore can particularize the experience of an individual, as his response to some event, in a way which can attract the reader; even though he or she may know nothing of the experience, or reject the response. We recognize a certain individual—or even more general—truth, without necessarily identifying ourselves with it. It is enough for the poem to be a work of art. 'It is a commonplace to observe', T. S. Eliot wrote, 'that the meaning of a poem may wholly escape paraphrase. It is not quite so commonplace to observe that the meaning of a poem may be something larger than its author's conscious purpose, and something remote from its origin . . . If, as we are aware, only a part of the meaning can be conveyed by paraphrase, that is because the poet is occupied with frontiers of consciousness beyond which words fail, though meanings still exist. A poem may appear to mean very different things to different readers, and all of these meanings may be different from what the author thought he meant . . . there may be much more in a poem than the author was aware of.'[30]

In its own way—but a rather different way—a hymn has also to be a work of art. Two views of this fact are reflected in the current debates over the wisdom of making substantial changes to texts which form part of our traditional inheritance of hymnody.[31] They are exemplified by the views of Wesley and Watts towards editorial alterations to their finished texts. Wesley (who, as an editor, did his share of altering existing texts) wrote in his famous Preface:

'Many gentlemen have done my brother and me (though without naming us) the honour to reprint many of our hymns. Now, they are perfectly welcome to do so, provided they print them just as they are. But I desire they would not attempt to mend them; for they really are not able. None of them is able to mend either the sense or the verse. Therefore I must beg of them one of these two favours; either to let them stand just as they are; to take them for better or for worse: or to add the true reading in the margin, or at the bottom of the page; that we may no longer be accountable either for the nonsense or for the doggerel of other men.'[32]

Here speaks (as we know from the Preface) the artist, the writer conscious that he wears the mantle of a poet. Isaac Watts, by contrast, makes no such high claim:

'If any expressions occur to the reader, that savour of an opinion different from his own, yet he may observe that these are generally such as are capable of an extensive sense, and may be used with a charitable latitude . . . However, where any unpleasing word is found, he that leads the worship may substitute a better; for (blessed be God) we are not confined to the words of any man in our public solemnities.'[33]

Few poets would feel that they could, with integrity, issue such an invitation. And yet there lies behind it a distinct philosophy, which found its fuller expression much more recently, in the words of Fred Pratt Green. Himself an established poet before he became a hymn-writer, he is clear that as poet he would not look kindly on emendations of his lyrics by well-meaning persons. But he adds of his newer role:

'I had no doubt at all that if, as a poet, I had complete liberty to choose my themes, my forms, and language, to please myself, now, as a hymn-writer, I must become a servant of the Church, writing what was suitable to be sung in an act of worship . . . I have come to regard myself much as an architect does . . . the hymn-writer needs to be humbler than the poet.'[34]

Let me say in passing that I do not think Watts's invitation to 'substitute a better word', nor Pratt Green's view of the hymn-writer as a servant of the Church, provides a mandate for sweeping editorial changes in the established text of older hymns. It is perfectly true that, in a number of instances, the text in most hymnbooks is not exactly what the author wrote; earlier editorial emendations have come to stay. But for older hymns we surely have, and are familiar with, a *received text*, one that has come down to us and achieved its present form as a generally accepted definitive version. In a very few cases, there may still be cause and opportunity for 'invisible mending'; for the rest, once a hymn has been for some time in common use, I am not generally in favour of editorial emendations.

The classic example here is A. M. Toplady, best known today for his hymn 'Rock of Ages, cleft for me'. His most recent biographer writes:

> 'The liberties which he took with other men's compositions are hardly believable. He paid deference to very few original patterns. Lines, stanzas, whole hymns, are chopped up, scattered and reassembled with fantastic freedom. To mutilate and dismember the heart-children of authors honoured as well as little known gave him neither pause nor qualm. He took the deepest utterances of men good and great, and turned them upside down and inside out. In some cases he so manipulated their language as to make them say what they never meant, and what they did not believe.'[35]

Such treatment would horrify any hymn writer. But there remain nevertheless the two viewpoints which I have illustrated from Watts and from Wesley, as between a text which is in a sense 'given' and unalterable, and one which is, in a sense, 'constructed'. Clearly they are not irreconcilable. A good hymn should exist (as, in Manning's comparison, a communion cup exists) in its own right as the product of craftsmanship and the artist's ear and eye. But it must also be a vehicle for the congregational worship of God, expressing for the worshippers sentiments which they can honestly acknowledge and share: and providing a form which, at best, finds fitter words for their devotion and aspiration than they might find themselves. In Eric Linklater's fantasy *Rabelais Replies*, Bishop Grundtvig, the Danish educator, has this to say of the power of words to illuminate our spiritual pilgrimage:

> 'Teach him his own language in such a way that he will learn the spirit of it: not only because words are the principal condition of social life, but for this reason: whenever a man makes one of those lonely journeys into his own mind or the secret places of his will, he takes with him, like a lamp to explore them, his native language.'[36]

Do you recall how Jane Austen puts into the mouth of an unnamed young lady who is asked what she is reading, the reply

'Oh! it is only a novel!'?—and goes on, with every writer's *cri-de-coeur*, to add:

> 'Only some work in which the greatest powers of the mind are displayed, in which the most thorough knowledge of human nature, the happiest delineation of its variety, the liveliest effusions of wit and humour, are conveyed to the world in the best-chosen language.'[37]

May we not say something of the same of the best of our inheritance of hymnody? 'Only a hymn' the critics say: to which George Sampson gives us this reply:

> 'If his [Charles Wesley's] hymns had been addressed to Pan or Apollo or some other heathen figure, or if they were written in some foreign tongue, how loud the praise would be! But, alas, he addressed the Christian Deity in English, and his poems are dismissed as mere hymns.'[38]

'Lyric under a vow of renunciation' was Erik Routley's phrase. The renunciation includes Dr Johnson's 'paucity of its topics' (but of course it takes for its theme the most noble of all life and literature) and what he called 'the ornaments of figurative diction'. Part of the reason why hymns must renounce the over-elaborate figures is that they must stand the test of repetition. Few poems— but many hymns—arrive at such familiarity that without intending it we know them by heart. To retain and renew freshness and depth of meaning under such circumstances is not achieved by recondite, elaborate or fanciful imagery.

Other renunciations include metrical freedom, individualism, and the attributing of the sentiments of the poem to another 'persona'—as for example to 'Terence Hearsay' in Housman's *A Shropshire Lad*.[39] On the contrary, as I have affirmed above, the sentiments must be capable of being made their own by a wide variety of worshippers. Some of these renunciations do mean, of course, that good hymns can be written by those who lack some essential for the making of a poet: but they must have, to balance their loss, particular qualities theological and mystical, in religious experience, and in a certain craftsmanship (cf. Manning's description 'smooth') which many a poet manages without.

By way of illustration to this last point, consider the skill with which so many of our best hymns say what they have to say complete within the line. Charles Wesley is again a supreme example:

> 'He breaks the power of cancelled sin,
>   He sets the prisoner free:
> His blood can make the foulest clean,
>   His blood availed for me.'[40]

It is a skill to be found, certainly, in other poets besides the hymn-writers. A. E. Housman exercises it on page after page:

'Their shoulders held the sky suspended;
They stood, and earth's foundations stay;
What God abandoned, these defended,
And saved the sum of things for pay.'[41]

So does John Betjeman:

'Sand in the sandwiches, wasps in the tea,
Sun on our bathing-dresses heavy with the wet,
Squelch of the bladder-wrack waiting for the sea,
Fleas round the tamarisk, an early cigarette.'[42]

But that it is not a general characteristic of lyric poetry is amply demonstrated by a dip into most anthologies: it is a further example of the constraints, the 'renunciations', under which the hymn-writer begins his task.

And for the writer of today there are at least three further constraints which did not apply, or applied with less force, to writers of the past. The first concerns craftsmanship, and more especially the purity of rhyme. I may be wrong, but it seems to me that the hymnal abounds in well-known and dearly-loved hymns, over which, had the writers foreseen the popularity of their work, they would have laboured longer. This is Robert Bridges' point above, in connection with the vast output of Charles Wesley; but the same could be said of many others—as for example of Bishop Christopher Wordsworth.[43]

I would not wish to multiply examples, since many of these technical faults have ceased to disturb us by their very familiarity. But take as one instance Mrs Alexander's 'Once in royal David's city', sung across the English-speaking world every Christmas time. Would a writer today feel able to use the word 'lowly' three times in three consecutive verses, and again in the final verse? It is applied in turn to the stable, the poor, and to Mary herself. And had the author known that what she was writing for children (to illustrate the Article of the Creed, 'who was conceived by the Holy Ghost, born of the Virgin Mary') would achieve such popularity, would she not have wrestled longer—would her editor not have urged her to do so?—to remove all hint of bathos, and achieve a better climax, in the closing couplet of the hymn?[44]

I mention rhyme especially. Certain rhymes have suffered under the hand of time. 'Join' is a case in point, which we are told used to be pronounced 'Jine' and therefore to be a suitable rhyme for 'divine', as in:

'A thousand oracles divine
Their common beams unite,
That sinners may with angels join
To worship God aright;'[45]

But others were no rhyme from the beginning:

> 'He comes the broken heart to bind,
> The bleeding soul to cure,
> And with the treasures of His grace
> To bless the humble poor.'[46]

Wesley is a law unto himself; he stands above law in this respect. And I accept that there may be much more skill in the use of assonance in place of rhyme, when this is done by a master's hand. The full text of 'Soldiers of Christ, arise' will repay study here.

Equally, there are a number of accepted pairs which by consensus escape (I do not attempt to explain it) the charge of false-rhyme. 'Given (or forgiven)/heaven' is one such, as is the invaluable 'Lord/Word'; or that two-word poem by George Macdonald which he called 'the shortest and sweetest of songs':[47]

> 'Come
> Home.'

Examples could easily be multiplied from our hymnbooks; and for the most part they matter little. Sometimes indeed they may be that high art which conceals art. H. F. Lyte has 'favour/ever'[48]; William Cowper has 'frame/Lamb' and 'return/mourn' in the same hymn[49]; and what of 'laws/voice' in the National Anthem?[50] These are all in their own way false rhymes, even though of very different merit. My point remains that no contemporary hymn writer *concerned for rhyme* could regularly allow himself or herself the same liberties as those in which our older hymnbooks abound. It is a constraint of craftsmanship. A further contraint is in the use of archaisms, beloved by the versifiers of an older day, and metrically of great convenience. Take *o'er* for a case in point. How helpful to be able to write (as poets have written for four hundred years):

> 'As o'er each continent and island'[51]

or:

> 'The voice that breathed o'er Eden'[52]

or:

> 'And view that landscape o'er'[53]

And by the same token it must have solved numerous problems to be able to write quite naturally:

> 'At even ere the sun was set'[54]

or:

> 'Ere through the world our way we take'[55]

—a word of which Fowler explains that it is of a class of words which were:

'in the days of our youth seldom seen in prose, and they then consorted well with any passage of definitely elevated style, lending to it and receiving from it the dignity that was proper to them. Things are now so different that the elevated style shuns them as tawdry ornament.. . .'[56]

But the loss of such 'poetic' words is as nothing compared to the loss (I am speaking now of the hymn writer's craft) of 'Thou' language, with all its associations and (especially for older Christians brought up on an ancient liturgy) its sense of worship: but while I believe that most older hymns are not suitable for more than 'invisible mending', which can seldom include the transposition from 'Thou-forms' to 'You-forms', nevertheless for myself I would find a general return to writing texts in the 1980s using 'Thou-forms' a conscious and unnacceptable archaism.[57]

But to abandon 'Thou-forms', and especially 'Thee' and 'Thine', has serious consequences when it comes to rhyme. Seven out of the first ten hymns in *Hymns Ancient and Modern* (standard edition) employ such rhymes. And moreover, because 'you' is often not a fitting substitute for 'Thee', certain direct constructions of sentences must be largely avoided. The increase in the writer's difficulties is very real.

A third constraint which is felt with new force in contemporary writing is the issue of sexism. Certain editors, I understand, find unacceptable any use of the generic 'man', or derivatives such as 'mankind'. I am myself sufficiently persuaded that this is a question to which we should be more sensitive than perhaps we have been. But I do not believe we can wholly accept the suggestion that all uses of *Man* to mean the human race are necessarily offensive (our Lord himself,[58] and the writers of the New Testament, use it in this sense): or that, for example, Pauline language about 'Now are we the Sons of God . . .'[59] or the Johannine use of 'Sons'[60] must be invariably resisted. At the same time I believe I am now more careful not to use such language without proper consideration than probably any of us were when my first texts were written.

'The hymn is never a piece of private poetry' writes Arthur Pollard:

'. . . nor is its appeal limited to a narrow group. It is directed at a wide audience, differing vastly in background, education and sensibility. Furthermore, this audience must be able to share in the thoughts and emotions evoked by the hymn. That is one reason why the good hymn can never be a product of narrow sectarianism.'[61]

Yet the hymn is often the vehicle of private experiences and emotions. I do not mean the purely personal variations that are adapted from time to time by individuals (by Mrs Christopher Wordsworth, for example, who because her husband, the Bishop of Lincoln, disliked Heber's line 'and only man is vile' used to substitute her own invention: 'and all the pastures smile'[62]—but the personal association of individual hymns. Bright's communion hymn, 'And now, O Father, mindful of the love . . .' has been to me an aid to devotion over the years, even if my theological understanding of the author's sacramental language may differ from his own. Poetry, in that sense, can leap theological barriers. The more pity, therefore, that John Keble should have been induced on his deathbed to sanction a change in *The Christian Year*, in the interests of tractarian theology, which he had resisted for forty years.[63]

Perhaps the final word can come from a poet, not himself a believer, who bears testimony to the enduring influence of hymns which may be doubtful poetry but good religion. Professor Watson in his inaugural lecture already mentioned quotes from a newspaper article by D. H. Lawrence published two years before his death:

'The hymns which I learned as a child and never forgot,' Lawrence wrote, 'mean to me almost more than the finest poetry, and they have for me a more permanent value.. . .'[64]

Against such testimony, hymns do not need to press their claim to any special place within the ranks of poetry or literature. They have glory enough of their own.

NOTES

1 *The Name and Nature of Poetry* by A. E. Housman, Cambridge 1933, p. 46f.
2 Ibid p. 48f.
3 See p. 144 of this book.
4 See p. 113 of this book.
5 See p. 63 of this book.
6 Paragraph 6 of the Preface, dated 20 October 1779.
7 *The Hymns of Methodism in their literary relations* by Henry Bett, Epworth Press 1913.

The same principle can of course work in reverse; and echoes of hymns find their way (most often unconsciously) into poetry. Charles Wesley's *The Whole Armour of God* (from which the hymn 'Soldiers of Christ, arise' is extracted) was first published in his brother's *The Character of a Methodist* in 1742, more than thirty years before W. S. Landor was born. Verse 4 of Wesley's poem begins:

> Leave no Unguarded Place,
> No Weakness of the Soul,
> Take every Virtue, every Grace,
> And fortify the Whole . . .

Is it fanciful to see the echo of that third line in Landor's famous lyric *Rose Aylmer*, which begins:

> Ah, what avails the sceptred race!
> Ah, what the form divine!
> What every virtue, every grace!
> Rose Aylmer, all were thine.

8 p. 291 of my (undated) nineteenth-century combined edition of Watts' *Psalms and Hymns*.

9 *Lives of the English Poets* by Samuel Johnson, 10 volumes 1777–1780. For Isaac Watts, see vol II of the *Everyman* edition, p. 293.

10 *Olney Hymns* by William Cowper and John Newton, 1779. John Newton wrote the greater part; and the Preface.

11 *Hymns today and tomorrow* by Erik Routley, 1964. My reference is to the Libra edition (Darton, Longman and Todd, Ltd. 1966) p. 19.

12 *The Victorian Hymn*, an inaugural lecture by J. R. Watson, University of Durham 1981, p. 12f.

13 *The Hymns of Wesley and Watts* by Bernard Lord Manning, Epworth Press 1942, p. 109.

14 See *C. S. Lewis, Speaker and Teacher* edited by Carolyn Keefe, Hodder & Stoughton 1974 (Zondervan 1971); chapter three, *To the Royal Air Force* by Stuart Barton Babbage, p. 97. See also C. S. Lewis's autobiography, *Surprised by Joy*, Bles 1955, p. 221: 'Hymns were (and are) extremely disagreeable to me'. See also *Letters of C. S. Lewis* edited by H. W. Lewis, Bles 1966, p. 224: 'I naturally *loathe* nearly all hymns . . .'. For an informed assessment of his reasons, see Erik Routley, *Christian Hymns Observed*, Prestige Publications, Princeton 1982, p. 103.

15 *The Hymns of Wesley and Watts*, p. 109. Something of the same thought seems to lie behind Donald Davie's distinction between devotional verse and Christian poetry. He writes 'There is something called "devotional verse", to which it may seem that this criterion of artistry need not, and probably should not, apply. For it is not hard to think of verses which, though deficient in artistry, could well, because of the purity and sweetness of their spiritual sentiment, minister to the private worshipper in his devotions more effectively than verse which is a great deal better written.' (Introduction to the *New Oxford Book of Christian Verse*, edited by Donald Davie, Oxford 1981, p. xviii).

16 *Edward White Benson, Archbishop of Canterbury* by A. C. Benson, Macmillan 1899, Vol I, p. 592.
    A. C. Benson was the Archbishop's son as well as his biographer. He clearly shared a similar opinion of some hymns, describing those he had to sing at family prayers at his mother's house (after his father's death) as 'bearing the same relation to poetry and music that onions and toasted cheese do to claret and peaches'. (*On the Edge of Paradise*—see below—p. 127).

17 *On the Edge of Paradise* by David Newsome, John Murray 1981, p. 86.
    The texts of the hymns in question cannot be traced in the Royal Archives: King Edward VII's personal papers were destroyed after his death at his own request. They must however be the two confirmation hymns (for Prince Leopold of Battenberg and the Princess Patricia of Connaught) on pp. 20 and 21 of his privately printed *Hymns and Carols* (1907).

18 *Poetry and Hymns* by Christopher Driver, the *Congregational Quarterly*, October 1957, p. 340.

19 *Hymns and Human Life* by Erik Routley, John Murray 1952, p. 19.

20 *Seven Essays* by George Sampson, Cambridge 1947; No. vii 'The Century of Divine Songs' (the British Academy's Warton Lecture for 1943) p. 199.

21 It was estimated in 1960 that 'between the Reformation and the present day more than 400,000 hymns have been written in the English language' (*English Hymns* by Arthur Pollard, Longmans, Green & Co. 1960 p. 7). Pollard adds that Charles Wesley is said to have written over 6,500 and Watts over 600 hymns. Since the 1960s we have seen the contemporary 'hymn explosion' which must have added some thousands more to the grand total.

22 *A Practical discourse on some principles of Hymn Singing* by Robert Bridges, B. H. Blackwell, Oxford 1901, reprinted from the *Journal of Theological Studies*, October 1899.

23 See, for example, the notes to the text *Praise the Lord of heaven* on p. 251; and compare verse 4, line 4, of *O changeless Christ* (p. 122) with verse 5, line 4, of *He comes to us as one unknown* (p. 88). I was not fully aware of this when writing the latter (and later) text; but even if I had been, the line says what I want to say in what seems to me the best way I can find of saying it.

24 See *Scripture Union Choruses*, first published 1921; this chorus is No 269 of the 1965 edition, published by permission of Hall-Mack Co., Philadelphia.

25 See, for example, *Oxford Book of English Verse*, 1900, No. 365, under the title 'Friends departed'. Vaughan's dates are 1622–1695.

26 *The Hymns of Wesley and Watts*, p. 138.

27 Ibid, p. 30.

28 *Writers at work*: interviews from *Paris Review*, selected by Kay Dick, Penguin 1972, p. 90. The quotation is a transcript from an interview with Richard Poirier. Elsewhere Frost is recorded as saying 'I'd as soon write free verse as play tennis with the net down.'

29 *The Victorian Hymn*, p. 12.

30 *On Poetry and Poets* by T. S. Eliot, Faber 1957, p. 30 of the paperback edition.

31 The fullest apologia that I know in favour of 'updating' texts appears in *Hymns in Today's Language* by Christopher Idle (Grove Books, Nottingham 1982) in connection with the publication of *Hymns for Today's Church* (Hodder & Stoughton 1982) of which he was one of the compilers. The case he makes out, although I personally do not accept it, deserves more serious consideration than it always received from critics of the hymnbook out of sympathy with the policy adopted.

32 *A Collection of Hymns for the use of the People called Methodists*, 1779.

33 *Hymns and Spiritual Songs* by Isaac Watts, 1707; Preface.

34 *The Hymns and Ballads of Fred Pratt Green*, Stainer and Bell, London, and Hope Publishing Co., Illinois 1982, p. xv.

35 *Within the Rock of Ages* by George Lawton, James Clarke & Co., Cambridge 1983, p. 204.

36 *The Great Ship and Rabelais replies* by Eric Linklater, Macmillan 1944, p. 60.

37 *Northanger Abbey*, ch. 5.

38 *Seven Essays*, p. 219.

39 See *Housman 1897–1936* by Grant Richards, Oxford 1941, p. 14f.

40 Verse 4 of 'O for a thousand tongues to sing' by Charles Wesley.

41 Verse 2 of 'Epitaph on an army of mercenaries' by A. E. Housman, No XXXVII in *Last Poems*, The Richards Press 1922.

42 The last four lines of verse 1 of 'Trebetherick'; p. 59 in the *Collected Poems*, John Murray 1958.

43 Christopher Wordsworth, Bishop of Lincoln 1869–85, was a nephew of the poet William Wordsworth. He wrote a complete hymnbook, including some fine hymns. Inevitably others fell short—as for example 'Let us emulate the names/Of St Philip and St James.' Some of his children (so E. F. Benson recounts in *As we were*, Longmans, London 1932) tried their own hand at such composition: 'Let us try to be as good/As St Simon and St Jude.'

44 'When like stars His children crown'd
   All in white shall wait around'

45 By Charles Wesley. No. 262 in *A Collection of Hymns for the use of the People called Methodists*.

46 Verse 3 of 'Hark the glad sound! the Saviour comes' by P. Doddridge.

47 *Poetical Works* by George Macdonald, Chatto & Windus 1911, Vol. II p. 362 The poem stands last in his privately printed *A Threefold Cord*, 1883.

48 Verse 2 of 'Praise, my soul, the King of heaven'.

49 'O for a closer walk with God'.

50 In fact the rhyme is triple: Laws/cause/voice

51 Verse 3 of 'The day thou gavest Lord is ended' by J. Ellerton.

52 By John Keble.

53 Verse 6 of 'There is a land of pure delight' by Isaac Watts.

54 By H. Twells.

55 Verse 6 of 'Sun of my soul, Thou Saviour dear' by John Keble.

56 *Modern English Usage* by H. W. Fowler, Oxford 1926. The entry 'ere' has cross-references to INCONGRUOUS VOCABULARY and to VULGARIZATION. The quotation is from the latter, p. 698 of the 1937 edition.

57 For a discussion of this subject, see *Hymns in Today's Language* (note 31 above) p. 5f. As can be seen, I draw a major distinction between retaining 'Thou-forms' in hymns where they naturally belong and writing in 'Thou-forms' in the 1980s.

58 e.g. Matthew 4.19 '. . . fishers of men.' The word is *anthropos* which is used to mean a *male* (e.g. Matthew 9.9 '. . . a man, called Matthew') and also a *human being* (e.g. Matthew 6.14 'If ye forgive men their trespasses . . .'). In this dual sense it corresponds with the use of *man* in English.

59 e.g. Romans 8.14. Paul uses 'sons' in verse 14, 'children' in verse 16.

60 e.g. John 1.12; 1 John 3.2.

61 *English Hymns* by Arthur Pollard, p. 8.

62 See *The Leaves of the Tree* by A. C. Benson, Smith, Elder & Co 1912, p. 275.

63 See *John Keble* by Walter Lock, Methuen 1893, p. 56. The poem is that added to the third edition in 1828 entitled *An Address to Converts from Popery*. This ran in the thirteenth stanza:

> O come to our Communion Feast!
> There, present in the heart,
> Not in the hands, the eternal Priest
> Will his true self impart.

It appears that Pusey originally suggested the change from *Not* in line 3 to *As*. The alteration was carried out after Keble's death by his executor. Many later editions have restored the original reading.

64 The *Evening News* (London) 13 October 1928; included in *Selected Literary Criticism: D. H. Lawrence* edited by Anthony Beal, Heinemann 1956, p. 6f.

O CHANGELESS CHRIST

O changeless Christ, for ever new,
　　who walked our earthly ways,
still draw our hearts as once you drew
the hearts of other days.

As once you spoke by plain and hill
or taught by shore and sea,
so be today our teacher still,
O Christ of Galilee.

As wind and storm their Master heard
and his command fulfilled,
may troubled hearts receive your word,
the tempest-tossed be stilled.

And as of old to all who prayed
your healing hand was shown,
so be your touch upon us laid,
unseen but not unknown.

In broken bread, in wine outpoured,
your new and living way
proclaim to us, O risen Lord,
O Christ of this our day.

O changeless Christ, till life is past
your blessing still be given;
then bring us home, to taste at last
the timeless joys of heaven.

USA © 1984 in LIFT EVERY HEART by Hope Publishing Company, Carol Stream, IL 60188
World outside USA © 1981 by Timothy Dudley-Smith

'O changeless Christ'
—the making of a hymn-text

Is there any purpose in trying to describe the process by which a hymn comes to be written? Clearly there are several good reasons *against* attempting it. First, it is not really possible, short of some kind of 'stream of consciousness' recorder. The thoughts and feelings, and the process of association, selection, rejection, comparison, trial and error, which make up the greater part of the creative process, are transitory in the extreme. To note them down as they occur would mean, I believe, that no finished text would ever result. To recapture them later is like trying to get the feathers back into the pillow. And the heart of the matter, the uprising of the thought, the concept, the phrase, which forms the final selection— no one can say (except perhaps an analyst) where this has come from or why.

Secondly, there is no knowing how far what I shall try to write here bears any relationship to a general description of how a text is made. It is not even *generally* true of my own work. My most-used text 'Tell out, my soul' was finished—as far as I can recall— in about three-quarters of an hour. What follows is therefore the best description I can manage of the writing of this one text, 'O changeless Christ'. Thirdly, I am not sure whether a text can survive the public analysis of how it was composed. If, in its finished form, it offers words with a certain inevitability, and a certain freshness, which worshippers may be glad to make their own, will such worshippers be able to use the text as a vehicle for their own prayers and praises if they retain the recollection that this line was originally written to express something quite different, or this verse added as an afterthought? R. L. Stevenson a hundred years ago was reminding readers of the *Contemporary Review* (April, 1885) that 'There is nothing more disenchanting than to be shown the springs and mechanism of any art.'

I do not know the answers to these questions: but I try the experiment, which has been in my mind for some time, and which others have tried before me, for three reasons. First, in the hope that some who read this may come to feel they too could follow such a process, and begin to write hymn texts. Second, that those who do write texts should see that they are not alone in the false-starts, the clichés and banalities of early drafts: and take heart to go on polishing, revising, correcting—which in most cases (more and more, as I grow older) seems the way my texts are written. Thirdly, I am a learner: and perhaps by this analysis I shall contribute to the general discussion of how to write better.

I see from my MS book that in the middle of August 1981 I copied a fair draft of the text, on completion: and at the same time, with just such a purpose as this in mind, I made two pages of notes on the construction of the text. It is from these notes, coupled with the rough versions of the different stanzas, and from drafts and letters on the subsequent corrections which were made some weeks later, that I am able to put together this account.

'O changeless Christ'—you will find the final version on page 30—is one of eight texts written on my summer holiday in August 1981.

Picture then a sunny morning in Cornwall, with Cadgwith Cove blue in the distance as seen from the sitting room window. I take my wife a tray of breakfast, lay a second tray for myself and take it to the sitting room or the garden, and begin to think about hymns. My starting point for 'O changeless Christ' was the thought of 'Christ our contemporary'; and the first line I set down was:

'Christ in our world today. . .'

A note at the side suggests that I had in mind a strongly-structured hymn, with the final line in each of four verses (so far of unknown length or metre, let alone tune) being:

v. 1 Christ be my Lord
2 Christ be my friend
3 Christ be my all
4 Christ be my King

At the same time, I was meditating on three words (which I had been using the previous Autumn in writing a small booklet on Confirmation): the words *turn*, *trust* and *true*. These thoughts found their fruition a year later in the Confirmation hymn 'We turn to Christ anew' written in August 1982.

I began by linking my thoughts of the centrality of Christ, and of Christ our contemporary with this trio of words; using one as the final word of the penultimate line of each of 3 verses, with the last line sketched in thus:

v. 1   . . . turn
to Christ alone.

v. 2   . . . trust
to Christ by faith.

v. 3   . . . be true
to Christ my Friend.

with 'Lord' as an alternative for the final word in verse 3.

It seems that at this early stage the tune MOSCOW (664.6664) was in my mind (or at least a metre following the hymn 'Thou, whose almighty word', often set to MOSCOW) since there comes next a set of four lines (little more than a metrical doodle) thus:

                    Called to follow Christ today
                    Called to walk his narrow way
                    Called to be his own
                    Let me, Lord, your lessons learn . . .

—changed in the final line to:

                    May we your lessons learn.

In spite of the fact that these lines are 77.57 the rhyme scheme is
clearly meant to lead up to the conclusion already noted in rough
on the opposite side of the page (and quoted above).

                        v. 1 . . . turn
                        to Christ alone.

Finally on this first page comes this:

                    Christ be our King today
                    friends of his narrow way
                    called as his own
                    May we his lesson learn
                    his saving truth discern
                    and in repentance turn
                    to Christ alone

    This is indeed 664.6664. As yet there is no punctuation. 'Friends
of' in line 2 was substituted for something illegible crossed out, and
replaced by 'Walking', which in turn gave place to this line as it
appears above. Clearly this has begun to move from the original
conception of 'Christ our contemporary' towards a Confirmation
hymn (which indeed I had been hoping some day to attempt) in
which the thought of 'turning to Christ . . . in repentance' would
echo two of the three responses in the renewal of baptismal vows: 'I
turn to Christ' and 'I repent of my sins'. But on the next page the
original theme returns with:

                    Christ who is ever new
                    calls us his work to do
                    his will obey
                    Christ of the saving Name
                    Christ who in meekness came
                    Christ who is still the same
                    Christ of our day.

the '. . . ame' rhyme is clearly meant to lead up to the echo of
Hebrews 13.8 in line 6. An alternative for lines 4–6 appears across
the page:

                    Trust in your saving Name
                    your word of truth proclaim
                    and prove you still the same

with 'find' as an alternative to 'prove'.

                        — 33 —

It is not possible to recapture the order of the three versions on this page; nor can I now suggest the reasoning behind them. But one more attempt in this metrical form appears here. The opening line

Jesus the ever new

is crossed out in favour of:

Christ who is always new
We come to follow you
Walk in your way
Your word of truth proclaim
trust in your saving Name
and prove you still the same
Christ of our day

Line 6 began with 'and find', changed to 'finding', and then to 'and prove'.

This is the last we see of the 664.6664 metre. At the foot of the page, with no real indication of how it was derived, comes the line:

O changeless Christ, for ever new

itself an alteration from:

O Christ unchanged, for ever new.

Even at that stage there seems to have been alongside the basic thought of 'Christ our Contemporary' the idea of 'As in Galilee . . . so now'.

This seems to have occupied my hymn-writing during 48 hours, no doubt much of that time taken up with visits to the beach, picnic suppers, swimming and surfing—in fact, having a family holiday.

In my experience an opening line is very real progress. Usually it contains within itself—or within my mind, when eventually I set it down—some clue as to how the rest of the hymn will follow. It does not fully determine the metre, of course; but it does limit very considerably the possible choices of metrical form. It is not unusual for an opening line to require this sort of process before it finally emerges. When it does, there is a certain confidence—not invariably fulfilled—that a first verse, and then a final text will follow.

On a new page of my MS book, then, I set the line:

O changeless Christ, for ever new

with the words 'view' and 'drew' (and 'knew', crossed out as a false rhyme) in the margin. An attempt at a second and fourth line of a 4-line stanza are added to give

line 1 O changeless Christ, for ever new

2 be present while we pray

3

4 who hear your call (voice?) today.

But before this is finished a second verse is coming into being.
The line

> 'As once you walked in Galilee'

gives way to

> 'As once you spoke on plain and hill
> and taught by shore and sea
> so be today our teacher still
> O Christ of Galilee'.

'Spoke' in the first line took the place of 'taught' (which I foresaw
would be needed in line 2) and 'walked', both crossed out. With
punctuation, and the later change in line 1 from 'on' to 'by', this is
verse 2 in its final form. A later analysis shows something of the
sounds built into its structure. Sibilants appear in all four lines and
labials in three: and there is an alliterative 't' in 'taught', 'today'
(both words including a second dental) and 'teachers', echoed also
within 'still' and 'Christ'. Again, '. . . or' dominates line 2 (not only
in 'or' and 'shore' but also in 'taught') and the short i is always
found with the letter l: till, still, and lil (of 'Ga*lil*ee').

But verse 1 is still unfinished, and a new start follows:

> O changeless Christ, for ever new
> come near in power again
> and draw our hearts as once you drew
> the hearts who heard you then.

Line 2 was the problem, just as 'drew' was the key-word, offering a
rhyme to line 1, and determining the fourth line, which must
contain 'drew's' object. Line 2 indeed began in this version as:

> among us move again

which was crossed out.

At this stage the single line:

> Unseen but not unknown

is jotted in the margin for future use. Line 2 was to continue to give
trouble through successive revision, partly because the obvious
rhyme to conclude it, 'men', is a difficult word to use in current
hymnody without raising the vexed question of 'inclusive language'.

First drafts of two more verses appear on this page, scribbled in
pencil (as these pages mostly are) with doodles in the margin. Verse
3 began:

> As once in power to those who prayed

changed to:

> And as of old to those who prayed

and then to:

> And as of old in all who prayed

with a second line:

> His healing touch was shown.

This in turn is changed to read 'Your' for 'His'—and 'hand' for 'touch', presumably when it became clear that 'touch' would be needed in line 3. Line 3 began:

> His healing touch upon us laid

changed to 'be on us laid' and then to:

> So be your touch upon us laid

with a possible variant:

> Your touch be still upon us laid.

There are signs of a new line, fitting the '. . . aid' rhyme, in a marginal addition:

> 'As wind and storm his word obeyed'

but this thought was put aside till later. Meanwhile line 4 was rescued from the margin where it had been jotted at an earlier stage (the rhyme-scheme of line 2 having been adapted to make room for it) to give:

> And as of old on all who prayed
> Your healing hand was shown
> so be your touch upon us laid
> unseen but not unknown.

This, though written as verse 3, becomes verse 4 in the finished hymn, with a single change ('on' becomes 'to' in line 1). At the very foot of this third page in my MS book comes a hasty scribble of another verse, drawing inspiration from:

> As wind and storm his word obeyed.

But 'obeyed' is not possible, since it follows the rhyme of the verse above. So we have:

> As wind and storm (wave?) obeyed his word

or

> As wind and storm (wave?) their Master heard
> Above the stormy seas

with a few odd suggestions jotted down:

> All creatures tempest-tossed . . .

and:

> Your promised peace prevail . . .

and:

> O Lord of wind and storm . . .

So to a new page, and a new stage. When enough of a text is written in a first draft, I like to transfer it in ink on to a clean MS page, so that I can see what it looks like. New verses can then be added in pencil at the foot. This is what I wrote in ink:

> 1 O changeless Christ, for ever new,
>   come near in power again
>   and draw our hearts, as once you drew
>   the hearts that heard you then.

> 2 As once you spoke on plain and hill
>   and taught by shore and sea
>   so be today our teacher still
>   O Christ of Galilee.

> 3 And as of old to all who prayed
>   your healing hand was shown
>   so be your touch upon us laid
>   unseen but not unknown.

> 4 As wind and storm their Master heard
>   and his command fulfilled
>   may restless hearts receive your word
>   the tempest-tossed be stilled.

At this time, I fancy I was pleased with the repetition of 'st' in verse 4. It comes once in the first line, but no less than six times in lines 3 and 4 if one includes the 'ts' sound of 'hearts' and 'tossed'.

Two more verses are now added in pencil, with little sign of their construction. As often happens, after a laborious and almost painful period when 'nothing seems to come', the hymn is flowing better. We have:

> In broken bread, in wine outpoured proclaim . . .

but 'proclaim' is crossed out, to give:

> In broken bread, in wine outpoured
> your new and living way
> you still proclaim, O risen Lord
> O Christ of this our day.

'O' in line 3 replaces 'Our' crossed out. The final line is meant to echo and contrast the final line of verse two above:

> O Christ of Galilee.

I think I had a certain uneasiness over the precise sacramental emphasis that might be conveyed by these lines: and, as we shall see, returned to them at a later stage.

The final verse had by this time begun to take shape in my mind. I had running in my head the lovely prayer from the Leonine

Sacramentary (dating back to the seventh century) often used in the Office of Compline:

> Be present, O merciful God, and protect us through the silent hours of this night, so that we who are wearied by the changes and chances of this fleeting world, may repose upon thy eternal changelessness; through Jesus Christ our Lord.

The final verse therefore became

> O changeless Christ, till life is past
> walk with us still to bless
> and bring us home to taste at last
> eternal changelessness.

In line 2, two earlier versions were tried and rejected: 'Be with us still to bless' and 'Be ever near to bless'. In line 3 'share' was crossed out in favour of 'taste'.

Here, then, recopied in full, in ink on a clean page was the full draft of the text. My main problem in the next revision was verse 1, which then read:

> O changeless Christ, for ever new,
> come near in power again
> and draw our hearts, as once you drew
> the hearts that heard you then.

There were two failings here, it seemed to me. First, 'again' is a difficult word as the first of a pair of rhymes: different people pronounce it differently. Secondly, the word 'then' has very little by way of antecedents in the verse to look back to, except the word 'once'. So various alternatives were tried for line 2:

> reveal your power again . . .

or:

> by faith be known again . . .

or:

> among us move again . . .

(this last had in fact been tried and rejected at an earlier stage). None of these dealt adequately with the weaknesses noted, so I turned to line 4, to see if the two rhyming lines, 2 and 4 should both be re-written. Suppose line 4 becomes:

> the hearts of long ago . . .

with line 2 changed to:

> your ancient glories show . . .

or:

> who lived on earth below

or:

> your call again bestow

—but none of these seemed on the right track. Suppose I try for line 4:

> the hearts that heard your call

with line 2 as:

> although our faith be small

or:

> the timeless Lord of all

—but that seems no better. Could we then have for line 4:

> the hearts that heard your voice?

But the rhymes for 'voice' are very limited. 'Choice' and 'rejoice' would appear hackneyed in this context (they have to be used, I find, with great care, and with more sensitivity than I always achieve). And, besides, we today do still (inwardly) hear the voice of Christ.

The next attempt was:

> the hearts that heard your word

—but apart from the unwanted internal rhyme (for rhymes out of place can be as damaging as false rhymes) this conflicts with the rhyme-scheme of verse 4.

So, still following the same general pattern, we have next:

> the hearts that heard you speak

—but this is in conflict with 'spoke' in verse 2. An alternative version might be:

> the hearts of days gone by

—but that seems 'fairy-tale' language and a little precious here. So at last there comes a more promising line 4:

> the hearts of earlier days

and this might have, as line 2:

> receive your people's praise

—weak, but possible: or something with 'ablaze': or a better use of 'praise' (always an overworked word in my hymnody) as in:

> whom endless ages praise.

This became in fact the text of my next fair copy (page 6 of the MS book), and only in jotting down notes on the completion of that draft, in case some day I should come to write this present account, did I see a better way:

> O changeless Christ for ever new
> who walked our earthly ways
> still draw our hearts, as once you drew
> the hearts of earlier days.

Line 2 here is less predictable (to my mind, verse should aim for lines that seem 'inevitable' but avoid those which seem 'predictable') and introduces the idea of 'walk' which will re-appear in the final verse.

The page 6 draft, which is dated 17 August was written with the idea that it was the final version. This was not in fact to be; and three small amendments appear in the margin of this copy:

> Verse 1, line 4: 'Other' in place of 'earlier'

(It is a moot point—but this text depends upon a certain simplicity, and 'other' is metrically the simpler word here);

> Verse 2, line 1: 'Or' in place of 'and'

(otherwise three 'ands' follow rather closely on each other's heels);

> Verse 4, line 4: 'troubled' for 'restless'

(to ease the overuse of st and ts).

In addition, in verse 5, line 4 there is a marginal suggestion, never in fact adopted, that 'every' should replace 'this our' in the line:

> O Christ of this our day.

After six pages of such drafting, my MS book turns to another subject entirely; with eight pages of prayers for a new collection, a page given to the first thoughts of a hymn on prayer (later to become 'O Lord yourself declare') and five pages of work on the text 'O Child of Mary, hark to her', taking us up to 28 August.

So, in the last days of my holiday, I wrote yet another fair copy, once again in ink on a clean page, of 'O changeless Christ'. It incorporates the marginal changes of the last draft: but moves the verse beginning 'In broken bread' to become verse 3, giving the contrast of the final line of verse 2:

> O Christ of Galilee

with the final line of verse 3:

> O Christ of this our day.

Line 3 is also changed in that verse to give:

> In broken bread, in wine outpoured
> your new and living way
> proclaim to us, O risen Lord,
> O Christ of this our day

in the belief that this verse, like the others, should be cast in the form of a prayer rather than a declaration. I was also anxious to make clearer the foundation truth that 'the new and living way' into the holiest (Hebrews 10.19) is by the shed blood of Jesus Christ, of which the sacrament is the 'sure witness and effectual sign': by that, in fact, to which the sacrament points, and not by the sacrament itself. Indeed, until I hit on the revision of the verse shown above, I had thought it might be better to discard it.

So I returned from holiday with this completed draft and put it in the typewriter. It is my practice, as I mentioned in the Foreword, to send all my drafts, soon after completion, to Derek Kidner for comment, criticism and advice. Chiefly, according to my note attached to the draft, I wanted to ask him about the sacramental verse, now returned to position as verse 5.

But in addition I raised with him my growing doubt about the final (and very key) line of the hymn, asking

'Is "eternal changelessness" (from Compline, I think!) a scriptural view of some aspect of the life of heaven? I hope so!'

In a careful reply, Derek Kidner wrote that 'Eternal changelessness bothered me even before I read of your own misgivings'—and went on to ask whether the concept is not more Greek than Christian. He wrote: 'I find the prospect of the marriage feast, or of "reigning with him" or "serving him" more biblical as well as more exhilarating!' He also added, with some sympathy: 'But metrically it makes a well-groomed ending which you will be loth to sacrifice.' Finally, he suggested, as suitable tunes, BALLERMA or ST BOTOLPH.

I was indeed reluctant to abandon the text, which had (as you can see) taken some thought and labour, and which seemed to me to have something worth saying and not too often said in hymns, however familiar the 'as then, so now' parallel may be. But my unease about the final verse was confirmed: and since a hymn must (in my view) be informed by Scripture, I could not let the last line stand. To say this is not necessarily to criticize a prayer of the Church for the last thirteen centuries: there is a difference between resting in (or upon) God's changelessness, and 'tasting' it for ourselves. And what matters in a text, besides the strict interpretation of the words, is the impression they convey to the singer of them—which would undeniably be a very static view of heaven! To suggest that we shall be changeless in heaven is certainly to suggest more than I know.

The text therefore appears once more, in full, in my MS book, written yet again in ink on a clean page, dated 13 October, 1981. By this time I was taking three days away from home to do some writing and reading, and was free enough of day-to-day preoccupations to look at the text once more. I could find no way (some reader of these lines may well do so, but I could not) to retain 'eternal changelessness' as a final line (which I dearly wanted to do) and avoid the problems discussed above. In the event, I turned from the concept of 'changelessness' to that of 'timelessness' where we seem to be on surer ground. And that gave, quite quickly, a new second and fourth line. The rhyme used, 'given/heaven', is hardly original and perhaps less than technically perfect; but it can claim many noble precedents. To take two examples, the first hymn in *A Collection of Hymns for the use of the People called Methodists* is Charles Wesley's magnificent 'O for a thousand tongues to sing', headed (in his *Hymns and Sacred Poems* of 1740) 'For the Anniversary Day of One's Conversion'. As written, it had eighteen verses, including this:

> With me, your chief, ye then shall know,
> Shall feel your sins forgiven;
> Anticipate your heaven below,
> And own that love is heaven.

And, as Wesley, so Francis Lyte:

> Praise, my soul, the King of Heaven,
> To his feet thy tribute bring;
> Ransomed, healed, restored, forgiven . . .

This final revision brought my text to its finished form; as it stands at the head of this chapter. In some strange way, while it differs considerably from what might have resulted from some of my earlier beginnings, it is to me recognizably the text I sat down to write as 'Christ in our world today'. It was completed just in time to find a place in the collection *Hymns for Today's Church* where it is set to BALLERMA. At the time of writing, I have yet to hear it sung!

Part Two

THE HYMNS

A PURPLE ROBE

A purple robe, a crown of thorn,
  a reed in his right hand;
before the soldiers' spite and scorn
I see my Saviour stand.

He bears between the Roman guard
the weight of all our woe;
a stumbling figure bowed and scarred
I see my Saviour go.

Fast to the cross's spreading span,
high in the sunlit air,
all the unnumbered sins of man
I see my Saviour bear.

He hangs, by whom the world was made,
beneath the darkened sky;
the everlasting ransom paid,
I see my Saviour die.

He shares on high his Father's throne,
who once in mercy came;
for all his love to sinners shown
I sing my Saviour's Name.

A SONG WAS HEARD AT CHRISTMAS

A song was heard at Christmas
  to wake the midnight sky;
a Saviour's birth, and peace on earth,
  and praise to God on high.
The angels sang at Christmas
  with all the hosts above,
and still we sing the newborn King,
  his glory and his love.

A star was seen at Christmas,
  a herald and a sign,
that men might know the way to go
  to find the child divine.
The wise men watched at Christmas
  in some far eastern land,
and still the wise in starry skies
  discern their Maker's hand.

A tree was grown at Christmas,
  a sapling green and young;
no tinsel bright with candlelight
  upon its branches hung.
But he who came at Christmas
  our sins and sorrows bore,
and still we name his tree of shame
  our life for evermore.

A child was born at Christmas
  when Christmas first began;
the Lord of all a baby small,
  for love of men made man.
For love is ours at Christmas,
  and life and light restored,
and so we praise through endless days
  the Saviour, Christ the Lord.

ALL FLOWERS OF GARDEN, FIELD AND HILL

ALL flowers of garden, field and hill
this borrowed beauty find:
what Jesus taught they teach us still,
and bring our Lord to mind.

Where sheaves of Galilean corn
their whitened harvest yield,
where blue and purple robes adorn
the lilies of the field,

Where meadow grasses green and tall
await the reapers' hands,
or sheltered by the sunlit wall
a barren fig-tree stands—

We hear his voice; as in their turn
those first disciples heard:
in nature's picture-book we learn
to read the Master's word.

The thorn that scars a Saviour's head,
the palms the people wave,
the balsam wrapped about the dead,
the myrrh to mark his grave,

Or Joseph's plot where olives bloom
and tangled branches twine
to bear above the empty tomb
the true and living vine—

They speak of him; and with one voice
lift silent songs above:
'All creatures of our God, rejoice,
his saving Name is Love!'

USA © 1984 in LIFT EVERY HEART by Hope Publishing Company, Carol Stream, IL 60188
World outside USA © 1978 by Timothy Dudley-Smith

ALL GLORY BE TO GOD ON HIGH

based on the Gloria in Excelsis

ALL glory be to God on high,
his peace on earth proclaim;
to all his people tell abroad
the grace and glory of the Lord,
and bless his holy Name.

In songs of thankfulness and praise
our hearts their homage bring
to worship him who reigns above,
almighty Father, Lord of love,
our God and heavenly King.

O Christ, the Father's only Son,
O Lamb enthroned on high,
O Jesus, who for sinners died
and reigns at God the Father's side,
in mercy hear our cry.

Most high and holy is the Lord,
most high his heavenly throne;
where God the Father, God the Son,
and God the Spirit, ever One,
in glory reigns alone.

ALL MY SOUL TO GOD I RAISE

based on Psalm 25

ALL my soul to God I raise;
　　Be my guardian all my days.
Confident in hope I rest,
Daily prove your path is best.
Ever work in me your will,
Faithful to your promise still.

Graciously my sins forgive;
Help me by your truth to live.
In your footsteps lead me, Lord,
Joy renewed and hope restored,
Knowing every sin forgiven,
Learning all the ways of heaven.

Mercies manifold extend,
Not as judge but faithful friend.
O my Saviour, hear my prayer,
Pluck my feet from every snare;
Quietude be mine at last,
Rest from all my guilty past.

Sheltered safe when troubles fret,
Trusting God I triumph yet!
Undismayed in him I stand,
Victor only by his hand.
Worship, homage, love and praise,
All my soul, to God I raise.

USA © 1984 in LIFT EVERY HEART by Hope Publishing Company, Carol Stream, IL 60188
World outside USA © 1982 by Timothy Dudley-Smith

ALL SHALL BE WELL

ALL shall be well!
    For on our Easter skies
see Christ the Sun
    of Righteousness arise.

All shall be well!
The sacrifice is made;
the sinner freed,
    the price of pardon paid.

All shall be well!
The cross and passion past;
dark night is done,
    bright morning come at last.

All shall be well!
Within our Father's plan
death has no more
    dominion over man.

Jesus alive!
Rejoice and sing again,
'All shall be well
    for evermore, Amen!'

USA © 1984 in LIFT EVERY HEART by Hope Publishing Company, Carol Stream, IL 60188
World outside USA © 1976 by Timothy Dudley-Smith

AND SLEEPS MY LORD IN SILENCE YET

AND sleeps my Lord in silence yet,
    within the darkness laid away;
where none remember nor forget,
    where breaks no more the sunlit day?
And sleeps my Lord in silence yet,
    where cold his lifeless body lay?

And does the sting of death remain
    to work unchanged its bitter will?
Were cross and passion all in vain,
    no battle won on Calvary's hill?
And does the sting of death remain,
    and gapes the grave in triumph still?

Have faith in Christ, the risen Son,
    who reigns eternal, glorified!
Who death destroyed, who triumph won,
    who flung the gates of heaven wide!
Have faith in Christ, the risen Son,
    the living Lord of Eastertide!

USA © 1984 in LIFT EVERY HEART by Hope Publishing Company, Carol Stream, IL 60188
World outside USA © 1982 by Timothy Dudley-Smith

AS FOR OUR WORLD

As for our world we lift our hearts in praise,
  for gifts unnumbered from our childhood days,
  now, in God's Name
stir our compassions; give us eyes to see
the orphaned child, the starved and refugee,
  the sick and lame:
for sad and needy children everywhere—
for this our world, we lift our hands in prayer.

As for our world we lift our hearts in praise,
the joy of home with lights and hearth ablaze,
  the welcome plain;
so we recall the homeless and the cold,
the destitute, the prisoners, and the old
  who lie in pain:
for all who grieve, for all who know despair—
for this our world, we lift our hands in prayer.

As for our world we lift our hearts in praise,
recount the blessings that our life displays
  in every part,
so look in mercy, Lord, where shadows rest,
the ravaged homes by want and wars oppressed,
  the sick at heart:
with burdens more than we were meant to bear—
for this our world, we lift our hands in prayer.

As for our world we lift our hearts in praise,
the love of God on all our works and ways,
  so we commend
all those who loveless live and hopeless mourn,
who die at last uncomforted, forlorn,
  without a friend:
who own no Saviour's love, no Father's care—
for this our world we lift our hands in prayer.

As for our world we lift our hearts in praise,
so with our songs of thankfulness we raise
  this ageless plea,
that darkened souls who have no song to sing
may find in Christ the living Lord and King
  he came to be:
and in his cross and resurrection share—
for this our world we lift our hands in prayer.

AS WATER TO THE THIRSTY

A s water to the thirsty,
    as beauty to the eyes,
as strength that follows weakness,
as truth instead of lies,
as songtime and springtime
and summertime to be,
    so is my Lord,
    my living Lord,
so is my Lord to me.

Like calm in place of clamour,
like peace that follows pain,
like meeting after parting,
like sunshine after rain,
like moonlight and starlight
and sunlight on the sea,
    so is my Lord,
    my living Lord,
so is my Lord to me.

As sleep that follows fever,
as gold instead of grey,
as freedom after bondage,
as sunrise to the day,
as home to the traveller
and all he longs to see,
    so is my Lord,
    my living Lord,
so is my Lord to me.

AT CANA'S WEDDING, LONG AGO

for a marriage

AT Cana's wedding, long ago,
    they knew his presence by this sign,
a virtue none but Christ could show,
to turn their water into wine—
    and still on us his blessing be
    as in the days of Galilee.

What if the way be far to go
and life at times a weary load?
Yet may our hearts within us glow
as theirs on that Emmaus road—
    the risen Christ become our guest,
    with him to walk, in him to rest.

O Lord of all our life below,
O risen Lord of realms above,
eternal joy be theirs to know,
united in the bond of love—
    one in the faith, with one accord,
    one with each other and the Lord.

BE STRONG IN THE LORD

based on Ephesians 6. 10–18

B E strong in the Lord
   in armour of light!
With helmet and sword,
with shield for the fight;
on prayer be dependent,
be belted and shod,
in breastplate resplendent—
the armour of God.

Integrity gird
you round to impart
the truth of his word
as truth in your heart:
his righteousness wearing
as breastplate of mail,
his victory sharing,
be strong to prevail.

With eagerness shod
stand firm in your place,
or go forth for God
with news of his grace:
no foe shall disarm you
nor force you to yield,
no arrow can harm you
with faith as your shield.

Though Satan presume
to test you and try,
in helmet and plume
your head shall be high:
beset by temptation
be true to your Lord,
your helmet salvation
and Scripture your sword.

So wield well your blade,
rejoice in its powers!
Fight on undismayed
for Jesus is ours!
Then in him victorious
your armour lay down,
to praise, ever glorious,
his cross and his crown.

BEHOLD, AS LOVE MADE MANIFEST

BEHOLD, as love made manifest,
the Lamb of God divine:
redeeming love perceived, possessed,
in sacrifice and sign.

A sign of saving grace displayed,
a sign of sinners' worth;
by wood and nails a ransom paid
for all the sins of earth.

A sign of love beyond belief
where every failing breath
affirms through agony and grief
a love that conquers death.

A sign of mercy's wide extent
and universal sway;
the evil powers of darkness spent
for Christ has won the day.

A sign of triumph over sin
and dread devouring grave,
a sign of all he died to win
for all he longs to save.

Herein is love beyond all price,
the Lamb of God divine:
his all-sufficient sacrifice,
his all-prevailing sign.

USA © 1984 in LIFT EVERY HEART by Hope Publishing Company, Carol Stream, IL 60188
World outside USA © 1983 by Timothy Dudley-Smith

BEYOND ALL MORTAL PRAISE

based on Daniel 2. 20–23

Beyond all mortal praise
      God's Name be ever blest,
unsearchable his ways,
his glory manifest;
      from his high throne
      in power and might
      by wisdom's light
      he rules alone.

Our times are in his hand
to whom all flesh is grass,
while as their Maker planned
the changing seasons pass.
      He orders all:
      before his eyes
      earth's empires rise,
      her kingdoms fall.

He gives to humankind,
dividing as he will,
all powers of heart and mind,
of spirit, strength and skill:
      nor dark nor night
      but must lay bare
      its secrets, where
      he dwells in light.

To God the only Lord,
our fathers' God, be praise;
his holy Name adored
through everlasting days.
      His mercies trace
      in answered prayer,
      in love and care,
      and gifts of grace.

USA © 1984 in LIFT EVERY HEART by Hope Publishing Company, Carol Stream, IL 60188
World outside USA © 1981 by Timothy Dudley-Smith

BLESS THE LORD AS DAY DEPARTS

based on Psalm 134

Bless the Lord as day departs,
   let your lamps be brightly burning,
lifting holy hands and hearts
   to the Lord till day's returning;

As within the darkened shrine,
   faithful to their sacred calling,
sons and priests of Levi's line
   blessed the Lord as night was falling;

So may we who watch or rest
   bless the Lord of earth and heaven;
and by him ourselves be blest,
   grace and peace and mercy given.

BORN BY THE HOLY SPIRIT'S BREATH

based on selected verses from Romans 8

BORN by the Holy Spirit's breath,
loosed from the law of sin and death,
now cleared in Christ from every claim
no judgment stands against our name.

In us the Spirit makes his home
that we in him may overcome;
Christ's risen life, in all its powers,
its all-prevailing strength, is ours.

Sons, then, and heirs of God most high,
we by his Spirit 'Father' cry;
that Spirit with our spirit shares
to frame and breathe our wordless prayers.

One is his love, his purpose one;
to form the likeness of his Son
in all who, called and justified,
shall reign in glory at his side.

Nor death nor life, nor powers unseen,
nor height nor depth can come between;
we know through peril, pain and sword,
the love of God in Christ our Lord.

BY LOVING HANDS

By loving hands the Lord is laid,
   no voice or pulse or breath;
as close within the shuttered gloom,
the sealed and silent garden tomb,
   he sleeps the sleep of death.

There through the dark of Easter dawn
   before the break of day,
before the dew was off the grass,
with none to see their footsteps pass,
   the women make their way.

No seal, no stone, secures the tomb,
   as low within the cave
they stoop to find, beyond belief,
where late the Lord was laid with grief,
   there stands an empty grave.

An empty grave! A risen Lord!
   A ransomed world reborn,
to see upon the shining skies
the Sun of Righteousness arise
   on that first Easter morn!

CHILD OF THE STABLE'S SECRET BIRTH

CHILD of the stable's secret birth,
the Lord by right of the lords of earth,
let angels sing of a King new-born—
the world is weaving a crown of thorn:
a crown of thorn for that infant head
cradled soft in the manger bed.

Eyes that shine in the lantern's ray;
a face so small in its nest of hay—
face of a child, who is born to scan
the world of men through the eyes of man:
and from that face in the final day
earth and heaven shall flee away.

Voice that rang through the courts on high
contracted now to a wordless cry,
a voice to master the wind and wave,
the human heart and the hungry grave:
the voice of God through the cedar trees
rolling forth as the sound of seas.

Infant hands in a mother's hand,
for none but Mary may understand
whose are the hands and the fingers curled
but his who fashioned and made our world;
and through these hands in the hour of death
nails shall strike the wood beneath.

Child of the stable's secret birth,
the Father's gift to a wayward earth,
to drain the cup in a few short years
of all our sorrows, our sins and tears—
ours the prize for the road he trod:
risen with Christ; at peace with God.

CHILL OF THE NIGHTFALL

CHILL of the nightfall,
lamps in the windows,
letting their light fall
clear on the snow;
  bitter December
  bids us remember
Christ in the stable
long, long ago.

Silence of midnight,
voices of angels,
singing to bid night
yield to the dawn;
  darkness is ended,
  sinners befriended,
where in the stable
Jesus is born.

Splendour of starlight
high on the hillside,
faint is the far light
burning below;
  kneeling before him
  shepherds adore him,
Christ in the stable
long, long ago.

Glory of daybreak!
Sorrows and shadows,
suddenly they break
forth into morn;
  sing out and tell now
  all shall be well now,
for in the stable
Jesus is born!

CHRIST BE MY LEADER

CHRIST be my leader by night as by day;
safe through the darkness for he is the way.
Gladly I follow, my future his care,
darkness is daylight when Jesus is there.

Christ be my teacher in age as in youth,
drifting or doubting, for he is the truth.
Grant me to trust him; though shifting as sand,
doubt cannot daunt me; in Jesus I stand.

Christ be my Saviour in calm as in strife;
death cannot hold me, for he is the life.
Nor darkness nor doubting nor sin and its stain
can touch my salvation: with Jesus I reign.

USA © 1964 by Hope Publishing Company, Carol Stream, IL 60188
World outside USA © 1961 by Timothy Dudley-Smith

CHRIST BE THE LORD OF ALL OUR DAYS

CHRIST be the Lord of all our days,
   the swiftly-passing years:
   Lord of our unremembered birth,
   heirs to the brightness of the earth;
Lord of our griefs and fears.

Christ be the source of all our deeds,
the life our living shares;
   the fount which flows from worlds above
   to never-failing springs of love;
the ground of all our prayers.

Christ be the goal of all our hopes,
the end to whom we come;
   guide of each pilgrim Christian soul
   which seeks, as compass seeks the pole,
our many-mansioned home.

Christ be the vision of our lives,
of all we think and are;
   to shine upon our spirits' sight
   as light of everlasting light—
the bright and morning star.

CHRIST FROM HEAVEN'S GLORY COME

a carol for our time

CHRIST from heaven's glory come,
    in a stable make your home.
Helpless new-born babe-in-arms,
dream of terror's night-alarms.
Lullaby, my little love,
Herod's troops are on the move.

Cradled on a mother's knee,
immigrant and refugee,
talking, walking hand in hand,
homeless in a foreign land,
Child of Mary, full of grace,
exile of an alien race.

Christ whose hand the hungry fed,
stones were yours in place of bread;
Christ whose love our ransom paid,
by a kiss at last betrayed;
friendless now, and nothing worth,
join the outcasts of the earth.

Soon the soldiers' jest is done,
'They will reverence my Son.'
On the gallows hang him high,
'By our law he ought to die.'
Perished, all the flower of youth:
Wash your hands, for what is truth?

*

Christ who once at Christmas came,
move our hearts who name your Name.
By your body, bring to birth
truth and justice, peace on earth,
sinners pardoned, love restored—
Reign among us, risen Lord!

USA © 1984 in LIFT EVERY HEART by Hope Publishing Company, Carol Stream, IL 60188
World outside USA © 1983 by Timothy Dudley-Smith

CHRIST HIGH-ASCENDED

CHRIST high-ascended, now in glory seated,
    throned and exalted, victory completed,
death's dread dominion finally defeated,
    we are his witnesses.

Christ from the Father every power possessing,
who on his chosen lifted hands in blessing,
sends forth his servants, still in faith confessing,
    we are his witnesses.

Christ, who in dying won for us salvation,
lives now the first-born of the new creation;
to win disciples out of every nation,
    we are his witnesses.

Christ in his splendour, all dominion gaining,
Christ with his people evermore remaining,
Christ to all ages gloriously reigning,
    we are his witnesses.

As at his parting, joy shall banish grieving,
faith in his presence strengthen our believing;
filled with his Spirit, love and power receiving,
    we are his witnesses.

USA © 1984 in LIFT EVERY HEART by Hope Publishing Company, Carol Stream, IL 60188
World outside USA © 1983 by Timothy Dudley-Smith

COME, LET US PRAISE THE LORD

based on the Venite, Psalm 95

COME, let us praise the Lord,
    with joy our God acclaim,
his greatness tell abroad
and bless his saving Name.
    Lift high your songs
    before his throne
    to whom alone
    all praise belongs.

Our God of matchless worth,
our King beyond compare,
the deepest bounds of earth,
the hills, are in his care.
    He all decrees,
    who by his hand
    prepared the land
    and formed the seas.

In worship bow the knee,
our glorious God confess;
the great Creator, he,
the Lord our Righteousness.
    He reigns unseen:
    his flock he feeds
    and gently leads
    in pastures green.

Come, hear his voice today,
receive what love imparts;
his holy will obey
and harden not your hearts.
    His ways are best;
    and lead at last,
    all troubles past,
    to perfect rest.

USA © 1984 in LIFT EVERY HEART by Hope Publishing Company, Carol Stream, IL 60188
World outside USA © 1981 by Timothy Dudley-Smith

COME NOW WITH AWE

COME now with awe, earth's ancient vigil keeping;
cold under starlight lies the stony way.
Down from the hillside see the shepherds creeping,
hear in our hearts the whispered news they say:
   'Laid in a manger lies an infant sleeping,
   Christ our Redeemer, born for us today.'

Come now with joy to worship and adore him;
hushed in the stillness, wonder and behold—
Christ in the stable where his mother bore him,
Christ whom the prophets faithfully foretold:
   High King of ages, low we kneel before him,
   starlight for silver, lantern-light for gold.

Come now with faith, the age-long secret guessing,
hearts rapt in wonder, soul and spirit stirred—
see in our likeness love beyond expressing,
all God has spoken, all the prophets heard;
   born for us sinners, bearer of all blessing,
   flesh of our flesh, behold the eternal Word!

Come now with love; beyond our comprehending
love in its fulness lies in mortal span!
How should we love, whom Love is so befriending?
Love rich in mercy since our race began
   now stoops to save us, sighs and sorrows ending,
   Jesus our Saviour, Son of God made man.

DEAR LORD, WHO BORE OUR WEIGHT OF WOE

DEAR Lord, who bore our weight of woe
   and for our pardon died,
incline our hearts to feel and know
   those arms yet open wide.

Those loving arms enfold us still
   nor turn one soul away;
to him who welcomes all who will
   we come anew today.

In penitence and faith we come
   on Jesus' promise stayed:
of all our sin, the final sum
   for love alone he paid.

He paid what none may comprehend;
   what all have lost, restored;
the sinner's advocate and friend,
   our gracious loving Lord.

Our loving Lord! We rest within
   that Name all names above,
for vaster far than all our sin
   is Christ our Saviour's love.

DONKEY PLOD AND MARY RIDE

DONKEY plod and Mary ride,
    weary Joseph walk beside,
theirs the way that all men come,
dark the night and far from home—
    down the years remember them,
    come away to Bethlehem.

Mary's child, on Christmas Eve,
none but ox and ass receive;
theirs the manger and the stall
where is laid the Lord of all—
    down the years remember them,
    come away to Bethlehem.

Angels throng the midnight sky:
'Glory be to God on high'.
Theirs the song that sounds abroad,
'Born a Saviour, Christ the Lord'—
    down the years remember them,
    come away to Bethlehem.

Shepherds haste the watch to keep
where their Maker lies asleep;
theirs the angels' promised sign,
'Born for us a child divine'—
    down the years remember them,
    come away to Bethlehem.

Ancient kings from eastern skies
trace the way of all the wise,
theirs the shining star, to find
light to lighten all mankind—
    down the years remember them,
    come away to Bethlehem.

Shepherds, kings and angel throngs,
teach us where our joy belongs:
souls restored and sins forgiven,
Christ on earth the hope of heaven—
    down the years rejoice in them,
    come away to Bethlehem.

USA © 1984 in LIFT EVERY HEART by Hope Publishing Company, Carol Stream, IL 60188
World outside USA © 1976 by Timothy Dudley-Smith

EVERY HEART ITS TRIBUTE PAYS

based on Psalm 65

EVERY heart its tribute pays,
    every tongue its song of praise;
sin and sorrow, guilt and care,
brought to him who answers prayer;
there by grace may all mankind
full and free forgiveness find;
called and chosen, loved and blest,
in his presence be at rest.

Ever while his deeds endure
our salvation stands secure;
He whose fingers spun the earth,
gave the seas and mountains birth,
tamed the ocean, formed the land,
spread the skies with mighty hand—
far-off shores revere his Name,
day and night his power proclaim.

Year by year, the seasons' round
sees the land with blessing crowned,
where caressed by sun and rain
barren earth gives life again;
sunlit valleys burn with gold,
nature smiles on field and fold,
byre and barn with plenty stored—
All things living, Praise the Lord!

USA © 1984 in LIFT EVERY HEART by Hope Publishing Company, Carol Stream, IL 60188
World outside USA © 1979 by Timothy Dudley-Smith

FAITHFUL VIGIL ENDED

*based on the New English Bible
translation of the Nunc Dimittis,
Luke 2, 29–32*

FAITHFUL vigil ended,
    watching, waiting cease;
Master, grant thy servant
his discharge in peace.

All the Spirit promised,
all the Father willed,
now these eyes behold it
perfectly fulfilled.

This thy great deliverance
sets thy people free;
Christ their light uplifted
all the nations see.

Christ, thy people's glory!
watching, doubting cease;
grant to us thy servants
our discharge in peace.

FAITHFUL VIGIL ENDED

*based on the New English Bible
translation of the Nunc Dimittis,
Luke 2, 29–32*

(alternative version)

FAITHFUL vigil ended,
   watching, waiting cease;
Master, grant your servant
his discharge in peace.

All the Spirit promised,
all the Father willed,
now these eyes behold it
perfectly fulfilled.

This your great deliverance
sets your people free;
Christ their light uplifted
all the nations see.

Christ, your people's glory!
watching, doubting cease;
grant to us your servants
our discharge in peace.

FATHER, NOW BEHOLD US

for the baptism of a child

FATHER, now behold us
and this child, we pray:
in your love enfold us,
wash our sins away.

Christ's eternal blessing
for this life we claim:
faith, by ours, professing;
signed in Jesus' Name.

By the Spirit tended
childhood grow to youth,
from all ill defended,
full of grace and truth.

God of all creation,
stoop from heaven's throne,
and by Christ's salvation
make this child your own.

FATHER OF LIGHTS, WHO BROUGHT TO BIRTH

FATHER of lights, who brought to birth
    from waste of waters, ordered earth;
from void and darkness, sunlit day;
    let there be light for us who pray.

Let there be light of faith and love,
    perpetual radiance from above,
assuring faith that God is good
    and love secure in Fatherhood.

He does not change; his splendour bright
    no turning shadow fades to night.
His glories burn, his mercies shine,
    one pure unvaried light divine.

Let there be light of heart and mind,
    the narrow path of truth to find;
the Spirit's light that all obey
    who walk with Christ in wisdom's way.

Father of lights, whose glory lies
    in light unseen by mortal eyes,
let there be light for us who call
    till Christ our Light be all in all.

USA © 1984 in LIFT EVERY HEART by Hope Publishing Company, Carol Stream, IL 60188
World outside USA © 1976 by Timothy Dudley-Smith

FATHER ON HIGH TO WHOM WE PRAY

FATHER on high to whom we pray
and lift our thankful hearts above,
for all your mercies day by day,
for gifts of hearth and home and love—
protect them still beneath your care:
Lord in your mercy, hear our prayer.

O Christ who came as man to earth
and chose in Egypt's land to be
a homeless child of alien birth,
an exile and a refugee—
for homeless people everywhere,
Lord in your mercy, hear our prayer.

Spirit divine, whose work is done
in souls renewed and lives restored,
strive in our hearts to make us one,
one faith, one family, one Lord—
till at the last one home we share:
Lord in your mercy, hear our prayer.

FATHER WHO FORMED THE FAMILY OF MAN

based on the Lord's prayer

FATHER who formed the family of man,
    high throned in heaven, evermore the same,
our prayer is still, as Christian prayer began,
that hallowed be your Name.

Lord of all lords, the only King of kings,
before whose countenance all speech is dumb,
hear the one song the new creation sings—
your promised kingdom come.

Father of mercy, righteousness and love,
shown in the sending of that only Son,
we ask on earth, as in the realms above,
your perfect will be done.

Lord of the harvest and the living seed,
the Father's gift from which the world is fed,
to us your children grant for every need
this day our daily bread.

Father, whose Son ascended now in heaven
gave once himself upon a cross to win
man's whole salvation, as we have forgiven,
forgive us all our sin.

Lord of all might and majesty and power,
our true Deliverer and our great Reward,
from every evil, and the tempter's hour,
deliver us, good Lord.

Father who formed the family of man,
yours is the glory heaven and earth adore,
the kingdom and the power, since time began,
now and for evermore.

FILL YOUR HEARTS WITH JOY AND GLADNESS

based on Psalm 147

FILL your hearts with joy and gladness,
sing and praise your God and mine!
Great the Lord in love and wisdom,
might and majesty divine!
He who framed the starry heavens
knows and names them as they shine!

Praise the Lord, his people, praise him!
Wounded souls his comfort know.
Those who fear him find his mercies,
peace for pain and joy for woe;
humble hearts are high exalted,
human pride and power laid low.

Praise the Lord for times and seasons,
cloud and sunshine, wind and rain;
spring to melt the snows of winter
till the waters flow again;
grass upon the mountain pastures,
golden valleys thick with grain.

Fill your hearts with joy and gladness,
peace and plenty crown your days;
love his laws, declare his judgments,
walk in all his words and ways,
he the Lord and we his children;
praise the Lord, all people, praise!

FROM AFAR A COCK IS CROWING

FROM afar a cock is crowing,
  every star is paler showing,
  night is on the wane;
dark is done, the dawn is breaking,
with the sun the world is waking,
  life is come again!

Gone is gloom and grief despairing!
See the tomb the truth declaring
  as the Saviour said:
Christ at last, his work completed,
passion past and death defeated,
  risen from the dead!

All the powers of darkness broken,
life is ours, from death awoken,
  born to joy again.
Open lies our ancient prison:
come, arise, with Jesus risen,
  and with Jesus reign!

FRUITFUL TREES, THE SPIRIT'S SOWING

based on Galatians 5. 22, 3

FRUITFUL trees, the Spirit's sowing,
  may we ripen and increase,
fruit to life eternal growing,
rich in love and joy and peace.

Laden branches freely bearing
gifts the Giver loves to bless;
here is fruit that grows by sharing,
patience, kindness, gentleness.

Rooted deep in Christ our Master,
Christ our pattern and our goal,
teach us, as the years fly faster,
goodness, faith and self-control.

Fruitful trees, the Spirit's tending,
may we grow till harvests cease;
till we taste, in life unending,
heaven's love and joy and peace.

USA © 1984 in LIFT EVERY HEART by Hope Publishing Company, Carol Stream, IL 60188
World outside USA © 1981 by Timothy Dudley-Smith

GLORY TO GOD IN THE HIGHEST

based on the Gloria in Excelsis

GLORY to God in the highest,
  rejoice in the praise of his worth!
Glory to God in the highest,
  all creatures of heavenly birth!
Glory to God in the highest,
  and peace to his people on earth!

Worship the Lord, the Almighty;
  devotion and thankfulness bring.
'Praise be to God for his glory
  and peace to his people', we sing;
'Glory to God in the highest,
  the Father and heavenly King.'

Jesus, the Christ, the Redeemer,
  the Son of the Father on high;
led as a lamb to the slaughter,
  the Lord who was willing to die;
God in the heavenly places,
  'Have mercy upon us', we cry.

Christ and he only is holy,
  the Lord whose dominion we own;
one with the Father and Spirit,
  most high, everlasting, alone;
reigning eternal in glory,
  the glory of God on his throne.

GOD IS KING! THE LORD IS REIGNING

based on Psalm 93

GOD is King! The Lord is reigning,
  might and majesty his robe;
to his seat on high ascended,
girded round with glory splendid,
there in time and space sustaining
  this our star-encircled globe.
Foreordained and founded fast,
evermore his throne shall last!

God is King! In storm and thunder
  wind and tide their warfare wage;
bursting seas and breakers towering,
pounding surge the rocks devouring,
lightning rending skies asunder,
  ocean's roar and tempest's rage.
Mightier far than sea or sky
stands the throne of God on high!

God is King! Let earth adore him,
  changeless still his sure decree.
Throned beyond our mortal telling,
holiness and truth his dwelling,
come with trembling hearts before him,
  bow the head and bend the knee,
where the ransomed ever raise
God's imperishable praise!

GOD IS MY GREAT DESIRE

based on Psalm 63

GOD is my great desire,
his face I seek the first;
to him my heart and soul aspire,
for him I thirst.
As one in desert lands,
whose very flesh is flame,
in burning love I lift my hands
and bless his Name.

God is my true delight,
my richest feast his praise,
through silent watches of the night,
through all my days.
To him my spirit clings,
on him my soul is cast;
beneath the shadow of his wings
he holds me fast.

God is my strong defence
in every evil hour;
in him I face with confidence
the tempter's power.
I trust his mercy sure,
with truth and triumph crowned:
my hope and joy for evermore
in him are found.

GOD OF ETERNAL GRACE

G OD of eternal grace
  in whom our spirits move,
we come to seek a Father's face—
  to rest within his love.

God of all truth and light
  from everlasting days,
who formed and lit the starry height,
  enlighten all our ways.

God of all joy and peace
  to whom all peace belongs,
our faith renew, our hope increase,
  and praise be all our songs.

God of all power and might,
  give us whom Christ has freed
the Spirit's strength to walk aright
  in thought and word and deed

God of unchanging love
  who wears a Father's face—
we sing with all the saints above
  his glory and his grace.

GOD OF GODS, WE SOUND HIS PRAISES

based on the Te Deum

God of gods, we sound his praises,
  highest heaven its homage brings;
earth and all creation raises
glory to the King of kings.
  Holy, holy, holy name him,
  Lord of all his hosts proclaim him,
to the everlasting Father
  every tongue in triumph sings.

Christians in their hearts enthrone him,
tell his praises wide abroad;
prophets, priests, apostles own him
martyrs' crown and saints' reward.
  Three in one his glory sharing,
  earth and heaven his praise declaring,
praise the high majestic Father,
  praise the everlasting Lord.

Hail the Christ, the King of glory,
he whose praise the angels cry,
born to share our human story,
love and labour, grieve and die.
  By his cross his work completed,
  sinners ransomed, death defeated,
in the glory of the Father
  Christ ascended reigns on high.

Lord, we look for your returning,
teach us so to walk your ways,
hearts and minds your will discerning,
lives alight with joy and praise.
  In your love and care enfold us,
  by your constancy uphold us,
may your mercy, Lord and Father,
  keep us now and all our days.

USA © 1973 by Hope Publishing Company, Carol Stream, IL 60188
World outside USA © 1970 by Timothy Dudley-Smith

GOD OF OLD, WHOM SAINTS AND SAGES

G OD of old, whom saints and sages,
    priests and prophets, trembling heard,
at whose voice, in distant ages
    hearts with dread and wonder stirred,
still to us in Scripture's pages
    speaks his true and living word.

Word of grace and peace, extending
    mercy to our souls' despair,
word of firm assurance, lending
    wings of faith to fervent prayer,
word of loving power, defending
    children of our Father's care.

Word of God in flesh declaring
    love that stoops to human aid,
Lamb of God our burden bearing
    till the price of sin was paid,
Son of God our nature sharing,
    in the Scriptures stand portrayed.

Gracious word of invitation,
    promised pledge of hope restored,
royal law for all creation,
    lamp of life and Spirit's sword,
tell of Christ, our souls' salvation,
    Christ the Scriptures' theme and Lord.

USA © 1984 in LIFT EVERY HEART by Hope Publishing Company, Carol Stream, IL 60188
World outside USA © 1979 by Timothy Dudley-Smith

HAD HE NOT LOVED US

HAD he not loved us
     he had never come,
yet is he love
     and love is all his way;
low to the mystery
     of the virgin's womb
Christ bows his glory—
     born on Christmas Day.

Had he not loved us
     he had never come;
had he not come
     he need have never died
nor won the victory
     of the vacant tomb,
the awful triumph
     of the Crucified.

Had he not loved us
     he had never come;
still were we lost
     in sorrow, sin and shame,
the doors fast shut
     on our eternal home
which now stand open—
     for he loved and came.

USA © 1984 in LIFT EVERY HEART by Hope Publishing Company, Carol Stream, IL 60188
World outside USA © 1969 Timothy Dudley-Smith

HE COMES TO US AS ONE UNKNOWN

H E comes to us as one unknown,
    a breath unseen, unheard;
as though within a heart of stone,
or shrivelled seed in darkness sown,
    a pulse of being stirred.

He comes when souls in silence lie
    and thoughts of day depart;
half-seen upon the inward eye,
a falling star across the sky
    of night within the heart.

He comes to us in sound of seas,
    the ocean's fume and foam;
yet small and still upon the breeze,
a wind that stirs the tops of trees,
    a voice to call us home.

He comes in love as once he came
    by flesh and blood and birth;
to bear within our mortal frame
a life, a death, a saving Name,
    for every child of earth.

He comes in truth when faith is grown;
    believed, obeyed, adored:
the Christ in all the Scriptures shown,
as yet unseen, but not unknown,
    our Saviour and our Lord.

USA © 1984 in LIFT EVERY HEART by Hope Publishing Company, Carol Stream, IL 60188
World outside USA © 1982 by Timothy Dudley-Smith

HE WALKS AMONG THE GOLDEN LAMPS

based on Revelation 1. 12–18

H E walks among the golden lamps
on feet like burnished bronze;
his hair as snows of winter white,
his eyes with fire aflame, and bright
his glorious robe of seamless light
surpassing Solomon's.

And in his hand the seven stars
and from his mouth a sword:
his voice the thunder of the seas;
all creatures bow to his decrees
who holds the everlasting keys
and reigns as sovereign Lord.

More radiant than the sun at noon,
who was, and is to be:
who was, from everlasting days;
who lives, the Lord of all our ways;
to him be majesty and praise
for all eternity.

HEAVENLY HOSTS IN CEASELESS WORSHIP

from Revelation 4 & 5

HEAVENLY hosts in ceaseless worship
'Holy, holy, holy' cry;
'he who is, who was and will be,
God Almighty, Lord most high.'
Praise and honour, power and glory,
be to him who reigns alone;
we, with all his hands have fashioned,
fall before the Father's throne.

All creation, all redemption,
join to sing the Saviour's worth;
Lamb of God, whose blood has bought us,
kings and priests, to reign on earth.
Wealth and wisdom, power and glory,
honour, might, dominion, praise,
now be his from all his creatures
and to everlasting days.

HERE WITHIN THIS HOUSE OF PRAYER

HERE within this house of prayer
   all our Father's love declare;
love that gave us birth, and planned
days and years beneath his hand:
   praise to God whose love and power
   bring us to this present hour!

Here, till earthly praises end,
tell of Christ the sinner's friend;
Christ whose blood for us was shed,
Lamb of God and living bread,
   life divine and truth and way,
   light of everlasting day.

Here may all our faint desire
feel the Spirit's wind and fire,
souls that sleep the sleep of death
stir to life beneath his breath:
   may his power upon us poured
   send us out to serve the Lord!

Here may faith and love increase,
flowing forth in joy and peace
from the Father, Spirit, Son,
undivided, three in one:
   his the glory all our days
   in this house of prayer and praise!

HIGH PEAKS AND SUNLIT PRAIRIES

HIGH peaks and sunlit prairies,
  earth's silent places, hark!
Lost caves where nothing varies
the dank and secret dark:
to oceans depths unseeing,
to circling planets dumb,
the source of all your being,
your absent Lord, is come!

Earth's countless living creatures,
all nature's legions, hark!
The myriad forms and features
that peopled Noah's ark.
In creaturehood, and sharing
the narrow gate of birth,
the news goes forth declaring
your King has come to earth!

And nature's child and master,
have we no news to hark?
No cheer against disaster,
no comfort through the dark?
A lost world's new beginning—
a dark night's blaze of morn—
to hearts grown old in sinning,
to us, a child is born.

USA © 1984 in LIFT EVERY HEART by Hope Publishing Company, Carol Stream, IL 60188
World outside USA © 1974 Timothy Dudley-Smith

HOLY CHILD

HOLY child, how still you lie!
   safe the manger, soft the hay;
faint upon the eastern sky
breaks the dawn of Christmas Day.

Holy child, whose birthday brings
shepherds from their field and fold,
angel choirs and eastern kings,
myrrh and frankincense and gold:

Holy child, what gift of grace
from the Father freely willed!
In your infant form we trace
all God's promises fulfilled.

Holy child, whose human years
span like ours delight and pain;
one in human joys and tears,
one in all but sin and stain:

Holy child, so far from home,
sons of men to seek and save,
to what dreadful death you come,
to what dark and silent grave!

Holy child, before whose Name
powers of darkness faint and fall;
conquered, death and sin and shame—
Jesus Christ is Lord of all!

Holy child, how still you lie!
safe the manger, soft the hay;
clear upon the eastern sky
breaks the dawn of Christmas Day.

USA © 1969 by Hope Publishing Company, Carol Stream, IL 60188
World outside USA © 1966 by Timothy Dudley-Smith

HOW FAINT THE STABLE-LANTERN'S LIGHT

How faint the stable-lantern's light
    but in the East afar
upon the darkness burning bright
there shines a single star.

A homeless child is brought to birth,
yet love and faith shall find
a candle lit for all the earth,
the hope of humankind;

A flame to warm the barren hearth,
a lamp for all who roam,
to shine upon the heavenward path
and light our journey home.

USA © 1983 by Hope Publishing Company, Carol Stream, IL 60188
World outside USA © 1979 by Timothy Dudley-Smith

HOW SHALL THEY HEAR, WHO HAVE NOT HEARD

'*How shall they hear*,' who have not heard
  news of a Lord who loved and came;
nor known his reconciling word,
nor learned to trust a Saviour's Name?

'*To all the world*,' to every place,
neighbours and friends and far-off lands,
preach the good news of saving grace;
go while the great commission stands.

'*Whom shall I send?*' Who hears the call,
constant in prayer, through toil and pain,
telling of one who died for all,
to bring a lost world home again?

'*Lord, here am I:*' Your fire impart
to this poor cold self-centred soul;
touch but my lips, my hands, my heart,
and make a world for Christ my goal.

Spirit of love, within us move:
Spirit of truth, in power come down!
So shall they hear and find and prove
Christ is their life, their joy, their crown.

USA © 1984 in LIFT EVERY HEART by Hope Publishing Company, Carol Stream IL 60188
World outside USA © 1979 by Timothy Dudley-Smith

HUSH YOU, MY BABY

Hush you, my baby,
    the night wind is cold.
The lambs from the hillside
are safe in the fold.
Sleep with the starlight
and wake with the morn,
    the Lord of all glory
a baby is born.

Hush you, my baby,
so soon to be grown,
watching by moonlight
on mountains alone,
toiling and travelling
so sleep while you can,
    till the Lord of all glory
is seen as a man.

Hush you, my baby,
the years will not stay;
the cross on the hilltop
the end of the way.
Dim through the darkness,
in grief and in gloom,
    the Lord of all glory
lies cold in the tomb.

Hush you, my baby,
the Father on high
in power and dominion
the darkness puts by.
Bright from the shadows,
the seal and the stone,
    the Lord of all glory
returns to his own.

Hush you, my baby,
the sky turns to gold;
the lambs on the hillside
are loose from the fold.
Fast fades the midnight
and new springs the morn,
    for the Lord of all glory
a Saviour is born.

USA © 1968 by Hope Publishing Company, Carol Stream, IL 60188
World outside USA © 1968 by Timothy Dudley-Smith

I LIFT MY EYES

based on Psalm 121

I lift my eyes
    to the quiet hills
in the press of a busy day;
    as green hills stand
    in a dusty land
so God is my strength and stay.

I lift my eyes
to the quiet hills
to a calm that is mine to share;
    secure and still
    in the Father's will
and kept by the Father's care.

I lift my eyes
to the quiet hills
with a prayer as I turn to sleep;
    by day, by night,
    through the dark and light
my Shepherd will guard his sheep.

I lift my eyes
to the quiet hills
and my heart to the Father's throne;
    in all my ways
    to the end of day
the Lord will preserve his own.

IN ENDLESS EXULTATION

IN endless exultation
    all earth unites to raise
her chorus of creation,
her ancient hymn of praise.
To tell abroad his wonders
the very stones give tongue;
by ocean's mighty thunders
the praise of God is sung.

Unnumbered creatures share it,
they make their homage heard;
the wind and storm declare it
fulfilling all his word.
Earth's varied voices blending
give praise to God on high,
one anthem never-ending
from earth and sea and sky.

In solemn high thanksgiving
his Name be now adored,
and bless with all things living
our Saviour and our Lord.
Sing out with all creation
the song of saints above,
to God our great salvation
whose very Name is Love.

USA © 1984 in LIFT EVERY HEART by Hope Publishing Company, Carol Stream, IL 60188
World outside USA © 1980 by Timothy Dudley-Smith

IN MY HOUR OF GRIEF OR NEED

based on Psalm 10

IN my hour of grief or need
  when a friend is friend indeed,
now, when Satan walks abroad,
be not far from me, O Lord.

When the powers of evil ride
through the world in open pride
flaunted sins and boasted shame
bring contempt upon your Name—

When the godless man is strong,
when his mouth is filled with wrong,
bitterness, deceit and fraud,
be not far from me, O Lord.

When the poor becomes his prey,
when the weak are led astray,
right is wrong and truth is lies—
then, O Lord our God, arise!

Powers of darkness bring to grief,
break the hold of unbelief,
sound anew the quickening word—
rise and come among us, Lord!

Then shall vice and falsehood fail,
truth and righteousness prevail,
all his ransomed people sing
God, their everlasting King!

JESUS IS THE LORD OF LIVING

JESUS is the Lord of living,
   all creation's bright array:
hearts for loving and forgiving,
ordered round of work and play—
   Jesus is the Lord of living,
   year by year and day by day.

Jesus is the Man for others,
love of God in man made plain:
those whom God created brothers
now in Christ are one again—
   Jesus is the Man for others,
   ours the pardon, his the pain.

Jesus is the Prince of glory,
love and praise to him be shown:
love for our salvation's story
praise for his eternal throne—
   Jesus is the Prince of glory,
   glory be to him alone.

USA © 1984 in LIFT EVERY HEART by Hope Publishing Company, Carol Stream, IL 60188
World outside USA © 1974 by Timothy Dudley-Smith

JESUS MY BREATH, MY LIFE, MY LORD

JESUS my breath, my life, my Lord,
   take of my soul the inmost part;
let vision, mind and will be stored
   with Christ the Master of my heart,
my breath, my life, my Lord.

Jesus my Lord, my breath, my life,
   my living bread for every day,
in calm and comfort, storm and strife,
   Christ be my truth, as Christ my way,
my Lord, my breath, my life.

Jesus my life, my Lord, my breath,
   the pulse and beat of all my years,
constant alike in life and death—
   and when eternal day appears
my life, my Lord, my breath.

USA © 1981 by Hope Publishing Company, Carol Stream, IL 60188
World outside USA © 1979 by Timothy Dudley-Smith

JESUS, PRINCE AND SAVIOUR

Jesus, Prince and Saviour,
    Lord of life who died:
Christ, the friend of sinners,
sinners crucified.
For a lost world's ransom
all himself he gave,
lay at last death's victim
lifeless in the grave.

Lord of life triumphant,
risen now to reign!
King of endless ages,
Jesus lives again!

In his power and Godhead
every victory won,
pain and passion ended,
all his purpose done:
Christ the Lord is risen!
sighs and sorrows past,
death's dark night is over,
morning comes at last!

Resurrection morning!
sinners' bondage freed.
Christ the Lord is risen—
he is risen indeed!
Jesus, Prince and Saviour,
Lord of life who died,
Christ the King of glory
now is glorified!

USA © 1984 in LIFT EVERY HEART by Hope Publishing Company, Carol Stream, IL 60188
World outside USA © 1974 by Timothy Dudley-Smith

LET HEARTS AND VOICES BLEND

L ET hearts and voices blend
the praise of Christ to sing;
our ever-living friend,
our Saviour and our King;

Our Saviour and our King,
who left his home on high,
for sinners life to bring—
a sinner's death to die;

A sinner's death to die
our rebel souls to save,
and at the last to lie
within the silent grave.

Within the silent grave
his risen power to claim:
eternal life he gave
when forth to life he came;

When forth to life he came,
whose kingdom knows no end—
to praise our Saviour's Name
let hearts and voices blend!

USA © 1984 in LIFT EVERY HEART by Hope Publishing Company, Carol Stream, IL 60188
World outside USA © 1975 by Timothy Dudley-Smith

LIGHT OF THE MINDS THAT KNOW HIM

based on a prayer from St. Augustine

LIGHT of the minds that know him,
　may Christ be light to mine!
My sun in risen splendour,
　my light of truth divine;
my guide in doubt and darkness,
　my true and living way,
my clear light ever shining,
　my dawn of heaven's day.

Life of the souls that love him,
　may Christ be ours indeed!
The living bread from heaven
　on whom our spirits feed;
who died for love of sinners
　to bear our guilty load,
and make of life's brief journey
　a new Emmaus road.

Strength of the wills that serve him,
　may Christ be strength to me,
who stilled the storm and tempest,
　who calmed the tossing sea;
his Spirit's power to move me,
　his will to master mine,
his cross to carry daily
　and conquer in his sign.

May it be ours to know him
　that we may truly love,
and loving, fully serve him
　as serve the saints above;
till in that home of glory
　with fadeless splendour bright,
we serve in perfect freedom
　our Strength, our Life, our Light.

USA © 1984 in LIFT EVERY HEART by Hope Publishing Company, Carol Stream, IL 60188
World outside USA © 1976 by Timothy Dudley-Smith

LIGHTEN OUR DARKNESS

LIGHTEN our darkness now the day is ended:
   Father in mercy, guard your children sleeping;
from every evil, every harm defended,
safe in your keeping;

To that last hour, when heaven's day is dawning,
far spent the night that knows no earthly waking;
keep us as watchmen, longing for the morning,
till that day's breaking.

LIVING LORD, OUR PRAISE WE RENDER

based on Romans 6. 5–11

Living Lord, our praise we render!
His the blood for sinners shed.
In the Father's power and splendour
Christ is risen from the dead.

Death's dominion burst and broken
by that Life which no more dies;
we to whom the Lord has spoken,
one with Christ, in freedom rise.

One with Christ, both dead and risen;
dead to self and Satan's claim,
raised from death and sin's dark prison,
sons of God through Jesus' Name.

USA © 1984 in LIFT EVERY HEART by Hope Publishing Company, Carol Stream, IL 60188
World outside USA © 1972 by Timothy Dudley-Smith

LONG BEFORE THE WORLD IS WAKING

based on John 21

Long before the world is waking,
    morning mist on Galilee,
from the shore, as dawn is breaking,
Jesus calls across the sea;
    hails the boat of weary men,
    bids them cast their net again.

So they cast, and all their heaving
cannot haul their catch aboard;
John in wonder turns, perceiving,
cries aloud, 'It is the Lord!'
    Peter waits for nothing more,
    plunges in to swim ashore.

Charcoal embers brightly burning,
bread and fish upon them laid:
Jesus stands at day's returning
in his risen life arrayed;
    as of old his friends to greet,
    'Here is breakfast; come and eat.'

Christ is risen! Grief and sighing,
sins and sorrows, fall behind;
fear and failure, doubt, denying,
full and free forgiveness find.
    All the soul's dark night is past,
    morning breaks in joy at last.

Morning breaks, and Jesus meets us,
feeds and comforts, pardons still;
as his faithful friends he greets us,
partners of his work and will.
    All our days, on every shore,
    Christ is ours for evermore!

LOOK, LORD, IN MERCY AS WE PRAY

Look, Lord, in mercy as we pray
  on tasks as yet undone;
fire us anew to seek the day
  that makes our churches one;
heirs to one work of grace divine,
  one Spirit freely given,
one pledge in sacrament and sign,
  one cross the hope of heaven.

One living faith be ours to learn
  with saints in every age,
one timeless word of truth discern
  in Scripture's sacred page.
Make us, with new resolve, begin
  one common call to own;
to be one church one world to win,
  and make one Saviour known.

Hear us who join in praise and prayer
  one act of faith to bring,
children who own one Father's care,
  soldiers who serve one King:
your kingdom come, O Lord, we pray,
  your will on earth be done;
our sins and errors purge away
  and make our churches one.

49
97
168

s the day begins
o our hearts in praise;
s all our sins,
all our ways.
step direct and guide
t in all be glorified.

work and skill,
other's need;
thought and will,
word and deed.
be set on things above
peace, in faith and love.

Spirit's strength,
lk his way;
at length
se of day.
o hour sustain and bless,
ong be thankfulness.

y begins
make it the best of days;
take from us all our sins,
guard us in all our ways.
Our every step direct and guide
that Christ in all be glorified.

USA © 1984 in LIFT EVERY HEART by Hope Publishing Company, Carol Stream, IL 60188
World outside USA © 1980 by Timothy Dudley-Smith

LORD, FOR THE YEARS

LORD, for the years your love has kept and guided,
   urged and inspired us, cheered us on our way;
sought us and saved us, pardoned and provided,
Lord of the years, we bring our thanks today.

Lord, for that word, the word of life which fires us,
speaks to our hearts and sets our souls ablaze;
teaches and trains, rebukes us and inspires us,
Lord of the word, receive your people's praise.

Lord, for our land, in this our generation,
spirits oppressed by pleasure, wealth and care;
for young and old, for commonwealth and nation,
Lord of our land, be pleased to hear our prayer.

Lord, for our world, when men disown and doubt him,
loveless in strength, and comfortless in pain;
hungry and helpless, lost indeed without him,
Lord of the world, we pray that Christ may reign.

Lord, for ourselves; in living power remake us—
self on the cross and Christ upon the throne—
past put behind us, for the future take us,
Lord of our lives, to live for Christ alone.

USA © 1969 by Hope Publishing Company, Carol Stream, IL 60188
World outside USA © 1967 by Timothy Dudley-Smith

LORD, GIVE US EYES TO SEE

a hymn for Embertide

L ORD, give us eyes to see
 in earth's unnumbered lands
today, as once in Galilee,
 the ripening harvest stands.

Lord, give us ears to heed
 and wills intent to share
that call to lay the harvest's need
 before its Lord in prayer.

Lord, give us hearts to pray
 according to his will,
that God may grant his church today
 the men to serve him still.

LORD OF THE CHURCH,
WE PRAY FOR OUR RENEWING

LORD of the church, we pray for our renewing:
Christ over all, our undivided aim.
Fire of the Spirit, burn for our enduing,
wind of the Spirit, fan the living flame!
We turn to Christ amid our fear and failing,
the will that lacks the courage to be free,
the weary labours, all but unavailing,
to bring us nearer what a church should be.

Lord of the church, we seek a Father's blessing,
a true repentance and a faith restored,
a swift obedience and a new possessing,
filled with the Holy Spirit of the Lord!
We turn to Christ from all our restless striving,
unnumbered voices with a single prayer—
the living water for our souls' reviving,
in Christ to live, and love and serve and care.

Lord of the church, we long for our uniting,
true to one calling, by one vision stirred;
one cross proclaiming and one creed reciting,
one in the truth of Jesus and his word!
So lead us on; till toil and trouble ended,
one church triumphant one new song shall sing,
to praise his glory, risen and ascended,
Christ over all, the everlasting King!

USA © 1984 in LIFT EVERY HEART by Hope Publishing Company, Carol Stream, IL 60188
World outside USA © 1976 by Timothy Dudley-Smith

LORD, WHO LEFT THE HIGHEST HEAVEN

LORD, who left the highest heaven
    for a homeless human birth
and, a child within a stable,
came to share the life of earth—
    with your grace and mercy bless
    all who suffer homelessness.

Lord, who sought by cloak of darkness
refuge under foreign skies
from the swords of Herod's soldiers,
ravaged homes, and parents' cries—
    may your grace and mercy rest
    on the homeless and oppressed.

Lord, who lived secure and settled,
safe within the Father's plan,
and in wisdom, stature, favour
growing up from boy to man—
    with your grace and mercy bless
    all who strive for holiness.

Lord, who leaving home and kindred,
followed still as duty led,
sky the roof and earth the pillow
for the Prince of glory's head—
    with your grace and mercy bless
    sacrifice for righteousness.

Lord, who in your cross and passion
hung beneath a darkened sky,
yet whose thoughts were for your mother,
and a thief condemned to die—
    may your grace and mercy rest
    on the helpless and distressed.

Lord, who rose to life triumphant
with our whole salvation won,
risen, glorified, ascended,
all the Father's purpose done—
    may your grace, all conflict past,
    bring your children home at last.

MERCY, BLESSING, FAVOUR, GRACE

based on Psalm 67, Deus Misereatur

MERCY, blessing, favour, grace,
    saving power to us be shown;
brightness of the Father's face
to the nations now be known.

Shout in triumph, sing in praise!
Peoples all, proclaim his worth.
Just and righteous are his ways,
sovereign Lord of all the earth.

Harvests year by year proclaim
blessings new in plenty poured;
all the earth shall fear his Name,
all his people praise the Lord.

NAME OF ALL MAJESTY

Name of all majesty,
    fathomless mystery,
King of the ages
by angels adored;
    power and authority,
    splendour and dignity,
    bow to his mastery—
Jesus is Lord!

Child of our destiny,
God from eternity,
love of the Father
on sinners outpoured;
    see now what God has done
    sending his only Son,
    Christ the beloved One—
Jesus is Lord!

Saviour of Calvary,
costliest victory,
darkness defeated
and Eden restored;
    born as a man to die,
    nailed to a cross on high,
    cold in the grave to lie—
Jesus is Lord!

Source of all sovereignty,
light, immortality;
life everlasting
and heaven assured;
    so with the ransomed, we
    praise him eternally,
    Christ in his majesty—
Jesus is Lord!

USA © 1984 in LIFT EVERY HEART by Hope Publishing Company, Carol Stream, IL 60188
World outside USA © 1979 by Timothy Dudley-Smith

NO TEMPLE NOW, NO GIFT OF PRICE

based on Hebrews 10. 1–25

No temple now, no gift of price,
  no priestly round of sacrifice,
    retain their ancient powers.
As shadows fade before the sun
the day of sacrifice is done,
    the day of grace is ours.

The dying Lord our ransom paid,
one final full self-offering made,
    complete in every part.
His finished sacrifice for sins
the covenant of grace begins,
    the law within the heart.

In faith and confidence draw near,
within the holiest appear,
    with all who praise and pray;
who share one family, one feast,
one great imperishable Priest,
    one new and living way.

For Christ is ours! With purpose true
the pilgrim path of faith pursue,
    the road that Jesus trod;
until by his prevailing grace
we stand at last before his face,
    our Saviour and our God.

NO TRAMP OF SOLDIERS' MARCHING FEET

No tramp of soldiers' marching feet
   with banners and with drums,
no sound of music's martial beat—
   'The King of glory comes!'
To greet what pomp of kingly pride
no bells in triumph ring,
no city gates swing open wide:
   'Behold, behold your King!'

And yet he comes. The children cheer;
with palms his path is strown.
With every step the cross draws near—
   the King of glory's throne.
Astride a colt he passes by
as loud hosannas ring,
or else the very stones would cry
   'Behold, behold your King!'

What fading flowers his road adorn;
the palms, how soon laid down!
No bloom or leaf but only thorn
   the King of glory's crown.
The soldiers mock, the rabble cries,
the streets with tumult ring,
as Pilate to the mob replies,
   'Behold, behold your King!'

Now he who bore for mortals' sake
the cross and all its pains
and chose a servant's form to take,
   the King of glory reigns.
Hosanna to the Saviour's Name
till heaven's rafters ring,
and all the ransomed host proclaim
   'Behold, behold your King!'

USA © 1984 in LIFT EVERY HEART by Hope Publishing Company, Carol Stream, IL 60188
World outside USA © 1979 by Timothy Dudley-Smith

NO WEIGHT OF GOLD OR SILVER

No weight of gold or silver
    can measure human worth;
no soul secures its ransom
with all the wealth of earth;
no sinner finds his freedom
but by the gift unpriced,
the Lamb of God unblemished,
the precious blood of Christ.

Our sins, our griefs and troubles,
he bore and made his own;
we hid our faces from him,
rejected and alone.
His wounds are for our healing,
our peace is by his pain:
behold, the Man of sorrows,
the Lamb for sinners slain.

In Christ the past is over,
a new world now begins.
With him we rise to freedom
who saves us from our sins.
We live by faith in Jesus
to make his glory known:
behold, the Man of sorrows,
the Lamb upon his throne!

USA © 1984 in LIFT EVERY HEART by Hope Publishing Company, Carol Stream, IL 60188
World outside USA © 1972 by Timothy Dudley-Smith

NOT IN LORDLY STATE AND SPLENDOUR

Not in lordly state and splendour,
lofty pomp and high renown;
infant-form his robe most royal,
lantern-light his only crown;
see the new-born King of glory,
Lord of all to earth come down!

His no rich and storied mansion,
kingly rule and sceptred sway;
from his seat in highest heaven
throned among the beasts he lay;
see the new-born King of glory
cradled in his couch of hay!

Yet the eye of faith beholds him,
King above all earthly kings;
Lord of uncreated ages,
he whose praise eternal rings—
see the new-born King of glory
panoplied by angels' wings!

Not in lordly state and splendour,
lofty pomp and high renown;
infant-form his robe most royal,
lantern-light his only crown;
Christ the new-born King of glory,
Lord of all to earth come down!

NOT TO US BE GLORY GIVEN

based on Psalm 115

NOT to us be glory given
　　but to him who reigns above:
Glory to the God of heaven
　　for his faithfulness and love!
What though unbelieving voices
　　hear no word and see no sign,
still in God my heart rejoices,
　　working out his will divine.

Not what human fingers fashion,
　　gold and silver, deaf and blind,
dead to knowledge and compassion,
　　having neither heart nor mind—
lifeless gods, yet some adore them,
　　nerveless hands and feet of clay;
all become, who bow before them,
　　lost indeed and dead as they.

Not in them is hope of blessing—
　　hope is in the living Lord!
High and low, his Name confessing,
　　find in him their shield and sword.
Hope of all whose hearts revere him,
　　God of Israel, still the same!
God of Aaron! Those who fear him,
　　he remembers them by name.

Not the dead, but we the living
　　praise the Lord with all our powers;
of his goodness freely giving—
　　his is heaven; earth is ours.
Not to us be glory given
　　but to him who reigns above:
Glory to the God of heaven
　　for his faithfulness and love!

NOW TO THE LORD WE BRING
THE CHILD HE GAVE US

for the baptism of a child

Now to the Lord we bring the child he gave us,
    for rain or shine, for laughter and for tears;
pledged to his service, who was born to save us,
    rich with the promise of the future years.

Into the threefold Name we here baptise you
    as Jesus bids by water and the word;
fast in his grace, when Satan sifts and tries you,
    child of the covenant of Christ the Lord!

True to believe and trust our living Master
    from life's bright morning to the twilight dim,
firm in the face of evil or disaster,
    Christ's faithful soldier, turned to follow him.

One with his church, though all the world deride you;
    signed with his cross, who once was sacrificed;
strong in his strength, for Jesus walks beside you,
    world without end, in company with Christ!

O CHANGELESS CHRIST, FOR EVER NEW

O changeless Christ, for ever new,
    who walked our earthly ways,
still draw our hearts as once you drew
the hearts of other days.

As once you spoke by plain and hill
or taught by shore and sea,
so be today our teacher still,
O Christ of Galilee.

As wind and storm their Master heard
and his command fulfilled,
may troubled hearts receive your word,
the tempest-tossed be stilled.

And as of old to all who prayed
your healing hand was shown,
so be your touch upon us laid,
unseen but not unknown.

In broken bread, in wine outpoured,
your new and living way
proclaim to us, O risen Lord,
O Christ of this our day.

O changeless Christ, till life is past
your blessing still be given;
then bring us home, to taste at last
the timeless joys of heaven.

O CHILD OF MARY, HARK TO HER

O Child of Mary, hark to her
and to the song she sings,
of gold and frankincense and myrrh,
the shepherds and the kings.
The light of love is in her eyes
and music on her breath,
that tells of Galilean skies,
and home, and Nazareth.

She sings of sunlight through the door,
the olive and the vine,
and shavings on the workshop floor
of resin-scented pine;
of winter stars, and fires alight,
and bed and hearth and board,
and only sometimes, in the night,
the shadow of a sword.

O sinless child, for sinners born
to suffering and loss,
the bitter nails, the cruel thorn,
the darkness and the cross;
no song, since ever time began,
can tell the path you trod,
O Son of Mary, Son of Man,
redeeming Son of God.

Yet have we songs: no death and grave,
no cross with all its pains,
can master him who died to save
and now in glory reigns;
to him, our ever-living Lord,
new songs are ours to sing:
the crown, the triumph and the sword
are yours, O Christ our King.

USA © 1984 in LIFT EVERY HEART by Hope Publishing Company, Carol Stream, IL 60188
World outside USA © 1981 by Timothy Dudley-Smith

O CHRIST THE SAME

O Christ the same, through all our story's pages,
   our loves and hopes, our failures and our fears;
eternal Lord, the King of all the ages,
unchanging still, amid the passing years—
O living Word, the source of all creation,
who spread the skies, and set the stars ablaze,
O Christ the same, who wrought our whole salvation,
we bring our thanks for all our yesterdays.

O Christ the same, the friend of sinners sharing
our inmost thoughts, the secrets none can hide,
still as of old upon your body bearing
the marks of love, in triumph glorified—
O Son of Man, who stooped for us from heaven,
O Prince of life, in all your saving power,
O Christ the same to whom our hearts are given,
we bring our thanks for this the present hour.

O Christ the same, secure within whose keeping
our lives and loves, our days and years remain,
our work and rest, our waking and our sleeping,
our calm and storm, our pleasure and our pain—
O Lord of love, for all our joys and sorrows,
for all our hopes, when earth shall fade and flee,
O Christ the same, beyond our brief tomorrows,
We bring our thanks for all that is to be.

USA © 1984 in LIFT EVERY HEART by Hope Publishing Company, Carol Stream, IL 60188
World outside USA © 1971 by Timothy Dudley-Smith

O CHRIST, WHO TAUGHT ON EARTH OF OLD

O Christ, who taught on earth of old,
  and fashioned in the tales you told
of life and truth the hidden key,
and windows on eternity,
    prepare our hearts, that in our turn
    we too may read and mark and learn.

The world of nature, death and birth,
the secrets of the fertile earth,
the ripened field, the garnered grain,
the seed that dies to live again,
    are doors in heaven, opened wide
    upon your kingdom's countryside.

Of wedding-feasts and pearls and flowers,
of debts, and half-completed towers,
of sunny slopes where vineyards grow,
we read more wisely than we know;
    for in your parables there shine
    the images of things divine.

A beggar's bowl, a robber band,
foundations built on rock or sand,
we mark them all; but one imparts
a dearer hope to human hearts:
    from that far country where we roam
    a Father's welcome calls us home.

USA © 1984 in LIFT EVERY HEART by Hope Publishing Company, Carol Stream, IL 60188
World outside USA © 1982 by Timothy Dudley-Smith

O LORD, YOURSELF DECLARE

O Lord, yourself declare,
　　our new and living way;
move all our hearts to love and prayer
and teach us how to pray:

In worship to be still,
in penitence confess,
to ask according to your will,
receive with thankfulness.

Your purposes to share,
your promises to claim,
move all our hearts to love and prayer
through faith in Jesus' Name.

O PRINCE OF PEACE

O Prince of peace whose promised birth
 the angels sang with 'Peace on earth',
peace be to us and all beside,
  peace to us all—
peace to the world this Christmastide.

O child who found to lay your head
no place but in a manger bed,
come where our doors stand open wide,
  peace to us all—
  peace to the world—
peace in our homes this Christmastide.

O Christ whom shepherds came to find,
their joy be ours in heart and mind;
let grief and care be laid aside,
  peace to us all—
  peace to the world—
  peace in our homes—
peace in our hearts this Christmastide.

O Saviour Christ, ascended Lord,
our risen Prince of life restored,
our Love who once for sinners died,
  peace to us all—
  peace to the world—
  peace in our homes—
  peace in our hearts—
peace with our God this Christmastide.

USA © 1980 by Hope Publishing Company, Carol Stream, IL 60188
World outside USA © 1978 by Timothy Dudley-Smith

O SAVIOUR CHRIST, BEYOND ALL PRICE

O Saviour Christ, beyond all price
   the debt you paid for me,
the full, sufficient sacrifice
that sets the prisoner free:
   I come to plead your saving Name,
   to make your cross my prayer,
   to own my guilt and sin and shame,
   and find forgiveness there.

O Christ, the sure and certain guide
to where my pathway lies,
the patient teacher at my side
immeasurably wise,
   I come those richest gifts to find
   that love and grace impart,
   a humble and responsive mind,
   a true and willing heart.

O Christ, companion of the way
till life's long journey ends,
you cheer us through the darkest day
and call your servants friends:
   I come to follow where you lead,
   to trust, obey, adore;
   walk with me as my friend indeed
   this day and evermore.

O sovereign Christ, the Lord of all
in loftier worlds than ours,
before whose feet in homage fall
dominions, thrones and powers,
   I come in faith before your throne,
   your ransomed child, to bring
   my very self to be your own,
   my sovereign Lord and King.

USA © 1984 in LIFT EVERY HEART by Hope Publishing Company, Carol Stream, IL 60188
World outside USA © 1978 by Timothy Dudley-Smith

OUR SAVIOUR CHRIST ONCE KNELT IN PRAYER

OUR Saviour Christ once knelt in prayer
  with none but three disciples there,
upon a lonely mountain high
beneath a blue expanse of sky—
    below them, far as eye could see,
    the little hills of Galilee.

There as he prays a radiance bright
transfigures all his form to light;
his robe in dazzling splendour shows
a purer white than sunlit snows,
    while on his countenance divine
    transcendent glories burn and shine.

So for a moment stands revealed
what human form and flesh concealed;
while Moses and Elijah share
in earth and heaven mingled there,
    with him whom prophecy foresaw,
    the true fulfiller of the law.

The shadowed summit, wrapped in cloud,
sounds to a voice that echoes loud:
'This is my true beloved Son,
listen to him, my chosen One.'
    The glory fades. With all its pains
    the road to Calvary remains.

Give to us, Lord, the eyes to see
as saw those first disciples three:
a teacher true, a friend indeed,
the risen Saviour sinners need,
    the Son whose praise eternal rings,
    the Lord of lords and King of kings!

USA © 1984 in LIFT EVERY HEART by Hope Publishing Company, Carol Stream, IL 60188
World outside USA © 1978 by Timothy Dudley-Smith

OUT OF DARKNESS LET LIGHT SHINE

based on 2 Corinthians 4.6 (NEB)

Out of darkness let light shine!
    Formless void its Lord obeyed;
at his word, by his design,
sun and moon and stars were made.

Still his brightness shines abroad;
darkened lives his light have known:
all the glories of the Lord
in the face of Christ are shown.

New creation's second birth
bids eternal night depart;
as the dawn of dawn on earth
morning breaks within the heart.

Out of darkness let light shine,
as it shone when light began;
earth be filled with light divine,
Christ be light for everyman!

USA © 1984 in LIFT EVERY HEART by Hope Publishing Company, Carol Stream, IL 60188
World outside USA © 1978 by Timothy Dudley-Smith

PRAISE BE TO CHRIST

based on Colossians 1.15–20

PRAISE be to Christ in whom we see
    the image of the Father shown,
the first-born Son revealed and known,
the truth and grace of deity;
through whom creation came to birth,
    whose fingers set the stars in place,
the unseen powers, and this small earth,
    the furthest bounds of time and space.

Praise be to him whose sovereign sway
    and will upholds creation's plan;
    who is, before all worlds began
and when our world has passed away:
Lord of the church, its life and head,
    redemption's price and source and theme,
alive, the first-born from the dead,
    to reign as all-in-all supreme.

Praise be to him who, Lord most high,
    the fulness of the Godhead shares;
    and yet our human nature bears,
who came as man to bleed and die.
And from his cross there flows our peace
    who chose for us the path he trod,
that so might sins and sorrows cease
    and all be reconciled to God.

PRAISE THE GOD OF OUR SALVATION

based on Psalm 146

Praise the God of our salvation,
   all life long your voices raise!
Stir your hearts to adoration,
set your souls to sing his praise!

Turn to him, his help entreating;
only in his mercy trust:
human pomp and power are fleeting;
mortal flesh is born for dust.

Thankful hearts his praise have sounded
down the ages long gone by:
happy they whose hopes are founded
in the God of earth and sky!

Faithful Lord of all things living,
by his bounty all are blest;
bread to hungry bodies giving,
justice to the long-oppressed.

For the strength of our salvation,
light and life and length of days,
praise the King of all creation,
set your souls to sing his praise!

PRAISE THE LORD OF HEAVEN

based on Psalm 148

Praise the Lord of heaven,
  praise him in the height;
praise him, all his angels,
praise him, hosts of light.
Sun and moon together,
shining stars aflame,
planets in their courses,
magnify his Name!

Earth and ocean praise him;
mountains, hills and trees;
fire and hail and tempest,
wind and storm and seas.
Praise him, fields and forests,
birds on flashing wings,
praise him, beasts and cattle,
all created things.

Now by prince and people
let his praise be told;
praise him, men and maidens,
praise him, young and old.
He, the Lord of glory!
We, his praise proclaim!
High above all heavens
magnify his Name!

REMEMBER, LORD, THE WORLD YOU MADE

REMEMBER, Lord, the world you made,
  for Adam's race to find
the life of heaven on earth displayed,
a home for humankind.

A home of peace: but war and strife
and hatred we confess;
where death is in the midst of life
and children fatherless.

A home of freedom: yet the flame
burns low for liberty;
and few will serve in Jesus' Name
that all men may be free.

A home of plenty: clothed and fed
our sturdy children play;
while other children cry for bread
not half the world away.

Renew our love, O Lord, and touch
our hearts to feel and care
that we who seem to have so much
so little seem to share.

For those who have no prayers to say,
who in despair are dumb,
teach us to live as well as pray
'O Lord, your kingdom come.'

SAFE IN THE SHADOW OF THE LORD

based on Psalm 91

SAFE in the shadow of the Lord
beneath his hand and power,
I trust in him,
I trust in him,
my fortress and my tower.

My hope is set on God alone
though Satan spreads his snare,
I trust in him,
I trust in him,
to keep me in his care.

From fears and phantoms of the night,
from foes about my way,
I trust in him,
I trust in him,
by darkness as by day.

His holy angels keep my feet
secure from every stone;
I trust in him,
I trust in him,
and unafraid go on.

Strong in the everlasting Name,
and in my Father's care,
I trust in him,
I trust in him,
who hears and answers prayer.

Safe in the shadow of the Lord,
possessed by love divine,
I trust in him,
I trust in him,
and meet his love with mine.

USA © 1973 by Hope Publishing Company, Carol Stream, IL 60188
World outside USA © 1970 by Timothy Dudley-Smith

SAVIOUR CHRIST

SAVIOUR Christ,
in praise we name him;
all his deeds
proclaim him:

Lamb of God
for sinners dying;
all our need
supplying:

Risen Lord
in glory seated;
all his work
completed:

King of kings
ascended, reigning;
all the world
sustaining:

Christ is all!
Rejoice before him:
evermore
adore him!

USA © 1984 in LIFT EVERY HEART by Hope Publishing Company, Carol Stream, IL 60188
World outside USA © 1982 by Timothy Dudley-Smith

SEE, TO US A CHILD IS BORN

a Christmas antiphon
based on Isaiah 9.6, 7

Choir
(or solo) See, to us a child is born—
All   *Glory breaks on Christmas morn!*

Choir Now to us a Son is given—
All   *Praise to God in highest heaven!*

Choir On his shoulder rule shall rest—
All   *In him all the earth be blest!*

Choir Wise and wonderful his Name—
All   *Heaven's Lord in human frame!*

Choir Mighty God, who mercy brings—
All   *Lord of lords and King of kings!*

Choir Father of eternal days—
All   *Every creature sing his praise!*

Choir Everlasting Prince of peace—
All   *Truth and righteousness increase!*

Choir He shall reign from shore to shore—
All   *Christ is King for evermore!*

SERVANTS OF THE LIVING LORD

based on Psalm 113

SERVANTS of the living Lord,
    bend in awe before his throne,
tell his majesty abroad,
know and name him God alone.
    Join to praise the Lord of grace,
    all who stand before his face.

Age to age, his Name be blest,
Ancient of eternal days.
Furthest bounds of east and west
echo his perpetual praise.
    Everliving Lord of grace,
    throned beyond all time and space.

Who like him in glory reigns
higher than the heavens are high?
He who world on world sustains,
sun and stars and sea and sky.
    He it is who, Lord of grace,
    hears from heaven his dwelling-place.

Lord of grace! In him we trust!
By his love the lost are found,
lowly lifted from the dust,
happy homes with children crowned.
    All who stand before his face,
    praise, O praise, the Lord of grace!

USA © 1984 in LIFT EVERY HEART by Hope Publishing Company, Carol Stream, IL 60188
World outside USA © 1983 by Timothy Dudley-Smith

SET YOUR TROUBLED HEARTS AT REST

from John 14.1 (NEB)

'SET your troubled hearts at rest'—
  hear again the word divine;
all our Father does is best;
  let his peace be yours and mine.

Trusting still in God above,
  set your troubled hearts at rest;
find within a Father's love
  comfort for a soul distressed.

When you come to make request
  know that God will answer prayer;
set your troubled hearts at rest,
  safe within a Father's care.

Be at peace, then, and rejoice,
  loved and comforted and blessed;
hear again the Saviour's voice;
  'Set your troubled hearts at rest.'

SING A NEW SONG TO THE LORD

based on Psalm 98, Cantate Domino

SING a new song to the Lord,
    he to whom wonders belong!
Rejoice in his triumph and tell of his power—
    O sing to the Lord a new song!

Now to the ends of the earth
see his salvation is shown;
and still he remembers his mercy and truth,
    unchanging in love to his own.

Sing a new song and rejoice,
    publish his praises abroad!
Let voices in chorus, with trumpet and horn,
    resound for the joy of the Lord!

Join with the hills and the sea
    thunders of praise to prolong!
In judgment and justice he comes to the earth—
    O sing to the Lord a new song!

SPIRIT OF GOD WITHIN ME

SPIRIT of God within me,
    possess my human frame;
fan the dull embers of my heart,
stir up the living flame.
Strive till that image Adam lost,
new minted and restored,
in shining splendour brightly bears
the likeness of the Lord.

Spirit of truth within me,
possess my thought and mind;
lighten anew the inward eye
by Satan rendered blind;
shine on the words that wisdom speaks
and grant me power to see
the truth made known to men in Christ
and in that truth be free.

Spirit of love within me,
possess my hands and heart;
break through the bonds of self-concern
that seeks to stand apart:
grant me the love that suffers long,
that hopes, believes and bears,
the love fulfilled in sacrifice
that cares as Jesus cares.

Spirit of life within me,
possess this life of mine;
come as the wind of heaven's breath,
come as the fire divine!
Spirit of Christ, the living Lord,
reign in this house of clay,
till from its dust with Christ I rise
to everlasting day.

STARS OF HEAVEN, CLEAR AND BRIGHT

STARS of heaven, clear and bright,
shine upon this Christmas night.
Vaster far than midnight skies
are its timeless mysteries.
Trampled earth and stable floor
lift the heart to heaven's door—
God has sent to us his Son,
earth and heaven meet as one.

Sleepy sounds of beast and byre
mingle with the angel choir.
Highest heaven bends in awe
where he lies amid the straw,
who from light eternal came
aureoled in candle-flame—
God has sent to us his Son,
earth and heaven meet as one.

Wide-eyed shepherds mutely gaze
at the child whom angels praise.
Threefold gifts the wise men bring,
to the infant priest and king:
to the Lord immortal, myrrh
for an earthly sepulchre—
God has sent to us his Son,
earth and heaven meet as one.

Heaven of heavens hails his birth,
King of glory, child of earth,
born in flesh to reign on high,
Prince of life to bleed and die.
Throned on Mary's lap he lies,
Lord of all eternities—
God has sent to us his Son,
earth and heaven meet as one.

'Glory be to God on high,
peace on earth,' the angels cry.
Ancient enmities at rest,
ransomed, reconciled and blest,
in the peace of Christ we come,
come we joyful, come we home—
God has sent to us his Son,
earth and heaven meet as one.

USA © 1984 in LIFT EVERY HEART by Hope Publishing Company, Carol Stream, IL 60188
World outside USA © 1983 by Timothy Dudley-Smith

TELL HIS PRAISE IN SONG AND STORY

based on Psalm 34

TELL his praise in song and story,
　　bless the Lord with heart and voice;
in my God is all my glory,
　　come before him and rejoice.
Join to praise his Name together,
　　he who hears his people's cry;
tell his praise, come wind or weather,
　　shining faces lifted high.

To the Lord whose love has found them
　　cry the poor in their distress;
swift his angels camped around them
　　prove him sure to save and bless.
God it is who hears our crying
　　though the spark of faith be dim;
taste and see! Beyond denying
　　blest are those who trust in him.

Taste and see! In faith draw near him,
　　trust the Lord with all your powers;
seek and serve him, love and fear him,
　　life and all its joys are ours—
true delight in holy living,
　　peace and plenty, length of days;
come, my children, with thanksgiving
　　bless the Lord in songs of praise.

In our need he walks beside us,
　　ears alert to every cry;
watchful eyes to guard and guide us,
　　love that whispers 'It is I'.
Good shall triumph, wrong be righted,
　　God has pledged his promised word;
so with ransomed saints united
　　join to praise our living Lord.

USA © 1984 in LIFT EVERY HEART by Hope Publishing Company, Carol Stream, IL 60188
World outside USA © 1976 by Timothy Dudley-Smith

TELL OUT, MY SOUL

based on the New English Bible
translation of the Magnificat
St. Luke 1. 46–55

TELL out, my soul, the greatness of the Lord!
　　Unnumbered blessings, give my spirit voice;
tender to me the promise of his word;
in God my Saviour shall my heart rejoice.

Tell out, my soul, the greatness of his Name!
Make known his might, the deeds his arm has done;
his mercy sure, from age to age the same;
his holy Name—the Lord, the Mighty One.

Tell out, my soul, the greatness of his might!
Powers and dominions lay their glory by.
Proud hearts and stubborn wills are put to flight,
the hungry fed, the humble lifted high.

Tell out, my soul, the glories of his word!
Firm is his promise, and his mercy sure.
Tell out, my soul, the greatness of the Lord
to children's children and for evermore!

THANKFUL OF HEART

THANKFUL of heart for days gone by,
    mirrored in memory's inward eye;
childhood and youth, their hopes and fears,
stored with the tale of all the years;
stilled from the storms of joy and pain
chiefly the sunlit hours remain—
    Come then, as Christian people should,
    give thanks to God: for God is good.

Thankful to welcome, day by day,
tokens of love about our way;
and from a Father's hand to trace
blessings of nature and of grace.
Treasures on earth let time destroy!
Christ is our love, our peace, our joy.
    Come then, as Christian people should,
    rejoice in God: for God is good.

Thankful we look for days to be,
part of a purpose none foresee;
firm in the faith of sins forgiven,
Christ and his cross our hope of heaven;
Christ at the last our great reward,
Christ over all, ascended Lord!
    Come then, as Christian people should,
    hope still in God: for God is good.

USA © 1984 in LIFT EVERY HEART by Hope Publishing Company, Carol Stream, IL 60188
World outside USA © 1979 by Timothy Dudley-Smith

THE DARKNESS TURNS TO DAWN

THE darkness turns to dawn,
    the dayspring shines from heaven,
for unto us a child is born,
to us a Son is given.

The Son of God most high,
before all else began,
a virgin's Son behold him lie,
the new-born Son of Man.

God's Word of truth and grace
made flesh with us to dwell;
the brightness of the Father's face,
the child Emmanuel.

How rich his heavenly home!
How poor his human birth!
As mortal man he stoops to come,
the light and life of earth.

A servant's form, a slave,
the Lord consents to share;
our sin and shame, our cross and grave,
he bows himself to bear.

Obedient and alone
upon that cross to die—
and then to share the Father's throne
in majesty on high.

And still God sheds abroad
that love so strong to send
a Saviour, who is Christ the Lord,
whose reign shall never end.

THE HEAVENS ARE SINGING

based on echoes of Isaiah 44 & 45

THE heavens are singing, are singing and praising,
the depths of the earth and the mountains rejoice;
the trees and the forests are raising, are raising
the song of creation in thunderous voice!

The sun in his rising, his rising and setting,
the stars in their courses, their Maker proclaim.
We only, his children, forgetting, forgetting
the love of our Father, have turned to our shame.

For he is the Father, the Father who made us,
who founded and fashioned the earth and the sky;
who stooped from his glory to aid us, to aid us
when yet we were sinners deserving to die.

O Father eternal, eternally living,
resplendent in glory, the Lord on his throne,
we praise and adore you, forgiving, forgiving,
none other beside you, in mercy alone!

THE HEAVENS ARE SINGING

based on echoes of Isaiah 44 & 45

(Alternative version)

THE heavens are singing, are singing and praising,
   the depths of the earth and the mountains rejoice;
the trees and the forests are raising, are raising
the song of creation in thunderous voice;
   for God has redeemed us,
   redeemed us and bought us,
remembered his people, and made us his choice!

The sun in his rising, his rising and setting,
the stars in their courses, their Maker proclaim.
We only, his children, forgetting, forgetting,
the love of our Father, have turned to our shame;
   yet God has redeemed us,
   redeemed us and bought us,
remembered his people, and called us by name!

For he is the Father, the Father who made us,
who founded and fashioned the earth and the sky;
who stooped from his glory to aid us, to aid us
when yet we were sinners deserving to die;
   our God has redeemed us,
   redeemed us and bought us,
remembered his people, and lifted us high!

O Father eternal, eternally living,
resplendent in glory, the Lord on his throne,
we praise and adore you, forgiving, forgiving,
none other beside you, in mercy alone;
   for God has redeemed us,
   redeemed us and bought us,
remembered his people, and made us his own!

THE LORD IN WISDOM MADE THE EARTH

THE Lord in wisdom made the earth,
    our sky and sea and land,
and gave the furthest stars their birth,
unnumbered as the sand:
    beyond all worlds, all stars and skies,
    he reigns all-loving and all-wise.

Beneath his hand the seasons turn,
he rules the wind and tide;
for him the fires of nature burn,
the cells of life divide.
    Creation moves as he decrees
    and wisely works its mysteries.

By him the lamps of reason shine,
the laws of life are told;
within his purposes divine
our destinies unfold.
    In love and wisdom, Lord, fulfil
    and work in us your perfect will.

So make us wise, in Christ to trust,
in truth to walk his ways,
the Wise, the Righteous and the Just
from everlasting days:
    redeeming Son, eternal Word,
    the Power and Wisdom of the Lord.

THE LORD MADE MAN

THE Lord made man, the Scriptures tell,
  to bear his image and his sign;
yet we by nature share as well
the ancient mark of Adam's line.

In Adam's fall falls every man,
with every gift the Father gave:
the crown of all creation's plan
becomes a rebel and a slave.

Herein all woes are brought to birth,
all aching hearts and sunless skies:
brightness is gone from all the earth,
the innocence of nature dies.

Yet Adam's children, born to pain,
by self enslaved, by sin enticed,
still may by grace be born again,
children of God, beloved in Christ.

In Christ is Adam's ransom met;
earth, by his cross, is holy ground;
Eden indeed is with us yet!
In Christ are life and freedom found!

THE SHINING STARS UNNUMBERED

THE shining stars unnumbered
    on Bethlehem looked down;
unnumbered too the travellers
    who thronged to David's town;
no place to rest, no room to spare,
but what the ox and ass may share
    for Mary's Son so tender;
she laid him in a manger there,
    the Crown of heaven's splendour!

While earth lies hushed and sleeping
    nor dreams of Jesus' birth,
hushed deep in new-born slumbers
    lies he who made the earth;
and from that stable through the night
there shines a lantern burning bright,
    a sign for mortals' seeing,
that Christ is come, the Light of light,
    the Lord of all our being!

A sound of angels singing
    the watching shepherds heard;
our songs of praise are bringing
    anew the promised word;
so let all hearts be joyful when
we hear what angels carolled then
    and tell the Christmas story,
of peace on earth, goodwill to men,
    through Christ the King of glory!

USA © 1983 by Hope Publishing Company, Carol Stream, IL 60188
World outside USA © 1976 by Timothy Dudley-Smith

THE STARS DECLARE HIS GLORY

based on Psalm 19

THE stars declare his glory;
   the vault of heaven springs
mute witness of the Master's hand
   in all created things,
and through the silences of space
   their soundless music sings.

The dawn returns in splendour,
   the heavens burn and blaze,
the rising sun renews the race
   that measures all our days,
and writes in fire across the skies
   God's majesty and praise.

So shine the Lord's commandments
   to make the simple wise;
more sweet than honey to the taste,
   more rich than any prize,
a law of love within our hearts,
   a light before our eyes.

So order too this life of mine,
   direct it all my days;
the meditations of my heart
   be innocence and praise,
my rock, and my redeeming Lord,
   in all my words and ways.

THE WILL OF GOD TO MARK MY WAY

based on selected verses from Psalm 119

THE will of God to mark my way,
  the word of God for light;
eternal justice to obey
  in everlasting right.

Your eyes of mercy keep me still,
  your gracious love be mine;
so work in me your perfect will
  and cause your face to shine.

With ordered step secure and strong,
  from sin's oppression freed,
redeemed from every kind of wrong
  in thought and word and deed—

So set my heart to love your word
  and every promise prove,
to walk with truth before the Lord
  in righteousness and love.

THIS CHILD FROM GOD ABOVE

for the baptism of a child

THIS child from God above,
the Father's gift divine—
to this new life of light and love
we give his seal and sign;

To bear the eternal Name,
to walk the Master's way,
the Father's covenant to claim,
the Spirit's will obey;

To take the Saviour's cross,
in faith to hold it fast;
and for it reckon all things loss
as long as life shall last;

To tell his truth abroad,
to tread the path he trod,
with all who love and serve the Lord—
the family of God.

THIS DAY ABOVE ALL DAYS

THIS day above all days
    glad hymns of triumph bring;
lift every heart to love and praise
and every voice to sing:
    for Jesus is risen
our glorious Lord and King!

Christ keeps his Eastertide!
The Father's power descends;
the shuttered tomb he opens wide,
the rock-hewn grave he rends:
    for Jesus is risen
and death's dominion ends!

What sovereign grace is found
in Christ for all our need!
The powers of sin and death are bound,
the ransomed captives freed:
    for Jesus is risen
the Prince of life indeed!

So lift your joyful songs
with all the hosts on high,
where angel and archangel throngs
his ceaseless praises cry:
    for Jesus is risen
and lives no more to die!

USA © 1984 in LIFT EVERY HEART by Hope Publishing Company, Carol Stream, IL 60188
World outside USA © 1977 by Timothy Dudley-Smith

TIMELESS LOVE! WE SING THE STORY

based on Psalm 89, verses 1–18

TIMELESS love! We sing the story,
   praise his wonders, tell his worth;
love more fair than heaven's glory,
love more firm than ancient earth!
   Tell his faithfulness abroad:
   who is like him? Praise the Lord!

By his faithfulness surrounded,
North and South his hand proclaim;
earth and heaven formed and founded,
skies and seas, declare his Name!
   Wind and storm obey his word:
   who is like him? Praise the Lord!

Truth and righteousness enthrone him,
just and equal are his ways;
more than happy, those who own him,
more than joy, their songs of praise!
   Sun and Shield and great Reward:
   who is like him? Praise the Lord!

TO CHRIST OUR KING

To Christ our King in songs of praise
    lift every heart and mind;
unfading light of all our days,
    true life of humankind.

O Christ our Light, draw near and fill
    this shadowed soul of mine;
renew my darkened heart and will
    to light and life divine.

O Christ our Life, from death and sin
    my forfeit soul set free;
that life laid down a world to win
    be life indeed for me.

O Christ our King, to whom we give
    again the life you gave,
tell out by us that all may live
    through Christ who died to save.

May Christ, our Light, our Life, our King,
    make all our hearts his own,
join all our lives his praise to sing,
    and make his glories known.

USA © 1984 in LIFT EVERY HEART by Hope Publishing Company, Carol Stream, IL 60188
World outside USA © 1976 by Timothy Dudley-Smith

TO HEATHEN DREAMS OF HUMAN PRIDE

based on Psalm 2

To heathen dreams of human pride
   rebellious nations cling:
the kindly rule of God defied,
and his anointed King.
   'Throw off your fetters, burst your chain'
   the dreamers call; and call in vain.

For God enthroned above the skies
shall laugh his foes to scorn:
'On Zion's hill your king shall rise,
My Son a King is born!
   Before his sceptre none can stand
   and all the world is in his hand.'

Let humble hearts this lesson learn
and bow before his throne;
in true and trembling homage turn,
and name him Lord alone.
   O happy hearts, with wisdom blest,
   who trust in him, and in him rest!

USA © 1984 in LIFT EVERY HEART by Hope Publishing Company, Carol Stream, IL 60188
World outside USA © 1982 by Timothy Dudley-Smith

WE COME AS GUESTS INVITED

WE come as guests invited
  when Jesus bids us dine,
his friends on earth united
  to share the bread and wine;
the bread of life is broken,
  the wine is freely poured
for us, in solemn token
  of Christ our dying Lord.

We eat and drink, receiving
  from Christ the grace we need,
and in our hearts believing
  on him by faith we feed;
with wonder and thanksgiving
  for love that knows no end,
we find in Jesus living
  our ever-present friend.

One bread is ours for sharing,
  one single fruitful vine,
our fellowship declaring
  renewed in bread and wine—
renewed, sustained and given
  by token, sign and word,
the pledge and seal of heaven,
  the love of Christ our Lord.

USA © 1984 in LIFT EVERY HEART by Hope Publishing Company, Carol Stream, IL 60188
World outside USA © 1975 by Timothy Dudley-Smith

WE SING THE LORD OUR LIGHT

based on Psalm 27

WE sing the Lord our light;
    our strength, who walk his way;
though full of fears the night,
though long and hard the day.
    His mercy kind
    we boldly claim
    who in his Name
    salvation find.

To him we make request.
This prayer alone we bring:
that in his presence blest
we may behold our King;
    by his free grace
    discern his will,
    and worship still
    before his face.

In trouble's darkest day
his strength is near at hand;
in danger or dismay
upon his rock we stand.
    O anxious heart,
    forsake your fear
    for God is here
    to take your part!

His love will still prevail,
his mighty hand uphold;
though kith and kin may fail
and dearest hearts grow cold.
    Be patient yet!
    His kingdom own,
    in whom alone
    our hopes are set!

WE TURN TO CHRIST ANEW

WE turn to Christ anew
    who hear his call today,
his way to walk, his will pursue,
    his word obey.
  To serve him as our King
  and of his kingdom learn,
from sin and every evil thing
    to him we turn.

  We trust in Christ to save;
  in him new life begins:
who by his cross a ransom gave
    from all our sins.
  Our spirits' strength and stay
  who when all flesh is dust
will keep us in that final day,
    in him we trust.

  We would be true to him
  till earthly journeys end,
whose love no passing years can dim,
    our changeless friend.
  May we who bear his Name
  our faith and love renew,
to follow Christ our single aim,
    and find him true.

USA © 1984 in LIFT EVERY HEART by Hope Publishing Company, Carol Stream, IL 60188
World outside USA © 1982 by Timothy Dudley-Smith

WHEN GOD THE SPIRIT CAME

WHEN God the Spirit came
    upon his church outpoured
in sound of wind and sign of flame
they spread his truth abroad,
    and filled with the Spirit
proclaimed that Christ is Lord.

What courage, power and grace
that youthful church displayed!
to those of every tribe and race
they witnessed unafraid,
    and filled with the Spirit
they broke their bread and prayed.

They saw God's word prevail,
his kingdom still increase,
no part of all his purpose fail,
no promised blessing cease,
    and filled with the Spirit
knew love and joy and peace.

Their theme was Christ alone,
the Lord who lived and died,
who rose to his eternal throne
at God the Father's side;
    and filled with the Spirit
the church was multiplied.

So to this present hour
our task is still the same,
in pentecostal love and power
his gospel to proclaim,
    and filled with the Spirit,
rejoice in Jesus' Name.

USA © 1984 in LIFT EVERY HEART by Hope Publishing Company, Carol Stream, IL 60188
World outside USA © 1977 by Timothy Dudley-Smith

WHEN HE COMES

based on I Thessalonians 4.14–17

WHEN he comes,
    when he comes,
we shall see the Lord in glory when he comes!
As I read the gospel story
we shall see the Lord in glory,
we shall see the Lord in glory when he comes!
    With the Alleluias ringing to the sky,
    with the Alleluias ringing to the sky!
    As I read the gospel story
    we shall see the Lord in glory
    with the Alleluias ringing to the sky!

When he comes,
when he comes,
we shall hear the trumpet sounded when he comes!
We shall hear the trumpet sounded,
see the Lord by saints surrounded,
we shall hear the trumpet sounded when he comes!
    With the Alleluias ringing to the sky,
    with the Alleluias ringing to the sky!
    We shall hear the trumpet sounded,
    see the Lord by saints surrounded,
    with the Alleluias ringing to the sky!

When he comes,
when he comes,
we shall all rise up to meet him when he comes!
When he calls his own to greet him
we shall all rise up to meet him,
we shall all rise up to meet him when he comes!
    With the Alleluias ringing to the sky,
    with the Alleluias ringing to the sky!
    When he calls his own to greet him
    we shall all rise up to meet him
    with the Alleluias ringing to the sky!

WHEN JESUS LIVED AMONG US

WHEN Jesus lived among us he came a child of earth
    to wear our human likeness, to share our human birth;
and after flight and exile, an alien refugee,
return in peace and safety at last to Galilee;
    through sunlit days of childhood a loving home to know;
    in wisdom and in favour with God and man to grow.

He came, the friend of sinners, to meet us in our need;
the gospel of his kingdom declare in word and deed;
to touch and cure the leper, the lost to seek and find,
to heal in signs and wonders the deaf and dumb and blind.
    The voice of their Creator the wind and waters heard;
    to those with ears to listen he spoke the living word.

'The Son of Man must suffer,' he taught by word and sign;
like bread his body broken, his blood poured out like wine.
His cross is for our pardon, our sacrifice for sins,
and by his resurrection our risen life begins.
    We come in faith to Jesus to follow where he trod;
    O Son of Man receive us, and make us sons of God.

WHEN JOHN BAPTISED BY JORDAN'S RIVER

WHEN John baptised by Jordan's river
in faith and hope the people came,
that John and Jordan might deliver
their troubled souls from sin and shame.
They came to seek a new beginning,
the human spirit's ageless quest,
repentance, and an end of sinning,
renouncing every wrong confessed.

There as the Lord, baptised and praying,
rose from the stream, the sinless one,
a voice was heard from heaven saying,
'This is my own beloved Son'.
There as the Father's word was spoken,
not in the power of wind and flame,
but of his love and peace the token,
seen as a dove, the Spirit came.

O Son of Man, our nature sharing,
in whose obedience all are blest,
Saviour, our sins and sorrows bearing,
hear us and grant us this request:
daily to grow, by grace defended,
filled with the Spirit from above;
in Christ baptised, beloved, befriended,
children of God in peace and love.

WHEN THE LORD IN GLORY COMES

WHEN the Lord in glory comes
    not the trumpets, not the drums,
not the anthem, not the psalm,
not the thunder, not the calm,
not the shout the heavens raise,
not the chorus, not the praise,
not the silences sublime,
not the sounds of space and time,
but his voice when he appears
shall be music to my ears—
    but his voice when he appears
    shall be music to my ears.

When the Lord is seen again
not the glories of his reign,
not the lightnings through the storm,
not the radiance of his form,
not his pomp and power alone,
not the splendours of his throne,
not his robe and diadems,
not the gold and not the gems,
but his face upon my sight
shall be darkness into light—
    but his face upon my sight
    shall be darkness into light.

When the Lord to human eyes
shall bestride our narrow skies,
not the child of humble birth,
not the carpenter of earth,
not the man by all denied,
not the victim crucified,
but the God who died to save,
but the victor of the grave,
he it is to whom I fall,
Jesus Christ, my All in all—
    he it is to whom I fall,
    Jesus Christ, my All in all,

WHEN TO OUR WORLD

WHEN to our world the Saviour came
    the sick and helpless heard his Name,
and in their weakness longed to see
the healing Christ of Galilee.

That good physician! Night and day
the people thronged about his way;
and wonder ran from soul to soul—
'The touch of Christ has made us whole!'

His praises then were heard and sung
by opened ears and loosened tongue,
while lightened eyes could see and know
the healing Christ of long ago.

Of long ago—yet living still,
who died for us on Calvary's hill;
who triumphed over cross and grave,
his healing hands stretched forth to save.

Those wounded hands are still the same,
and all who serve that saving Name
may share today in Jesus' plan—
the healing Christ of everyman.

Then grant us, Lord, in this our day,
to hear the prayers the helpless pray;
give to us hearts their pain to share,
make of us hands to tend and care.

Make us your hands! For Christ to live,
in prayer and service, swift to give;
till all the world rejoice to find
the healing Christ of all mankind.

USA © 1984 in LIFT EVERY HEART by Hope Publishing Company, Carol Stream IL 60188
World outside USA © 1977 by Timothy Dudley-Smith

WHO IS JESUS?

WHO is Jesus? Friend of sinners,
    whom in love the Father gave;
born within a borrowed stable,
laid within a borrowed grave,
Son of God and son of Mary,
sons of men to seek and save.

Who is Jesus? Man of sorrows!
see his glory all put by.
Prince of life and sinners' ransom
stumbles forth to bleed and die.
Lamb of God and Love immortal
hangs upon the cross on high.

Who is Jesus? Risen Saviour!
to his Father's throne restored,
firstborn of the new creation,
sun and star and saints' reward—
Prince of glory, King of ages,
Christ the ever-living Lord!

WHO IS THERE ON THIS EASTER MORNING

WHO is there on this Easter morning
    runs not with John to find the grave?
Nor sees how, death's dominion scorning,
Jesus is risen, strong to save?
    Who is there on this Easter morning
    runs not with John to find the grave?

Who has not stood where Mary grieving
to that first Easter garden came;
for very joy but half believing
whose is the voice that calls her name?
    Who has not stood where Mary grieving
    to that first Easter garden came?

Who is there doubts that night is ended?
Hear from on high the trumpets call!
Christ is in triumph now ascended,
risen and reigning, Lord of all!
    Who is there doubts that night is ended?
    Hear from on high the trumpets call!

USA © 1984 in LIFT EVERY HEART by Hope Publishing Company, Carol Stream, IL 60188
World outside USA © 1980 by Timothy Dudley-Smith

WITHIN A CRIB

WITHIN a crib my Saviour lay,
 a wooden manger filled with hay,
come down for love on Christmas Day:
 all glory be to Jesus!

Upon a cross my Saviour died,
to ransom sinners crucified,
his loving arms still open wide:
 all glory be to Jesus!

A victor's crown my Saviour won,
his work of love and mercy done,
the Father's high-ascended Son:
 all glory be to Jesus!

Part Three

EARLY POEMS

Early poems

The poems that follow are drawn from a rather larger number, many of which have appeared in print but have never been collected. Most of them were written when I was in my twenties, a few more recently. As can be seen, they represent generally a more personal viewpoint (and sometimes, especially in the more pessimistic ones, a more temporary viewpoint) than can be found in the hymns.

I include them for more than one reason. I hope, for example, that they may still have something to say which will strike a chord in another's experience, and that there may be readers who respond to them. If they lack, sometimes, the restraint and revision that belongs to hymn-texts, at least I can say that they sprang very directly from experiences and perceptions more vivid, more disturbing, than most that come to me now. I hope also that those who have an interest in the creation of hymn-texts may care to look on them as a kind of seed-bed from which later writing has sprung. They come, mostly, from the time referred to in the Foreword when I should have liked to write hymns, but seemed unable to do so.

Acknowledgement is gratefully made to those journals which first printed a number of these items. Some appeared in parish or diocesan magazines, in the *Battlement* (the journal of Ridley Hall, Cambridge), *Pilgrim*, *Crusade*, *The British Weekly*, and the *Church of England Newspaper*.

I

Necessity

More than all, I have loved earth's lonely places,
Where the winds of healing pass, and the air is sweet;
Free from the spell of the listless vacant faces,
Far from the jostling street.

The warm grey rocks that rise from the purple moorlands,
Deserted woods where the slanting sunbeams fall;
Wind-swept pines, austere upon distant forelands
Where only sea-birds call.

The grassy dunes where the line of the cliffs is broken,
And hilltops bright with the moon in a velvet sky;
These, not men, are my loves—but the Lord hath spoken,
Who can but prophesy?

II

Bethlehem

The lighted windows die, the night drifts down,
Faint on the wind the voices fade away;
And all the world, as one with David's town,
Silent in darkness waits for Christmas Day.

God's ancient promise perfectly fulfilled!
Dawns on our dark the Dayspring from on high!
The strife of nations for a moment stilled,
A new world wakens to a Baby's cry.

III

Night Sky

Think when you see the stars on high
That one alone sufficed
The three, to read upon the sky
The road to Christ.

Make one and every star beside,
Piercing the curtain dim,
No more to Bethlehem a guide
Yet still to Him.

IV

Visit of the Wise Men

Take, O Child,
The gift that I bring,
Rich and rare as befits a King:
Gold that glints as the star looks down—
Gold to gleam in a great king's crown.
When the kingdom comes, when the flags unfold,
Remember me, and my gift of gold.

Take, O Child,
The gift that I bring,
Rich and rare as befits a King:
I kneel as a king to a King divine,
Receive my praise, and this gift of mine
Which is frankincense for the altar fire
To burn in worship to the World's Desire.

Take, O Child,
The gift that I bring,
Rich and rare as befits a King:
Costliest myrrh from the East afar
For the tomb foretold by the travelling star.
When they bear you slow to your kingly grave
You shall lie at last with the gift I gave.

*

Strange are the gifts that the Wise Men bring
To so small a Child, to so strange a King.
Sovereign gold, but His brow was torn
When they hailed Him king, with a crown of thorn;
Frankincense, that they might provide
Perpetual praise to a God who died;
But none so strange as the myrrh they gave
To anoint the clothes of a three-day grave.

V

Faith

Kindled by light divine, faith's feeble spark
Glimmers, a pin-point, in my doubtful dark;
Glints on the nails that pin Him to the tree—
The Man of Sorrows in His agony.

Faint in the darkness springs the flickering fire
Guttering dim in gusts of self-desire,
But in the ghostly glow so dimly shed
Shadows divide around the thorn-crowned head.

Desire grows dim, while brighter burns the flame
Whose twisted tongues reveal the Prince of Shame:
God in His grace uplifted, stricken sore—
God in His mercy, knocking at my door.

VI

Encounter

Lord, as Thou art: Not as I think of Thee;
Not as the Babe upon the virgin's knee,
Not as the guiltless victim, pale in death;
Not as the Carpenter of Nazareth.

Lord, as Thou art, make Thyself known to me;
Not as the wandering Seer of Galilee;
Not the Anointed, whom the prophets showed,
Not as the Guest of the Emmaus road.

Lord, as Thou art, that I may meet with Thee;
Not the unearthly stiller of the sea;
Not as the Bread of Life, Incarnate Word,
But as Thou truly art. Who art Thou, Lord?

*

Thou needst not ask: Be thou content to find
To seek me with the heart and not the mind.
Seer, Rabbi, Babe, deny not: Only see
They in their turn were Christ, and I AM He.

VII

Fraud

'Wrong if you like,' he said; 'I could not choose;
A man in business has so much to lose.
This game of commerce cannot now be played
To rules that fit a small-town joiner's trade.
What if the sale was wrong? I have the yield.'

*

Profit enough to buy the Potter's Field.

VIII

Worldling

I loved this new religion
And I sought to hold it fast,
But a love more deeply rooted
Overcame me at the last.

And my epitaph is written
In a letter old and curled,
Saying 'Demas has deserted,
Having loved this present world.'

IX

A blind man healed by Christ

The gift that God withheld from me at birth
The Son of God has now bestowed on me.
These eyes which looked today upon the earth
Are shut, because I do not choose to see.

The old familiar things my fingers trace,
My feet discern the way the pavement lies;
And having seen the sunlight on His face
I have fulfilled the purpose of my eyes.

X

'One of thy hired Servants'

This is my home; here in my bed I ponder
All that my father would not let me say;
His head is resting on the pillow yonder,
And every hair is grey.

Again I see him stare, and wave to greet me;
A frail old figure, trembling and in pain.
Now he has started down the road to meet me,
And I am home again.

XI

Hands

Once in a raftered attic where I slept
I wrestled in an agony of prayer
My hands tight-locked before me, and I wept
For joy to see the stigmata were there.
    Proud tears! Should I have wept if I had known
    Another's hands were clasped about my own?

XII

Cathedral Builders

This ground is holy—walk unshod
We raise a monument to God:
And in us, since our life began,
He builds a monument to man.

Our grandsires' grandsires cleared the spot;
We raise the walls now they are not.
The men who crown this tower shall say
Their grandsires' grandsires wrought today.

We build it well; and God alone
Can quarry more enduring stone.
But though it stand till time be past,
God, and He only, builds to last.

For at the end the shifting ground
Shall take its toll of all we found.
With gaping arch and slanting wall
The temple that we build shall fall.

So much, at last, for all our pains;
But yet His work in us remains.
His temple, builded not with hands,
For ever firmly founded, stands.

XIII

Remembrance Sunday

The autumn sunlight, sharp and sweet,
Shares with the wind the empty street;
Only the clock's slow-moving hand
Bids silence to a silent land.

Here, while a nation bows its head,
Soft in the silence speak the dead:
'We shall not sleep' their crosses cry
'If you break faith with us who die.'

Their crosses cry? Not their's alone.
No graven cenotaph of stone
Stands monument to more than pride
If we break faith with Him who died.

XIV

The Heart of Man

If by your vision sin and doubt
Are sown within your mind,
The eyes God gave you, pluck them out,
And enter heaven blind.

If by your hand sin's web is spun
Shrink not from sword or knife.
Better, when all is said and done,
Helpless, to enter life.

Long since I severed hand and eye
But sin does not depart.
One thing remains—except I die
I must root out my heart.

XV

Fiat

'Let there be light'—and the light shone.
The darkness fled in that first hour.
And to this day the light shines on:
No word of God is void of power.

When will the sound I seek be heard,
And one divine command restore
The fallen image? Speak the word,
The word of power, 'Go sin no more.'

XVI

Treasures upon earth

Each passing moment measures
The mouldering slow decay,
As all my tarnished treasures
Dissolve to dust away.

The moth and rust infect them,
My stores so long laid by;
And powerless to protect them
And sick at soul am I.

For where, corrupt and blighted,
My treasures mould and fade,
In earthbound vaults benighted
My heart is also laid.

XVII

Bitter Harvest

Seedtime and harvest, while the world shall turn,
Compose together all life's little hours.
The seed, God's bounty, and your labour earn
At last, the flowers.

And seasons come for men as well as lands;
In young hearts' springtime there are sown the seeds.
Summer is ended: autumn's harvest stands—
Not flowers, but weeds.

Despair

Thou deepest reach of every human pain,
Charged with the bitterness of final woe,
Though I dispel thee, thou wilt come again—
I cannot bid thee go.

Here must I drink the dregs that still are left,
Travel the nightmare road as yet untrod;
And in the darkness, hopeless and bereft,
Cry out 'My God, My God.'

Down the last twisting steps I must descend,
To hell's extremities, to blank despair—
To find Thy work was finished to the end,
For Thou wast sometime there.

Escape

On breathless summer evenings
When moon and tides are high
We walk beside the water
Alone, myself and I.

Far out beyond the breakers
The dark horizons shine,
Split by the path of moonlight
One single silver line.

And here the sea-washed pebbles
Run grating through the foam,
And all the ocean's voices
Unite to call me home.

'Come out, come out' they call me;
Their cries are sweet and strong:
'Walk on the moonlit pathway
That knows not right from wrong.'

'Walk on the moonlit pathway
Set between East and West,
Come home to us, O anxious heart,
And we will give you rest.'

The land lies black behind me,
The surf, the waves, beat low.
From earth's dark shadows home to light
They call me: I will go.

But when I turn my footsteps
Their voices call in vain;
Oh, right and wrong possess me still,
I am myself again.

XX

Security

You shall not fall except it be His will,
Nor find your burden more than you can bear;
Not your good only, but your seeming ill,
Stands silent witness to a Father's care.

But if, not comforted, you tremble still,
Stand firm on this, unmoved by all alarms:
You shall not fall except it be His will
And underneath the everlasting arms.

XXI

Dusk

The sky was blue, unclouded;
And bright the sunlit day.
Tonight the sun is shrouded,
The sky is cloudy grey.
And night shall spread her awning,
Her velvet star-pierced veil,
And long before the dawning
The moon and stars shall fail.

And if for sweetness, sorrow
Shall come with grief for mirth,
The sun shall rise tomorrow
As onward spins the earth:
But spirits yet in prison,
The soul that Christless dies,
What if the sun be risen—
They shall not see it rise.

XXII

The Island

My careless heart, no longer light,
Was wounded unaware.
It was not sound nor scent nor sight
But Christ Himself was there.

To ease the ache I carry yet
No solace shall avail,
Till all my need in Thee is met,
In Thee desire fail.

XXIII

The Light of Reason

Once after illness, by the sea
I wandered strangely sad.
I made the world a mockery:
I thought that I was mad.

Till, with a heart too sick for speech,
Too dead for joy or pain,
I picked a pebble from the beach
And knew that I was sane.

XXIV

The Way

Lead me, O Lord, by paths I have not known,
Beyond resolve, past faith or thought or sense.
Let steadier vision, clearer light be shown,
Richer experience.

'Light is not sent except upon the road,
Nor is it knowledge I can chiefly bless.
Since on thy heart desire is bestowed
Desire faithfulness.'

XXV

Content

Content belongs, they say, to youth or health,
The friends of fortune or the favoured few,
Endowed alike with wisdom and with wealth,
It is not true.

Content belongs to those whose gain is loss,
Who carry burdens of distress and care;
Who lay them daily at a Saviour's cross,
And leave them there.

XXVI

Earth

The dark trees clustered black against the hill;
Night sky clear-shining through the briar and thorn;
The thin ghost-shadowed landscape lying still,
The dark chill wind before the dark chill dawn;

The pattering raindrops, and the dead leaves drifting,
One troubled star beyond the cloud-dark sky,
Wet crumbling earth between my fingers sifting
Stir deep enchantments: and I know not why.

XXVII

Reflection

I passed today a man upon the street
And in his face Thy features met my eye.
Teach me to see Thee, Lord, in all I meet—
Salute the Christ in every passer-by;
As in this muddy pool beneath my feet
I see the sunlit image of the sky.

XXXVIII

Pilgrimage

This is the road that leads to Eden,
To the garden long denied;
The road that leads to the grave of manhood,
The death that Adam died.

Follow the road to the fourfold river
That is flowing from Eden yet;
The waters that speak of the things forgotten
That God does not forget.

Ruined the garden, the garden of Eden,
Bereft of her children now;
And the tree of the knowledge of good and evil
Is scarred by a broken bough.

There you shall find in the land of Eden
When the burning sun has set,
And the cool of the evening scents the garden,
That God is walking yet.

There the Desire of men and nations,
King, Creator, Father, Lord,
Walks alone through the empty garden
Kept by the flaming sword.

XXIX

Jerusalem, Jerusalem

Why must He go to the great city,
Why must He choose today?
  Why is His face so firmly set
  And the eyes that have never been clouded yet—
Why are there shadows behind their pity?
  Why must He take this way?

Oh, faith must venture and love must cherish
And the pride of life condemn:
  The prince of this world must lose his power,
  His kingdom fall in the final hour—
And it cannot be that a prophet perish
  Out of Jerusalem.

XXX

Ecce Homo

I hear the voices of the crowds that cry
And in the tumult lift a stumbling prayer:
Though all the world be shouting 'Crucify!'
Let not my voice be there.

I cannot hear my voice among the crowd:
One sound alone rings clear above the din—
Voices demanding bloodshed, fierce and loud,
The voices of my sin.

XXXI

Simon

'This is the end, my sons; I'm sinking;
Looking my last on sky and sun.
There's little enough that I've seen, I'm thinking,
Little enough I've done.

'Only one thing that is worth recalling—
A cluster of people from out the town;
And a man in the midst of them, stumbling, falling,
A worn-out man who fell down.

'I was coming in from the country places,
The sun was hot on the dusty road;
I looked at the group of pitiless faces
And helped him up with his load.

'I meant no more than an act of kindness—
They made me follow against my will.
And I saw—and my soul was freed from blindness
As darkness covered the hill.

'This is the end, my sons; I'm sinking.
Life ebbs fast when the light grows dim.
But the Lord will know, when we meet, I'm thinking,
That I carried the cross for Him.'

XXXII

Trees

Upon a tree the sin of man
Found its primaeval root,
Where thick upon each burdened branch
There hung forbidden fruit.

The tree of knowledge rudely robbed,
The tree of life decayed,
Another tree was grown and hewn—
The tree of death was made.

And there the sin of Adam's race
Shall end as it began:
For high between the barren boughs
There hangs the Son of Man.

XXXIII

Gethsemane and Calvary

I

Across the torn apocalyptic sky
Thin tattered fragments of the sunset fly:
And deepest twilight, plunging, piercing, sees
A figure kneeling in the cypress trees.

II

Hard and cruel are the men who pass,
Callous the crowds that call:
Sharp and clear on the sunlit grass
Three twisted shadows fall.

XXXIV

Journey's End

Small and perfect and bare, the feet
Play in the dust of the village street;
Paddle and splash in the tingling chill
Of the springing stream at the foot of the hill.

Feet of a child that shall journey far
To the hammer and nails of Golgotha.

Brown and sandalled and hard, the feet
Walk where the wind and the water meet,
Tread the surf of the restless wave,
Swift and certain and strong to save.

Feet of a man that are travelling far
To the hammer and nails of Golgotha.

Tired and bleeding and torn, the feet
Came to a halt with their work complete:
For a moment firm on the hilltop stood
And were laid at last on a cross of wood.

The feet of God which have journeyed far
To the hammer and nails of Golgotha.

XXXV

Easter Sunrise

Thou who hast laid my light away
And overcast the sky,
Grant me deliverance with the day
Or in the dark to die.

Beneath night's shadow, ages long,
The stone secures the grave.
Oh, they were right and we were wrong,
Himself he could not save.

And I must bear, as best I may,
The life I would not live:
The night is merciful, but day
Has only truth to give.

But truth is more than judge's jest;
The stone is rolled away;
The skies are red from East to West
And Truth returns with day.

XXXVI

Walk to Emmaus

'Should have redeemed . . .'
Forlorn and plaintive words!
'We trusted . . .' and our confidence betrayed
Cries out to heaven; for the Master seemed,
Till that last evening, calm and unafraid:
And we had swords.
But now bereft we mourn as men that dreamed,
'Should have redeemed . . .'

'Slow to believe . . .'
Words of such mild rebuff!
Vision you trusted, rather than your Lord,
And from his triumph seeking his reprieve
You challenged God's foreknowledge with a sword.
Vain childish stuff!
'*Should have redeemed?*' Be humbled, bow, receive,
'Slow to believe!'

XXXVII

Resurrection

Alone before the heavenly gate
The radiant figure stands.
Approaching pilgrims see him wait:
The scars are in his hands.

They see the scars, their heads are bent,
His welcome brings relief:
'I too am but a penitent,
Who lived on earth a thief.'

XXXVIII

Unprofitable Servant

Oh, fond imagining!
That I should ever think to hear Him say
Standing in welcome at the judgment day
That long-sought-after thing.

How, 'faithful', and how 'good'?
I, who it seems a hundred times a day,
In all unwilling willingness, betray
Entrusted servanthood.

'I am among you still
As He that serveth'—so the words are said;
'To you my faithful good is reckonéd,
To Me, unfaithful ill.'

'O good and faithful one,
(Since what I judge, thou art)' he says, 'My loss
Is all thy virtue: By thy Servant's cross
Welcome thou home. Well done.'

XXXIX

Christ at the last

More silent than the twilight's tread,
Softer than shadow's fall,
Here in the dark beside my bed
There stands the Lord of all.

His are the realms of time and space,
The lands of endless day;
And I shall see His sunlit face
Where shadows flee away.

Part Four

NOTES ON THE HYMNS

In this collection the title of a hymn-text is always taken from the first line. Texts are given in alphabetical order both in the body of the book and in these notes.

A PURPLE ROBE   86 86 (CM)

Theme	Passiontide
Written	at Sevenoaks, October 1968
Suggested tune	A PURPLE ROBE by David G. Wilson
Published in	*Youth Praise 2*, 1969 to A PURPLE ROBE
	Thirty Hymns, CPAS 1972 (words only)
	UTC Hymnbook, Bangalore, 1975 (words only)
	Anglican Hymn Book Supplement, 1978 (words only)
	A Purple Robe (five choral settings in Chinese, translated and arranged by S. Y. Suen), 1982 to A PURPLE ROBE
	Hymns for Today's Church, 1982 to A PURPLE ROBE arranged by Noël Tredinnick
Recorded on	*Here is Youth Praise*, Reflection R1 308, 1975 to A PURPLE ROBE
	Hymns for Today's Church, Word WST 9623, 1982 to A PURPLE ROBE

This text was originally written for *Youth Praise 2*. Between writing and publication thirteen months later, I considered the addition of an extra line to each verse (the third or fourth line, in a rhyming scheme a b a a b, the present fourth line of each verse becoming the fifth line). But a tune had already been written and I abandoned the plan. In the summer of 1971 I returned to the idea in my MS book. The additional lines would be as follows:

    v.1 (as line 3)
        Their cruel jests in silence borne

    v.2 (as line 3)
        With failing steps and features marred

    v.3 (as line 4)
        Since first our fallen race began

    v.4 (as line 3)
        Our sins and griefs upon him laid

    v.5 (as line 4)
        By Christ redeemed, and Christ alone,

See Appendix 5, pp. 286ff.

A SONG WAS HEARD AT CHRISTMAS   76 86 D

Theme	Christmas
Written	at Ruan Minor and Porthoustock, August 1978
Suggested tune	ALFORD by J. B. Dykes

Published in   *Hymns for Today's Church*, 1982 to
                                   (1) CHERRY TREE CAROL (English Traditional)
                                   (2) HOLY APOSTLES by David G. Wilson
                           A Song was heard at Christmas (USA), 1983 to
                           ALFORD

Originally planned as 'A star there was at Christmas', this text was written and then extensively re-worked over a week-end while on holiday in Cornwall; verse 3 in particular being re-drafted on a walk to Porthoustock quarry.

These verses first appeared in print on the official Christmas card of the Lord Mayor of Norwich, Dr. J. P. English, December 1978.

See Appendix 5, pp. 286ff.

ALL FLOWERS OF GARDEN, FIELD AND HILL   86 86 (CM)

Theme   for a flower festival; harvest; nature; creation

Written   at Ruan Minor and at Stopham, Sussex, August 1977
                           and April 1978

Suggested tune   UNIVERSITY by Charles Collignon

Flower festivals are a feature of Norfolk country churches—and indeed country churches in many parts of England. This text sets out to evoke some of the ways in which the Lord Jesus Christ used the natural world around him in his teaching; or in which plants and flowers remind us of the gospel story. Originally eight verses, it proved particularly intractable in revision over a period of eight months, and found its present form by the omission of the original opening verse.

ALL GLORY BE TO GOD ON HIGH   86 88 6

Based on   the Gloria in Excelsis (see also: Glory to God in the
                           highest)

Theme   praise

Written   at Ruan Minor and at St Julian's, Coolham; August,
                           and October 1981

Suggested tune   REPTON by Hubert Parry (repeating the final line of
                           each verse)

This text represents a second attempt to cast the *Gloria in Excelsis* (which dates back at least to the 4th century) into metrical form. My first attempt, 'Glory to God in the highest', (q.v.) was two years earlier. This text began with verses of four lines; but Common Metre proved altogether too pedestrian for this purpose. Some months later an extensive revision added a fifth line, strengthening the rhyming scheme at the same time.

ALL MY SOUL TO GOD I RAISE

77 77 77

Based on   Psalm 25
Theme   trust in God
Written   at Ruan Minor, August 1982
Suggested tune   WELLS by Basil Johnson

Psalm 25, which has been called 'an alphabet of entreaty', is a Hebrew acrostic (a device used also in Psalm 34). Each verse starts with a successive letter of the Hebrew alphabet, in order. Few translations attempt to transpose this framework into the English version (one who does is R. A. Knox; and I have followed him to the extent of omitting the letters X, Y & Z; indeed the Hebrew scheme is not wholly regular) and there is a very real danger that an attempt to do so will sacrifice too much to this particular constraint—one found in English almost exclusively in comic verse. My notes suggest that I did not at first intend to try to follow the acrostic pattern, but over the three days in which the first draft was being written, it seemed to become possible to try. A hymn of 24 lines, without the three final letters of the alphabet, clearly needed one repetition; and I have come full circle to my opening line, re-punctuated to fit the syntax.

ALL SHALL BE WELL

46 46 *or* 10 10

Theme   Eastertide
Written   at Ruan Minor and St Anthony-in-Meneage, April
                    1976
Suggested tune   SONG 46 by Orlando Gibbons
Published in   *News Extra*, April 1977 (words only) and as the
                    words of an Anthem by Libby Larsen
                    commissioned by the Twin City Choristers Guild,
                    Minnesota USA, for their Third Annual Festival,
                    1979
                    Hymns for Today's Church, 1982 to (1) SONG 46
                    (2) EASTER SKIES by John Marsh

This text was written in Easter week on holiday in Cornwall, much of it walking beside Carne Creek. The words echo a meditation of the Lady Julian of Norwich in the thirty-first chapter of her *Revelations of Divine Love*: 'All shall be well, and all shall be well, and all manner of thing shall be well'—though they are not there applied to Christ's resurrection. I accept the comment that the hymn might read (and indeed, sing) better in 10 10 rather than in 4 6 4 6, but I prefer to print it as it appears, emphasising the repetition of the key line which appears in every verse.

For 'Sun of Righteousness' see Malachi 4.2; for verse 4 see Romans 6.9 and 2 Timothy 1.10.

In some editions of *Hymns for Today's Church* verse 3 is omitted in error.

See Appendix 5, pp. 286ff.

AND SLEEPS MY LORD IN SILENCE YET   88 88 88

Theme	Eastertide; especially Easter Eve
Written	at Durgan and Ruan Minor, August 1982
Suggested tune	EISENACH by J. H. Schein
Published in	*News of Hymnody*, January 1983 (words only)

A number of hymns begin with the word 'And' (for example, Charles Wesley's *And can it be* or W. Bright's *And now, O Father*) and this seems to have been one of the starting points of this text. Durgan is a tiny cluster of houses in a little bay on the Helford River; and the first four lines—in a rather different form—came into my head over a picnic supper on the beach. The device of question rather than affirmation, and the picture of the Lord still within the tomb, makes the text specially appropriate for Easter Eve; but the final verse requires a note of triumph and assurance suitable for other Easter occasions.

AS FOR OUR WORLD   10 10 4 10 10 4 10 10

Theme	social concern
Written	at Eastbourne, August 1968
Suggested tune	by Michael A. Baughen, arranged by David G. Wilson (see below)
Published in	*Youth Praise 2*, 1969 to a tune specially composed by Michael A. Baughen, arranged by David G. Wilson *Thirty Hymns*, CPAS 1972 (words only) *UTC Hymnbook*, Bangalore, 1975 (words only)

When *Youth Praise 2* was in preparation, there was a need for new hymns of social concern, but rooted in a personal and biblical spirituality. This text was an attempt at one such, in which the experiment in metre would alone be enough to make it almost unsingable. My MS reminds me that the most difficult word in the text comes second in the third line of the final verse. Ancient, common, single, final, urgent, deepest, heartfelt all appear; and the word is so crossed out and written over that one would not guess my final preference were it not for the fair copy.

See Appendix 5, pp. 286ff.

AS WATER TO THE THIRSTY   76 76 66 44 6

Theme	the Lord Jesus Christ
Written	at Bramerton, February 1975
Suggested tune	OASIS by T. Brian Coleman

Published in	*Partners in Praise*, 1979 to OASIS
	Anthem to music by Hal H. Hopson, Agape (USA), 1981
	Jesus Praise, 1982 to OASIS
	Word & Music, July–Sept 1982 to OASIS
	Hymns for Today's Church, 1982 to OASIS
Recorded on	*Hymns for Today's Church*, Word WST 9623, 1982 to OASIS

My notebook suggests that this text owes more to Simon and Garfunkel's classic phrase of the 1960s, 'Bridge over troubled water', than it does to Emma Bevan's 'As the bridgeroom to his chosen'. Erik Routley (*Hymns and Human Life*, p. 261) calls that 'one of the oldest of children's hymns', the translation by Mrs Bevan (daughter of Philip Shuttleworth, Bishop of Chichester 1840–42) being based on a 14th century original by John Tauler. A correspondent suggested to me that my own text must be an unconscious plagiarism of that hymn; but, on the contrary, I felt that there was room for a more modern hymn based on similes. It differs from Mrs Bevan's not only in date, but in metre, rhyming structure, and (of course) the imagery chosen. I hope that this imagery is no less biblical in tone, even if sometimes the likeness is to some other facet of Christian experience, rather than an explicit reference to the Lord Himself. Perhaps the following references will show what I mean:

Verse 1, line 1 Psalm 63.1
2 Psalm 27.4
3 Psalm 28.7
4 I Thessalonians 1.9
5 Exodus 15.2
6 Song of Songs, chapter 2

Verse 2, line 1 I Kings 19.11,12
2 Hebrews 13.20
3 John 20.11–18
4 Revelation 1.16
5 and 6 Psalm 104.2

Verse 3, line 1 Psalm 4.8
2 Matthew 17.2
3 Psalm 146.7
4 Malachi 4.2
5 and 6 Luke 16.11–24

See Appendix 5, pp. 286ff.

AT CANA'S WEDDING, LONG AGO   88 88 88

Based on	John 2.1–11 & Luke 24.13f.
Theme	marriage
Written	at Ruan Minor, August 1976
Suggested tune	WYCH CROSS by Erik Routley

Written to the tune WYCH CROSS, this began as 'O Christ at Cana long ago' and then 'As once at Cana long ago'. The opening line is a later correction on the first full draft; and I regret the loss of (but would not change back to) a fourth line in verse 1 reading 'their very water turned to wine'. As with many wedding hymns, there is an uneasiness about how far the words are for the couple and how far for the congregation. Yet there seems no logical reason why the congregational 'us' and 'our' of verses 1 and 2 should not become the intercessory 'their' of verse 3. It may be worth adding that commentators have suggested (there is no kind of evidence) that the second of the two disciples (Luke 24.13) was Cleopas's wife; making the Emmaus walk, and the wedding at Cana, favourite passages for wedding addresses.

Perhaps three names from the geography of the Gospels are too much for today? And yet one should not underestimate the evocative power of the proper name, not only in rooting the allusion within the gospel history, but in less expected ways. D. H. Lawrence once confessed ('Hymns in a man's life', *Evening News*, London 13 October 1928):

'To me the word Galilee has a wonderful sound. The Lake of Galilee! I don't want to know where it is. I never want to go to Palestine. Galilee is one of those lovely, glamorous words, not places, that exist in the golden haze of a child's half-formed imagination. And in my man's imagination it is just the same. It has been left untouched . . .'

There are losses as well as gains to be reckoned with in that account, of course. But the 'wonderful sound' of Galilee here receives testimony from an unexpected source.

BE STRONG IN THE LORD   10 10 11 11

Based on	Ephesians 6.10–18
Theme	the armour of God; pilgrimage & conflict
Written	at Ruan Minor, August 1982
Suggested tune	OLD 104TH from Thomas Ravenscroft's *Psalmes*, 1621

The *Alternative Service Book* of the Church of England, published in 1980, carries a table of suggested Sunday themes; and 'the whole armour of God' is the theme of the ninth Sunday after Pentecost. It had been in my mind to attempt a text on this passage since reading the account of it in Dr John Stott's *God's New Society* (IVP, London 1979, p. 275f). I had no copy with me on holiday; but in response to my letter a photostat of those pages reached me within a day or two; and the text above bears a close relationship to that exposition—see especially the first half of verses 2 & 3. 'Armour of light' in verse 1 is a reference to Romans 13.12; arguably a different image, but one I take to be related (or relatable) to the Ephesians passage. If, as I hope, the finished text gives an impression of simplicity, it may be worth adding that the original drafting occupies five pages in my MS book. The reference in the final line is to the cross of Christ as the source of all victory, and his crown as its symbol and reward.

It is easy to overlook the fact that this passage supplies the theme of one of Charles Wesley's greatest hymns, 'Soldiers of Christ arise', since the versions usually printed in the hymnals (including the Methodist Hymnal as John Wesley compiled it) often give only four of the sixteen verses, making of course *general* references to the armour (including the famous use of 'panoply' drawn directly from the Greek text) and omit references to individual items. The complete hymn contains explicit allusions to the girdle, the breastplate, 'the Gospel greaves', the shield, the helmet and the Spirit's sword.

I know of only two other texts on this specific theme: C. G. Hambly's 'Lord, we would put around ourselves' *in Partners in Praise*, and 'Take your stand with truth as your belt' in *Fresh Sounds*.

BEHOLD, AS LOVE MADE MANIFEST   86 86 (CM)

Theme	Passiontide; the cross of Christ; grace
Written	at Ruan Minor, August 1983
Suggested tune	BALLERMA by François H. Barthélémon

The theme of this text is what the cross of Christ *reveals*, though this is inseparably linked with the fact that it *redeems*. These two emphases come together in the words 'sacrifice' and 'sign' which conclude the first and the last verses. Starting from John the Baptist's 'Behold, the Lamb of God . . .' (John 1.36), the significance of the cross in terms of grace, love, mercy and victory forms the subject of the four central verses, returning to the declaration of 1 John 4.10 (AV) 'Herein is love . . .'

Verse 2 contains an allusion to the prayer 'O Jesus, Master Carpenter of Nazareth, who on the cross through wood and nails didst work man's whole salvation . . .' It appears in a number of collections, but I do not know its original source.

BEYOND ALL MORTAL PRAISE   66 66 88

Based on	Daniel 2.20–23
Theme	praise and worship
Written	at Ruan Minor, August 1981
Suggested tune	DARWALL'S 148TH by J. Darwall

One of two hymns written to this metre in August 1981, this is a metrical version of Daniel's prayer of thanksgiving and praise when God revealed to him King Nebuchadnezzar's dream in Daniel 2. This accounts for the reference to answered prayer in verse 4. A glance at the passage in most Bible translations will show why the first line was originally a variant of what is now line 2. It assumed its final shape on a grassy cliff above Poldhu Cove through a long and sunny afternoon.

Based on	Psalm 134
Theme	evening
Written	at Ruan Minor, August 1978
Suggested tune	awaiting a composer

Psalm 134 is not among the metrical versions collected in *Psalm Praise*, but as the last of the fifteen Songs of Ascents (sung by the pilgrims on their way to the Temple in Jerusalem) it makes a fitting evening psalm or hymn. See 1 Chronicles 9.33 for a reference to the Levitical singers 'day and night' about their work; and 1 Timothy 2.8 for a New Testament reference to 'lifting holy hands'. The reciprocal blessing (from man to God, in thankfulness, and God to man in benediction) is the keynote of the Psalm, as it is of verse 3 of this text. See further Derek Kidner's *Psalms 73–150* (IVP, London 1975) from which the notes above are drawn and which was beside me as I worked on this text. In spite of the simplicity of the metre, there does not seem to be a suitable tune available, which came as a surprise to me. I know of no explanation as to why 78.78 features so little among the many metres to which hymn tunes have been composed.

BORN BY THE HOLY SPIRIT'S BREATH   88 88 (LM)

Based on	selected verses from Romans 8
Theme	life in the Spirit; Whitsuntide; Pentecost
Written	at Sevenoaks, November 1972
Suggested tune	WHITSUN PSALM by Noël Tredinnick or FULDA from William Gardiner's 'Sacred Melodies' or BIRLING adapted by Geoffrey Shaw
Published in	*Psalm Praise*, 1973 to WHITSUN PSALM *Keswick Praise*, 1975 to EISENACH by J. H. Schein *Living Songs* (Africa Christian Press), 1975 to BRESLAU by Christian Gall *Songs of Worship*, 1980 to (1) WHITSUN PSALM and (2) FULDA *Hymns for Today's Church*, 1982 to (1) WHITSUN PSALM and (2) FULDA *Making Melody*, 1983 to (1) WHITSUN PSALM and (2) FULDA *Hymns and Psalms*, 1983 to CHURCH TRIUMPHANT by James William Elliott

This is one of a number of seasonal 'canticles' written for *Psalm Praise*—in this case with Pentecost in mind. It occupies only a single page in my MS book (which, as was my practice at the time, does not contain a fair copy). The original opening shows a different metre, and a rhyming scheme of a b a b:

In Jesus Christ all uncondemned we stand,
new life in Christ has conquered sin and death;
powerless indeed to meet the law's demand,
God now transforms us by the Spirit's breath.

I should be interested to hear this text sung to EASTER SONG, with the
appropriate 'Alleluias'. I believe it might make a joyful carol for Pentecost.

See Appendix 5, pp. 286ff.

BY LOVING HANDS   86 88 6

Theme	Eastertide
Written	at Bramerton, March 1975
Suggested tune	REPTON by C. H. H. Parry
Published in	News Extra, April 1976

My original fair copy is dated 29 March 1975; and the text was first
published under the title EASTER in the parish-magazine-inset News Extra.
Lines 3 & 4 of verse 2 then read:

> With none to see their footsteps pass
> As cold as dew across the grass . . .

I have been sorry to lose the impression of the icy dew of early morning,
while believing that the present version (revised at the request of the editor
of a hymnal as yet unpublished) is the better.

CHILD OF THE STABLE'S SECRET BIRTH   89 99 98

Theme	Christmas
Written	at Sevenoaks, February 1969
Suggested tune	MORWENSTOW by Christopher Dearnley
Published in	Crusade magazine, December 1969 (words only)
	English Praise, 1975 to MORWENSTOW
	Christmas Carols (Vine books carol sheet), 1978 (words only)
	Hymns for Today's Church, 1982 to (1) MORWENSTOW (2) SECRET BIRTH by Norman L. Warren
	A Song was heard at Christmas (USA), 1983 to MORWENSTOW
	Hymns and Psalms, 1983 to MORWENSTOW
Recorded on	Christmas Music, Philips 6833 157, 1975 to MORWENSTOW by the choir of St Paul's Cathedral, London

Originally written as a poem for our family Christmas card with no thought of a musical setting, this text was noticed by Christopher Dearnley, organist of St Paul's Cathedral, and set to his arrangement of MORWENSTOW, before I was aware that it might become a hymn or carol. It was included in *English Praise*, of which he was himself one of the editors, and recorded by his choir in a selection of Christmas carols. I like to think that had I been aware of this possibility earlier, I might have tidied up the metrical consistency of the verses—but there it is. My MS shows that verse 2 was written first, and indeed contains the original 'vision' of the text. The words *drive*, *pierce*, *sink*, *thrust* were tried and discarded in favour of *strike* in verse 4.

See Appendix 5, pp. 286ff.

CHILL OF THE NIGHTFALL   55 54 D

Theme	Christmas
Written	at Bramerton, December 1978
Suggested tune	BUNESSAN (Gaelic traditional)
Published in	*The Hymn* (Hymn Society of America), July 1980 (words only)
	Hal Hopson Choral Series (USA), 1982 as sheet music to GAELIC MELODY arranged by Hal. H. Hopson
	Beacon Choral Series (USA), 1982 as sheet music to a tune by Robert Kircher arranged by Dick Bolks
	Son of the highest (USA), 1983 to the tune by Robert Kircher arranged by Dick Bolks
	A Song was heard at Christmas (USA), 1983 to BUNESSAN
	Choristers Guild (USA), 1983 as sheet music to a tune by Richard E. Frey
Recorded on	*Son of the highest*, L-9044 (USA), 1983 to the tune by Robert Kircher arranged by Dick Bolks

Two texts were written (unusually for me) over the Christmas period, 1978. 'O Prince of peace' was completed on Christmas Eve; and this text begun a few days later, to be finally dated December 30th. The rhyming scheme differs in different texts to this tune; and it will be seen that lines 5 and 6 carry the rhyme here, rather than (as in 'Morning has broken' or 'Praise and thanksgiving') lines 5 and 7. The opening lines of the four verses were among the first to be written after the metrical form was apparent, the title-line being the last of the four. On publication in the journal of the Hymn Society of America, in July 1980, I received a quantity of letters from churches wishing to use the text in their Christmas worship, or from composers interested in settings or arrangements. The text first appeared on our family Christmas card in 1979.

CHRIST BE MY LEADER

10 10 10 10

Based on	John 14.6
Theme	youth; Christian living
Written	at Sevenoaks, July 1961
Suggested tune	SLANE (Irish traditional)
Published in	*Anglican Hymn Book*, 1965 to SLANE harmonized by Erik Routley
	* *Youth Praise 1*, 1966 to music by Michael A. Baughen, arranged by C. Roberts
	* *Renewal Songbook*, 1971 (words only)
	The Hymnal (of the Baptist Federation of Canada), 1973 to SLANE harmonized by Martin Shaw
	Keswick Praise, 1975 to SLANE harmonized by Erik Routley
	Grace Hymns, 1975 to SLANE (traditional)
	Concordia Choral Series (USA), 1978 as sheet music; set to SLANE harmonized by H. V. Gerike
	Lutheran Worship (USA), 1982 to SLANE
	Christian Hymns Observed, 1982 (words only)
	Hymns and Psalms, 1983 to TRISAGION by Henry Smart

At the time this was written, John 14.6 was a text much in my mind; and I have always been an admirer of the economy of Bishop Doane's hymn 'Thou art the Way'. This was one of two hymns written at the general invitation of Canon H. C. Taylor, the Chairman of the editorial committee of the *Anglican Hymn Book* (the other being 'Lord, who left the highest heaven') but on its inclusion a year later in *Youth Praise* I changed line 3 of verse 1 to read 'Fears for the future I trust to his care'; and this was followed by the editor of *Renewal Songbook* in 1971. This reading is now discontinued, since it loses the immediate thought of 'following' Christ the Way, paralleled by trusting him as the Truth in verse 2. Note the alliterative references to Christ as victor over darkness, doubt and death.

CHRIST BE THE LORD OF ALL OUR DAYS

86 88 6

Theme	Christian living
Written	at Ruan Minor, August 1975
Suggested tune	REPTON by C. H. H. Parry
Published in	*Hymns for Today's Church*, 1982 to GATESCARTH by Caryl Micklem

This text sprang from the single line 'Christ is the Lord of all our days' which had been running in my head through the weeks preceding our summer holiday in 1975. I had imagined a hymn with that title, and with

---

* incorporates an earlier version of the text in v.1, line 3, now discontinued.

each succeeding verse following the pattern of 'Christ is the Lord of all our . . .' Deeds, Hopes and Lives were all possible verses. At the same time I had been attracted by the metrical quality of the phrase 'the bright and morning star' (Revelation 22.16 in the AV) as a title of Christ. These came together in this text though originally with the statement 'is' in place of the prayer 'be' in each opening line. Line 4 of verse 1 is an echo of I Peter 3.7; and line 4 of verse 3 of the AV rendering of John 14.2

CHRIST FROM HEAVEN'S GLORY COME 77 77 77

Theme	Christmas; social concern
Written	at Ruan Minor, August 1983
Suggested tune	ENGLAND'S LANE (English traditional) or DIX by Conrad Kocher

Most summers, I try to write a Christmas hymn or carol for our family Christmas card. For 1983, I had in mind the familiar comparison of Christ unwelcomed and rejected, with those who experience disadvantage and rejection in our world today. But the note, almost of satire, which emerges in this text was certainly not in my mind when I sat down to begin work on it. I include it here for three reasons, even though I cannot see it finding a place in ordinary congregational worship: (a) because it might make an effective choir or group item, perhaps with an antiphonal 'echo' taking the alternate lines; (b) because the theme is a serious one, easily overlooked in our traditional inheritance of Christmas praise; and (c) because I am conscious that some of my own Christmas hymn-writing is self-contained in its biblical images; and not greatly related to the world we live in. I do not regret this; but I am glad of items like this present one, and like 'Lord, who left the highest heaven' (written more than twenty years ago) to show that the other side of the coin is not ignored.

Verse 1 is a picture of Bethlehem, verse 2 of Egypt (hence the reference to 'alien race'). In verse 4, the three quotations chosen for their ironic suitability come from Matthew 21.37, John 19.7, and the words and actions of Pontius Pilate in John 18.38 and Matthew 27.24.

The asterisk between verses 4 & 5 marks, of course, a change of mood (which might well be emphasized by a pause) and in the final verse ironic emphases should be replaced by a no less powerful sincerity of prayer and purpose.

CHRIST HIGH-ASCENDED 11 11 11 6

Theme	Ascensiontide; mission
Written	Ruan Minor, August 1983
Suggested tune	CHRISTE SANCTORUM (French traditional) as 11 11 11 6

I went on holiday in August 1983 hoping to write a hymn suitable for Ascensiontide; having done some preliminary work on the biblical passages in Acts and the Gospels, and in 1 Corinthians, Ephesians, Colossians and 1 Peter, as well as certain Old Testament references. The subject is one not over-represented in some hymnals, particularly for churches which wish to observe both Ascension Day and (as in the Church of England Calendar) the Sunday after Ascension.

Ascensiontide is inseparable from the giving of the Great Commission and the promise of the Spirit. The first is recognised in the five-times repeated final line which ends each verse, as well as more specifically in verses 2 & 3. The final verse looks forward to Pentecost.

The first line of verse 5 refers expressly to the final verse of St Luke's Gospel with its surprising testimony that 'he was parted from them' and they returned 'with great joy'—so exactly the contrary to what, by any human reckoning, the circumstances would suggest.

The tune suggested, CHRISTE SANCTORUM, is metrically 11 11 11 5; however, it will be found suitable for this text by allowing two full syllables—omitting the 'slur'—in the penultimate bar.

COME, LET US PRAISE THE LORD 66 66 88

Based on	Psalm 95, the Venite
Theme	praise and worship; morning; witness
Written	at Ruan Minor, 1981
Suggested tune	DARWALL'S 148TH by J. Darwall

In January 1972 Michael Baughen, editor of *Psalm Praise*, wrote to ask me for a metrical *Venite* (Psalm 95, so called from the opening word of the Latin title in the Book of Common Prayer, where it is set for daily use). I wrote one, but in the end withdrew it as unsuitable; and it was only nine years later that I returned to this Psalm. Verses 1 & 2 were begun over breakfast and into the morning; verses 3 & 4 in the later afternoon after lunch at the beach. Revisions were finished after supper, and final polishing the following day. This is one of two texts in this metre written in the same week.

COME NOW WITH AWE 11 10 11 10 11 10

Theme	Christmas
Written	at Ruan Minor, August 1975
Suggested tune	FINLANDIA by Jean Sibelius
Published in	*The Church of England Newspaper*, 12 December 1975 (words only)
	Digest (Association of Christian Teachers), September 1977 (words only)
	A Song was heard at Christmas (USA), 1983 to FINLANDIA

This text was intended as a Christmas hymn to FINLANDIA, for our family Christmas card 1975 (though actually written in August, on our summer holiday). It was written slowly, about a verse a day, over three or four days. Line 3 of verse 1 has been criticised as inconsistent with Luke 2.16, 'They came with haste . . .', but in my own mind I saw the picture of the shepherds following a rough and stony track, lit only by the stars; they would be the only figures moving in a midnight landscape. Whatever their haste, they would hardly have been striding out towards the sleeping town, and country-dwellers will not, I think, find the description 'creeping' untrue to experience. Until quite a late stage of revision, line 2 stood as 'Dark is the night and darker yet the way'.

DEAR LORD, WHO BORE OUR WEIGHT OF WOE   86 86 (CM)

Theme   Passiontide; penitence
Written   at Bramerton, October 1976
Suggested tune   BANGOR by William Tans'ur or
                   THIS ENDRIS NYGHT (English traditional)

This hymn was written at the request of the Roman Catholic International Commission on English in the Liturgy, who were seeking hymns to accompany their revision of the *Rite of Penance*. It did not in the event prove to be what they wanted; and verse 4 has always stood for me as an illustration of how difficult it is for a writer to be his own critic. I find the verse satisfying, and the parallelism and inversion of the first two lines meaningful. But I know this is not a general view, as compared, for example with the directness of the final two lines of the text. Whatever the merits of the hymn, the truths of which it speaks seem to me the most precious, and the nearest to the heart of our Christian faith.

See Appendix 5, pp. 286ff.

DONKEY PLOD AND MARY RIDE   77 77 77

Theme   Christmas
Written   at Bramerton, January 1976
Suggested tune   ARFON (Welsh traditional) or
                   ENGLAND'S LANE (English traditional)

A number of my texts begin with a line or couplet, arrived at with difficulty, sadly rejected, and then returned to as more satisfying than it had first appeared. This is one such instance. The hymn took its shape round the third line of each verse, linking an eternal truth which is our present possession to some part of the Christmas story that belonged especially to one group of participants. It was written in the days immediately following Christmas, and verse 1 had originally the two lines which now conclude it as part of the verse (i.e. as lines 3 & 4) in the form 'In your hearts draw near to them/On the road to Bethlehem'. The rest of the hymn followed when, on New Year's Day, the line 'Come away to Bethlehem' at last appeared as the key. The text was printed on our family Christmas card in December 1976.

See Appendix 5, pp. 286ff.

EVERY HEART ITS TRIBUTE PAYS   77 77 D

Based on	Psalm 65
Theme	praise and worship; creation; harvest
Written	at Ruan Minor, August 1979
Suggested tune	MAIDSTONE by W. B. Gilbert
Published in	*On the Move* (Australia), April 1980 (words only)
	Symphony, Autumn/Winter 1982/3 (words only)

Originally planned in verses of six lines rather than eight, it proved impossible to do justice to the theme of verse 2 in only six lines; and I believe that the final two lines of verse 1 are not such as fall under John Wesley's condemnation (in his famous preface to the *Collection* of 1779) '. . . no doggerel; no botches; nothing put in to patch up the rhyme; no feeble expletives.' The final verse was completed late at night, after a drive to Zennor; and is (to my mind) enhanced by the double alliteration of 'field and fold, byre and barn'. The psalm, and so this text, gives praise to God under the threefold division of the General Thanksgiving of the Book of Common Prayer; in which the Lord is recalled as the God of our Creation, our Preservation amid the blessings of this life, and of our Salvation through Christ.

See Appendix 5, pp. 286ff.

FAITHFUL VIGIL ENDED   65 65

Based on	The New English Bible translation of the Nunc Dimittis, Luke 2.29–32
Theme	fulfilment; consummation; conclusion
Written	at Eastbourne, in the garden of Holy Trinity Vicarage, August 1967: revised at Bramerton, February 1981
Suggested tune	FAITHFUL VIGIL by David G. Wilson or GLENFINLAS by K. G. Finlay
Published in	*Youth Praise 2*, 1969 to FAITHFUL VIGIL
	Thirteen Psalms, CPAS 1970 (words only)
	Family Worship, 1971 (words only)
	Psalm Praise, 1973 to FAITHFUL VIGIL (in two versions, unison and harmony)

English Praise, 1975 to (1) GLENFINLAS
    (2) PASTOR PASTORUM by P. F. Silcher
Pilgrim's Manual (Walsingham), 1979 (words only)
Songs of Worship, 1980 to FAITHFUL VIGIL
More Hymns for Today, 1980 to PASTOR PASTORUM
Hymns for Today's Church, 1982 to (1) FAITHFUL
    VIGIL arranged by John Barnard   (2) FAWLEY
    LODGE by Norman L. Warren
Hymns Ancient & Modern New Standard, 1983 to
    PASTOR PASTORUM
Hymns for Today, 1983 to PASTOR PASTORUM

On holiday in August 1967, I set myself to write a metrical version of these verses, sung as the *Nunc Dimittis* (from the Latin of the opening words) at Evening Prayer in the Book of Common Prayer. We had been lent by my brother-in-law his Vicarage of Holy Trinity Church, Eastbourne; and this text was written in the garden, working from the New English Bible, to be a companion to 'Tell out, my soul'. The New English Bible retains the use of 'thee' and 'thy' in references to the Deity; and I therefore wrote my text in that form. Over the years a number of editors asked if they might publish it with the small changes necessary to eliminate these archaisms but (for reasons explained in the Introduction) I felt bound to refuse. In 1981 however, when I was compiling my *Collection* of texts, it came home to me that there were only two in 'thee and thou' form, and that it would be possible to alter and improve the other ('Lord, who left the highest heaven') and to provide a 'You' alternative to this one, with little more than 'invisible mending'. Encouraged by the editors of *Hymns for Today's Church*, which was then in preparation, I provided the alternative text shown, though the original is still available for editors who prefer to follow more closely the usage of the NEB here.

FATHER, NOW BEHOLD US   65 65

Theme	the baptism of a child
Written	at Poldhu Cove and Ruan Minor, August 1980
Suggested tune	PASTOR PASTORUM by P. F. Silcher to which the words were written
Published in	*On the Move* (Australia), October 1981 (words only)
	Hymns for Today's Church, 1982 to NORTH COATES by T. R. Matthews

In the summer of 1980 we happened to sing at a Service in my local church T. B. Pollock's hymn 'Faithful Shepherd, feed me' to the tune PASTOR PASTORUM. In its simplicity it struck me as a specially suitable tune for a hymn intended for use at the baptism of a child; and I tried my hand at one on holiday that summer. This is the result.

    Baptism—especially infant baptism—is a large subject, and by no means simple. The text can only allude to various aspects, as indicated by the use of verbs: loving, washing, blessing, claiming, believing, signing, beginning, growing, saving, belonging. Verse two carries a highly-compressed, even elliptical reference to the place of parents, godparents and sponsors who declare their faith and repentance 'in the name of this child'; and verse three echoes both the traditional confirmation prayer, and the description of 'the Word made flesh' in John 1.14.

FATHER OF LIGHTS   88 88 (LM)

Theme	discipleship; light on the way
Written	at Ruan Minor, August 1976
Suggested tune	BODMIN by Alfred Scott-Gatty

The title comes from James 1.17, a passage picked up again in verse 3 of this text. Verse 1, speaking of the creation of light, is drawn from Genesis 1.2–4. Other references are to 1 Timothy 6.16 and to John 8.12.

FATHER ON HIGH TO WHOM WE PRAY   88 88 88

Theme	home and family
Written	at Ruan Minor, August 1977
Suggested tune	WYCH CROSS by Erik Routley or ST MATTHIAS by W. H. Monk
Published in	*Book of Worship*, Church of St Luke, St Paul, Minnesota, 1979 to STELLA (traditional) *Songs of Worship*, 1980 to HOLY FAITH by G. C. Martin *The Hymn* (Hymn Society of America), April 1981 (words only) *Hymns for Today's Church*, 1982 to ST MATTHIAS

Two elements combined to create this text. The final line of each verse, familiar as the response to intercessions since the first publication of the 'Alternative Services' of the Church of England, had long been in my mind for such a purpose. Then during 1977 I was asked for a further text on the theme of 'home'; and at last this seemed the opportunity to include this by now very well-known form of intercession. The trinitarian form of the hymn emerged as I went along; and the suggestion of the tune WYCH CROSS was because I had recently heard it sung and felt it fitted the mood. I sent the text to Erik Routley in the course of my 'summer letter' (an air-letter which I sent to him annually from Cornwall, chronicling our holiday doings, and hearing of his own in return). At that stage the second and third lines of verse 2 read:

> And in our nature chose to be
> an alien child of homeless birth . . .

Erik Routley suggested that this could give rise to misunderstandings; and that I could not assume that all who might sing the hymn would recognize the circumstances implicit in those lines. Hence the introduction of 'Egypt's land' to show the meaning of the description 'alien'.

I had hoped the text would include a reference to our Lord's words about himself in Matthew 8.20: 'Foxes have holes, and birds of the air have nests; but the Son of Man has nowhere to lay his head.' This thought took shape in two alternative couplets:

> A fox's den, a sparrow's nest,
> where weary hearts can be at rest.

and

> a sparrow's nest, a fox's lair—
> Lord, in your mercy, hear our prayer.

But both were overtaken in the course of writing.

FATHER, WHO FORMED THE FAMILY OF MAN   10 10 10 6

Based on	the Lord's Prayer
Theme	prayer
Written	at Sevenoaks in July 1968
Suggested tune	by Michael A. Baughen, arranged by David G. Wilson (see below) or MUNDAYS by Martin Shaw
Published in	*Youth Praise II*, 1969 to a tune specially composed by Michael A. Baughen, arranged by David G. Wilson
	Thirty Hymns, CPAS 1972 (words only)
	UTC Hymnbook, Bangalore, 1975 (words only)
	New Creation Song Book, Australia, 1983 (words only)

Originally written for *Youth Praise 2*, this hymn pre-dated the use of a MS book; it is however one of the few such for which the original MS survives. The alternating pattern at the start of each verse ('Father . . . Lord . . .') was not an original intention; verse 2, for instance, was originally drafted as 'Father of all the nations of the earth' and verse 3 as 'Ruler of all the ordered realms above'. The 'new song' of verse 2 is not yet the new song of Revelation 5.9, but rather of (for example) Psalm 40.3. The two titles in verse 6, line 2 are from the Psalms (18, 40, 70 and 144) and from Genesis 15.1.

See Appendix 5, pp. 286ff.

FILL YOUR HEARTS WITH JOY AND GLADNESS   87 87 87

Based on	Psalm 147
Theme	praise and thanksgiving; creation, harvest
Written	at Sevenoaks, March 1970, for *Psalm Praise*

Suggested tune	REGENT SQUARE by Henry Smart
Published in	*Psalm Praise*, 1973 to a tune specially composed by Robin Coulthard
	Come and Praise (BBC Radio for Schools), 1978 to (1) REGENT SQUARE (2) LAUS ET HONOR by Gordon Hartless
	Book of Worship; Church of St Luke, St Paul, Minnesota, 1979 to BEACH SPRING (Sacred Harp, 1844)
	BBC Radio: A Service for Schools, Teacher's Notes, Autumn 1980 (words only)
	Hymns for Today's Church, 1982 to REGENT SQUARE
	More Songs of the Spirit, 1982 to ODE TO JOY by Beethoven arranged by Michael Irwin*
	Sing Praise, 1982 to ODE TO JOY*

This is a psalm 'linking the wonders of creation with the glories of providence and grace'.† Verse 4 in the Coverdale version is one to touch the imagination: 'He telleth the number of the stars: and calleth them all by their names.' So in my first attempts to come to grips with this psalm I tried:

> Great is the Lord: His wisdom great;
> his might and power proclaim.
> He counts the number of the stars
> and calls them all by name.

Isaac Watts, I find, has in one of his versions:

> He form'd the stars, those heavenly flames,
> He counts their numbers, calls their names.

(In part 2 of the same Psalm he begins:

> O Britain, praise thy mighty God,
> and make his honours known abroad . . . !)

In the BBC Collection, verse 2 is omitted, which makes a hymn suited for use in schools under the general heading of 'The Created World'. But for congregational use the theme of the psalm (which is in any event compressed in these four verses) requires the second verse with its references to the inner experiences of the heart.

FROM AFAR A COCK IS CROWING   885 D

Theme	Eastertide
Written	partly on cliff walks near Land's End, and above Mullion; mainly at Ruan Minor, August 1983
Suggested tune	awaiting a composer; but see also below

* repeating the last two lines of each verse.
† See *Psalms 73–150* by Derek Kidner (IVP Tyndale Old Testament Commentaries, 1975) p. 485.

This text (the last of my summer holiday, 1983, and so the most recent in this Collection) took its origin from a desire to write on the theme of Easter, with an internal rhyme. The first couplet (now lines 4 & 5 of verse 1) set the shape for the whole.

Line 3 of verse 2 is a reference to our Lord's numerous prophecies to his disciples of his own resurrection (e.g. Matthew 20.19, though more are recorded in Mark and Luke).

Line 5 of verse 3 takes up the references in Colossians (2.12; 3.1) to the people of God as 'risen with Christ'. Line 6 is based on 2 Timothy 2.12 and numerous references in the book of Revelation.

Although there seems to be no existing hymn-tune to the metre 8 8 5 D, it has been suggested that the text would sing well to a modified version of J. B. König's tune EVANGELISTS, with the omission of the first half of the bars concerned, in lines 3 & 6.

FRUITFUL TREES, THE SPIRIT'S SOWING   87 87

Based on   Galatians 5.22,23
Theme   the fruit of the Spirit
Written   at Ruan Minor, August 1981
Suggested tune   ALL FOR JESUS by John Stainer
Published in   *On the Move* (Australia), April 1981 (words only)

In his booklet *Essentials for Tomorrow's Christians* (Scripture Union, London 1978, p. 9) John Stott writes:

> 'I long to see our evangelical faith exhibiting the fruit of the Spirit. For many years now I have recited to myself every day the ninefold fruit of the Spirit in Galatians 5.22,23, and have prayed for the fullness of the Spirit'.

Reading these words in the summer of 1981, I copied into my MS book an analysis of these fruits, from a variety of English translations of the New Testament. The AV, the RSV, J. B. Phillips, the New English Bible, the Jerusalem Bible, and R. A. Knox's translation all agree on *love, joy* and *peace*. The moderns all have *patience* and *kindness* for AV's *longsuffering* and *gentleness*, and mostly use *gentleness* where AV has *meekness*. On the other fruits there is a little more divergence of vocabulary. This metrical version of the passage follows the RSV (and therefore most of the moderns) with the one exception that it retains the AV *faith* where RSV (alone) has *faithfulness*, and the other versions give fidelity, trustfulness, forbearance. I think that this must be taken as poetic licence, a concession to the demands of metre!

The original versions of my text have 'Trees of life' in place of 'Fruitful trees'. My notes say that the text was 'begun cheerfully' one afternoon, after a morning on the beach, but later that evening nearly abandoned 'with dismay'. Further work began to resolve some of the intractable problems of verse 3; and a revision some days later gave line 2 of verse 2, and the resolution of verse 3 into its present form.

GLORY TO GOD IN THE HIGHEST

88 88 88 Dactylic

Based on	the Gloria in Excelsis
Theme	praise
Written	at Ruan Minor, August 1978
Suggested tune	RUSSWIN by Richard Proulx
Published	as sheet music by GIA Publications Inc. (USA) to RUSSWIN

This text was written at the suggestion of a friend, E. G. H. Saunders, the Vicar of St Michael's, Chester Square in London, who knew that I had written metrical versions of a number of canticles used in liturgical worship. But I am conscious that the greatness of the 'Gloria' is not so easily captured, going back as it does to the 4th century. I made a second attempt three years after writing this (see 'All glory be to God on high') and shall no doubt try again. This text is based on the version of the 'Gloria' in the Church of England *Alternative Service Book, 1980*, the text agreed by the International Consultation on English Texts, which covers all the main denominations in the English-speaking world and most of the principal nations involved. The final two lines of my verse 1 are in fact the opening lines of the ICET text, and they went far to determining structure and metre; though there exists in my MS book an attempt to write the hymn in verses of four rather than six lines. I rejected it for two reasons: because four lines (98 98) seemed less suitable for the majesty of the subject; and also because it became even more difficult to include all that should find a place in the hymn if it was indeed to be 'based on' (I claim no more) the original.

The hymn preserves the basic structure of the Gloria, described by ICET as 'an opening antiphon based on Luke 2.14, followed by the three stanzas of acclamation, the first addressed to God the Father, the second and third to God the Son'. It amplifies the reference to 'Lamb of God' in the third stanza and substitutes at times an indirect statement, rather than a direct address to God—notably in the final verse.

Richard Proulx's tune appears in GIA Choral Series No. G-2310, '*Two new Hymn Tunes* for unison voices and organ with SATB and Descants'.

GOD IS KING! THE LORD IS REIGNING

87 88 87 77

Based on	Psalm 93
Theme	praise and worship; the living God
Written	at Ruan Minor, August 1982
Suggested tune	awaiting a composer

The metre of this text is drawn from No. XXIX in A. E. Housman's *Last Poems*, 'Wake not for the world-heard thunder'. I chose it because of its unusual and attractive quality; and its suitability for such a theme as the Psalmist here expounds. The text owes more than its metre to the poem and its author: 'founded' is a word much used by Housman; thunder and lightning appear in both texts; even 'imperishable' is found in 'Parta Quies', No. XLVIII of *More Poems*. What is ringing or rooted in one's head is bound to find echoes in one's own writing.

I hesitated a little over rhyming 'ascended' with 'splendid' in verse 1. They sound the same in ordinary speech; but can one equate the final -ed of one with the -id of the other, without 'false rhyme'? Then I recalled Wordsworth's 'Intimations of Immortality' with the lines:

> And by the vision splendid
> Is on his way attended;

and took courage.

GOD IS MY GREAT DESIRE   66 84 D

Based on	Psalm 63
Theme	love for God; God our strength
Written	at Ruan Minor, August 1982
Suggested tune	LEONI (adapted from a Synagogue melody)

This is one of a small number of metrical psalms written at the request of David G. Preston, the compiler of a projected collection. As with the others, I had Derek Kidner's *Commentary* (IVP 1973) on the Book of Psalms with me; and the threefold division, with its headings of desire, delight and defence I owe to him.

In an early draft, line 3 of verse 1 ends with the word 'afire'—which is indeed true to the thought of the Psalmist; perhaps nearer his meaning than the text as it stands. But in a hymn for congregational use one must not put into the mouths of those who sing the words sentiments which are so far beyond their experience as to be quite unreal. I judge that many of us can speak (or sing) of a desire for God, and of aspirations towards him; whereas few, for any length of time together, can honestly sing that their heart is 'afire' with thirst for the Divine.

While other sounds are repeated in places, s & t (sometimes as st) echo through every verse. No doubt this was part of the attraction of 'trust' as the final word of the text. The combination st comes, I think, eight times in these 24 lines; while s & t appear in the same word on at least five other occasions.

GOD OF ETERNAL GRACE   66 86 (SM)

Theme	praise and worship; grace
Written	at Ruan Minor, Holy Week 1976
Suggested tune	DOMINICA by H. S. Oakeley

Part of the basis for this text is to be found in the line 'who formed and lit the starry height'; and part in the thought of the 'God of all grace' of

1 Peter 5.10. My notebook contains the line 'God of grace and King of glory'; with no indication that I was quoting unconsciously from H. E. Fosdick's 'God of grace and God of glory'; and I can also recall a few years after this text was written being attracted by the line 'who formed and lit the starry height' and wanting to incoporate it into a hymn; with no recollection that I had already done so. Originally 'grace' and 'love' (verses 1 & 5) were to be a couplet in the same form as e.g. 'truth and light' in verse 2. It will be noticed that the first and last verses speak of ourselves, turning to God and singing his praise; while the intermediate verses are prayers for divine guidance, inner renewal, and spiritual strength.

GOD OF GODS, WE SOUND HIS PRAISES 87 87 88 87

Based on	the Te Deum
Theme	praise and worship
Written	at Sevenoaks, April 1970
Suggested tune	GOD OF GODS by Christian Strover
Published in	*Psalm Praise*, 1973 to GOD OF GODS
	Hymns II (USA), 1976 to GOD OF GODS
	Anglican Hymn Book Supplement, 1978 (words only)
	Hymns for Today's Church, 1982 to GOD OF GODS
Recorded on	*Psalm Praise: Sing a new Song*, Word WST 9586, 1978 to GOD OF GODS

It was part of the conception of *Psalm Praise* that it should contain metrical canticles as well as metrical psalms. The *Te Deum* (from the opening words of the Latin version; translated as 'We praise thee, O God') is a very ancient hymn, thought to come originally from Niceta, Bishop of Remesiana in the fifth century; in the Book of Common Prayer it is part of the daily Service for Morning Prayer of the Church of England. This metrical version, though individual lines are much corrected in MS, assumed its present form from the start; and was fortunate to find a composer who provided it with a strong and attractive tune since it fits no hymn tune already extant. 'God of gods' is not an epithet drawn from the *Te Deum*; but is perfectly Scriptural (e.g. Daniel 2.47) and the similar phrase 'a great King above all Gods' comes in the canticle immediately preceding the *Te Deum* at Morning Prayer (Psalm 95).

GOD OF OLD, WHOM SAINTS AND SAGES 87 87 87

Theme	the Holy Scriptures
Written	at Bramerton, May 1979
Suggested tune	REGENT SQUARE by Henry Smart or RHUDDLAN (Welsh traditional)

| Published in | *On the Move* (Australia), April 1980 (words only) |
| | *Declare His Glory*, 1981 to REGENT SQUARE |

This text was written by request, for a hymn to be sung at the Norwich celebrations of the centenary of the Scripture Union—though the invitation to write it only confirmed a desire that had been with me for some time to write a text about the Scriptures. The tune REGENT SQUARE was in my mind and the text was written to that tune. Verse 4 was considerably altered at a late stage. Originally the first lines of verse 4 were:

> Love beyond all human caring,
> Aid beyond all mortal aid . . .

Reciting the text over to myself, I saw the opportunity of the three-fold description, Word of God, Lamb of God, Son of God (all three of which will be found in John 1) and changed the text to its present form.

HAD HE NOT LOVED US   10 10 10 10

Theme	the love of Jesus; the incarnation; Christmas
Written	at Iwerne Minster, Dorset in the 1940s; and
	completed at Sevenoaks in November 1969
Suggested tune	JULIUS by Martin Shaw or
	FARLEY CASTLE by Henry Lawes or
	ELLERS by E. H. Hopkins
Published in	*News Extra*, December 1976 (words only)
	Songs of Worship, 1980 to SURSUM CORDA by Alfred
	Smith
	Hymns for Today's Church, 1982 to SURSUM CORDA

This text has its origins earlier than any other in the Collection. Two of the three verses were written as a poem, in the late 1940s; and used, I think, as part of an address. I came across it in 1969; and brought it to completion with the addition of an extra verse. It appeared on our Christmas Card that year.

HE COMES TO US AS ONE UNKNOWN   86 88 6

Theme	the Lord Jesus Christ; faith
Written	at Ruan Minor and Poldhu beach, August 1982
Suggested tune	REPTON by Hubert Parry
Published in	*On the Move* (Australia), July 1983 (words only)

This hymn had its origin in the quotation of the first line by David Edwards, Dean of Norwich, in a lecture on the Gospels. It is part of a longer sentence from the closing pages of Albert Schweitzer's *The Quest of the Historical Jesus* (A & C Black, London, 3rd edition 1954, p. 401) which says of Christ:

> 'He comes to us as One unknown, without a name, as of old, by the lakeside, He came to those first men who knew Him not.'

Taking as its theme our perception of God's approach to the soul, and the 'sense of the divine' which is part of human experience, the first two verses were written at a sitting. The third is a reference to Revelation 1.15 and to 1 Kings 19; with the merest allusion to 1 Chronicles 14.15, when 'a sound of going in the tops of the mulberry trees' is a sign or signal from the Lord himself: the NEB translation is 'a rustling sound in the treetops'. By verse 4 the text is explicitly Christian in its reference both to incarnation and to atonement; and by verse 5 there is the personal response of faith to the Lord Jesus Christ of the New Testament (cf. Luke 24.27; 1 Peter 1.8).

HE WALKS AMONG THE GOLDEN LAMPS   86 88 86

Based on	Revelation 1.12–18
Theme	the vision of Christ
Written	at Sevenoaks, March 1972
Suggested tune	REVELATION by Noël Tredinnick or GOLDEN LAMPS by Norman Warren
Published in	*Psalm Praise*, 1973 to (1) REVELATION (2) GOLDEN LAMPS
	Grace Hymns, 1975 to GOLDEN LAMPS
	Hymns II (USA), 1976 to REVELATION
	Book of Worship; Church of St. Luke, St. Paul, Minnesota, 1979 to AUDEN by Alec Wyton
	Hymns for Today's Church, 1982 to REVELATION
Recorded on	*Here is Psalm Praise*, Reflection RL311, 1975 to REVELATION

The text of this hymn follows closely the vision of the aged John on the island of Patmos, described in the first chapter of the book of Revelation. The golden lamps are the churches: the one in the midst of them is described in terms recalling Daniel, chapter 7, as 'like a son of man'. In this text, the robe, the feet, the eyes, the hair, the voice are all drawn direct from John's vision; the description of the robe is an (I hope legitimate) extrapolation; the stars and the sword remind us that John's imagery is symbolic rather than pictorial. John is told 'Write what you see'—and the hymn takes up John's description and seeks to make of it an act of worship.

No existing hymn-tune known to me fitted the metre of this text—which is not in fact a complicated one. But as can be seen above, editors have been glad of the opportunity to use one or other of the two tunes composed to these words for *Psalm Praise*, the book for which the text was written.

HEAVENLY HOSTS IN CEASELESS WORSHIP

87 87 D

Based on	Revelation 4 & 5
Theme	Praise and worship
Written	at Sevenoaks, September 1972
Suggested tune	ABBOT'S LEIGH by Cyril V. Taylor or HYFRYDOL by R. H. Prichard
Published in	*Psalm Praise*, 1973 to (1) HEAVENLY HOSTS by Noël Tredinnick (2) music specially composed by Norman Warren
	Grace Hymns, 1975 to MAESYNEAUADD by W. R. Thomas
	Worship II (USA), 1975 to HEAVENLY HOSTS
	Sixty Hymns from Songs of Zion (USA), 1977 to LINCOLNWOOD by Keith Landis
	Book of Worship, Church of St Luke, St Paul, Minnesota, 1979 to LINCOLNWOOD
	Hymns for Today's Church, 1982 to (1) BLAENWERN by W. P. Rowlands (2) ABBOT'S LEIGH

The two verses of this hymn appear in my MS book substantially in their present form from the beginning. They occupy a single page, and the corrections are more to individual lines than to the construction or form of the text.

This hymn is based on what John describes in a vision through a door open into heaven (Revelation 4.1). He sees there the throne and 'One seated on the throne', worshipped by the elders and the living creatures round about him; with special reference not only to his glory, honour and power, but to his creation. And then John sees also the Lamb of God who by his blood 'did ransom men for God' (chapter 5. v.9) worshipped by 'myriads and myriads and thousands and thousands' of the citizens of heaven. Indeed, 'every creature in heaven and on earth and under the earth and in the sea' (verse 13) join in the chorus of praise: and the 'Glory, honour and power' of the first song swells to 'Power and wealth and wisdom and might and honour and glory and blessing . . . for ever and ever' (12,14).

HERE WITHIN THIS HOUSE OF PRAYER

77 77 77

Theme	anniversary, thanksgiving or special occasion; the Holy Trinity
Written	at Bramerton, January 1978
Suggested tune	DIX by Conrad Kocher
Published in	*Book of Worship*, Church of St Luke, St Paul, Minnesota, 1979 to DIX
	Hymns for Today's Church, 1982 to (1) ASHBURTON by R. Jackson (2) DIX

About the end of 1977, Canon Frank Colquhoun, then Vice-Dean of Norwich Cathedral (himself known as a hymnologist) asked me if I would write a hymn for the Installation of the Very Reverend David Edwards as Dean of Norwich, on 8 April 1978. Norwich Cathedral is dedicated to 'the Holy and Undivided Trinity'; so that a Trinitarian form seemed right. Because of this, even before its publication in any hymnal, the text was in use occasionally in other churches with a Trinitarian dedication.

As often happens, the opening line was the most difficult; and the reference to 'House of Prayer' which appears in early drafts as line 6, line 3, and line 2, crept upwards to create an opening. The first verse is designed to indicate a landmark or a milestone, without specifying at all closely the nature of the occasion thus celebrated. Verse 2 speaks of Christ as central to the ministry of both Word and Sacrament; and the final line of verse 3 is a deliberate echo of the concluding prayer at every Service of Holy Communion (in one of the modern alternatives): 'Send us out in the power of your Spirit to live and work to your praise and glory'. By the final line of the hymn, it will be seen that prayer has been lifted into praise.

HIGH PEAKS AND SUNLIT PRAIRIES   76 76 D

Theme	Christmas
Written	at Ruan Minor, August 1974.
Suggested tune	CRÜGER by Johannes Crüger

These verses appeared on our family Christmas card in 1974; and perhaps they are more in the nature of a Christmas poem than of a hymn. The three verses speak in succession of the natural world, the created earth—and indeed the universe to which it belongs; then of the living creatures, among whom the 'absent Lord' is content to be numbered; and finally of ourselves, men and women who are the crown of all God's creative work, in whose human form God comes to earth.

See Appendix 5, pp. 286ff.

HOLY CHILD   77 77

Theme	Christmas
Written	at Sevenoaks, September 1966
Suggested tune	HOLY CHILD by Michael A. Baughen
Published in	*News Extra*, December 1966 (words only)
	Youth Praise 2, 1969 to HOLY CHILD arranged by David G. Wilson
	Hear the Bells of Christmas (Manila), 1975 to HOLY CHILD
	Merrily to Bethlehem, 1978 to HOLY CHILD
	Christmas Carols (Vine books carol sheet), 1978 (words only)

Hymns for Today's Church, 1982 to (1) FAIRMILE by
David Peacock   (2) HOLY CHILD arranged by
Noël Tredinnick
A Song was heard at Christmas (USA), 1983 to
HOLY CHILD arranged by Noël Tredinnick

Recorded on   *Christmas Praise*, Fountain FTN 2501, 1976 to
HOLY CHILD

If an author is allowed favourite texts, this is one of mine. I recall writing it
in the days following the birth of our youngest child; and it appeared on
our family Christmas card that same year. No doubt much of its popularity
is due to the tune that Michael Baughen and David Wilson wrote for these
words.

The punctuation here shown is largely due to the careful work of the
editors of *Hymns for Today's Church*; and is, I think, an improvement on
the punctuation that appears in earlier hymnals or in my own *Collection,
1961–81*.

In singing the hymn, a change of mood should be emphasised as between
verse 5 and verse 6, where the thought moves from the cross to the
resurrection. If a choir is singing, a slight pause is then effective, before the
gentle *reprise* of the final verse.

See Appendix 5, pp. 286ff.

HOW FAINT THE STABLE-LANTERN'S LIGHT   86 86 (CM)

Theme   Christmas
Written   at Bramerton, 23 December 1979
Suggested tune   THIS ENDRIS NYGHT (Traditional) or
BALLERMA by François H. Barthélémon or
ST BOTOLPH by Gordon Slater
Published in   *A Song was heard at Christmas* (USA), 1983 to THIS
ENDRIS NYGHT arranged by R. Vaughan Williams

This text was written round a single word. A few years later, reading an
edition of Cecil Beaton's *Diaries* (edited by Richard Buckle, London 1979,
p. 91), I came across an entry which reminded me of the experience:

'Lunch with Cecil Day Lewis who talked about the way he writes poetry:
gets a clue line, writes it in a notebook. Later, when he has a
stomach-ache that denotes it is time for him to deliver, the poem is
evolved round this line. Half of the poem is due to the way he works it
out—half inspiration, half technique (or idiom).'

Apart from the stomach-ache, that accurately describes this text; the word
was 'candle' in a line originally written as 'A candle through the night' with

the note '(better, dark?)'. The order of the verses was changed in the course of revision, and an additional verse discarded:

> O Christ, our light of life divine,
> our Sun and Star ablaze,
> Within our spirits burn and shine
> for this and all our days;

Re-discovering it on writing these notes, it was clearly right to remove it as both too reminiscent of earlier work, and out of character with the hymn; which appeared first on our family Christmas card in December 1981.

HOW SHALL THEY HEAR, WHO HAVE NOT HEARD   88 88 (LM)

Based on	verses from Romans 10, Matthew 28, Isaiah 6
Theme	mission and evangelism
Written	at Bramerton, 27 December 1979
Suggested tune	BODMIN by Alfred Scott-Gatty or OMBERSLEY by W. H. Gladstone
Published in	*Consultation Program* (see below), June 1980 (words only)
	Programme and Information, National Assembly of the National Initiative in Evangelism, UK, September 1980 (words only)
	also in German translation by the Department of World Mission and Ecumenical Relations, Evangelical-Lutheran Church of Württemburg: translation by Johannes Jourdan, © 1980 by Hanssler-Verlag, D-7703 Neuhausen-Stuttgart.
	Declare His Glory, 1981 to OMBERSLEY

Late in 1979 the Reverend Dr John Stott asked me to try my hand at a hymn for the Consultation on World Evangelization arranged by the Lausanne Committee for World Evangelization to be held at Pattaya in Thailand in June 1980. The notes of my talk with him at the time indicates that he suggested, among possible themes, those of 'Resolve leading to strategy', of 'Penitence', of 'Recognition of the size and diversity of the task', of 'Prayer', and of what he called 'Costly incarnational evangelism'. All too few of those ideas find expression in this text.

'How shall they hear' was the theme of the Consultation, so Romans 10 furnished the first of the questions which begin each of the first four verses; but I did not see, when I began, that the other questions from Matthew 28 and Isaiah 6 would fit such a framework. The idea evolved as the text developed.

The text was used as the theme song of the Consultation, under the direction of Cliff Barrows of the Billy Graham Evangelistic Association, and was first printed in the Consultation Program.

Theme	Christmas
Written	at Sevenoaks, June 1968
Suggested tune	by Michael A. Baughen, arranged by David G. Wilson (see below)
Published in	*Crusade* magazine, 1969 (words only)
	Youth Praise 2, 1969 to a tune specially composed by Michael A. Baughen, arranged by David G. Wilson
	Hear the Bells of Christmas (Manila), 1975 to the tune by Michael A. Baughen
	Carols (USA), 1978 to a tune by H. M. Huffman
	A Song was heard at Christmas (USA), 1983 to the tune by Michael A. Baughen, arranged by David G. Wilson

Originally written on the back of a Christmas card bearing the text of 'Holy child', both texts have obvious similarities in their treatment of a Christmas theme, looking forward through the coming years at the life, and death, of Christ. The MS suggests comparatively few major revisions, save for an alternative quatrain to end verse 3, which has its own attractions:

> Saviour of others
> none other can save,
>   the Lord of all glory
> lies cold in the grave.

Though I have been a reader of Kipling for at least 45 years, it was only in the course of writing these notes that I became conscious of his poem, used as a chapter heading for 'the White Seal' in the *Jungle Book*, beginning

> 'Oh! hush thee, my baby, the night is behind us.'

But I must have read it more than once; and lodged it in my unconscious mind.

The text appeared on our family Christmas card in December 1968.

I LIFT MY EYES   4 5 8 4 5 7

Based on	Psalm 121
Theme	confidence and peace
Written	at Sevenoaks, December 1968
Suggested tune	by Michael A. Baughen and Elisabeth Crocker (see below)
Published in	*Psalm Praise*, 1973 to a tune specially composed by Michael A. Baughen and Elisabeth Crocker
	Hymns II (USA), 1976 to a tune by Michael A. Baughen and Elisabeth Crocker; including a choral setting

Book of Worship, Church of St Luke, St Paul,
    Minnesota, 1979 to CONSOLATION (Kentucky
    Harmony, 1816)
Partners in Praise, 1979 to UPLIFTED EYES by
    Michael A. Baughen and Elisabeth Crocker
Songs of Worship, 1980 to LIFT MY EYES by Michael
    A. Baughen

Recorded on   Here is Psalm Praise, Reflection RL 311, 1975 to the
    tune by Michael A. Baughen and Elisabeth
    Crocker
I lift my eyes to the quiet hills, IVR TM (USA), 1976
    to the tune by Michael A. Baughen and Elisabeth
    Crocker

This is one of a pair of 'metrical psalms' written for Psalm Praise when
recovering from an attack of 'flu (the other is 'Safe in the shadow of the
Lord'). Its popularity must be attributed to the haunting tune which
Michael Baughen wrote for it when he was Vicar of Holy Trinity, Platt (the
hymn was first sung at a televised Service from that church in October
1970, over two years before Psalm Praise was published); it was also
among the hymns sung at his consecration as Bishop of Chester in York
Minster in June 1982.

The imagery of the hymn in my own mind owes something to my
affection for a hill called 'Caesar's Camp' (which indeed it once was) above
the town of Folkestone, where we lived before and after the 1939–45 war.

The text is a good example of why I prefer the description 'based on . . .'
for my metrical psalms; it indicates that they make no claim to be
'translations' (I have no Hebrew) or even versions of the inspired originals;
but hymns which owe their form, theme and content to the psalm. This is
in some degree the case with the majority of our traditional metrical
versions.

Note that while the keeping, guarding and preserving are all objective,
'secure and still' (v.2) are subjective. See R. C. Trench, A Select Glossary
(London, 1859) for the distinction between safe and secure—literally, sine
cura, without anxiety. Trench gives a good example of this, the more
ancient meaning, from Judges 18.7 in the Authorised Version where the
people of Laish are described as 'careless . . . quiet and secure'.

IN ENDLESS EXULTATION   76 76 D

Theme   praise
Written   at Ruan Minor, August 1980
Suggested tune CRÜGER by Johannes Crüger
Published in   On the Move (Australia), October 1981 (words only)

Successive drafts of this hymn are entered in my MS book under the title
The Song of the Earth, which rightly indicates the starting place of the text.
Perhaps in consequence the first verse 'wrote itself'; the only change from

the jottings with which I began is that the original line 7 read 'and by the ocean's thunders'. The second half of the hymn proved much more intractable.

The thought of earth rejoicing is a recurring theme in Scripture—for example in Isaiah 44.23: 'Sing, O heavens . . . shout, O depths of the earth . . .' Luke 19.40 and Psalm 96.11 exemplify the ideas which end verse 1; and the wind and storm of verse 2 is from Psalm 148.8 in the Prayer Book version. The last line owes, I think, a debt to the last line of Charles Wesley's magnificent 'Wrestling Jacob', the hymn 'Come, O thou Traveller unknown'.

IN MY HOUR OF GRIEF OR NEED   77 77

Based on	Psalm 10
Theme	deliverance
Written	at Sevenoaks, March 1970
Suggested tune	by Michael A. Baughen, arranged by Elisabeth Crocker and David G. Wilson (see below); or HEINLEIN by Martin Herbst
Published in	*Psalm Praise*, 1973 to a tune specially composed by Michael A. Baughen, arranged by Elisabeth Crocker and David G. Wilson
	Grace Hymns, 1975 to THEODORA from G. F. Handel

I think this must be one of the first 'metrical psalms' which I attempted especially for *Psalm Praise*; it would be the first on a list in order of number. If memory serves, I wrote much of it on a train journey (I think to Chipping Campden).

Psalm Praise provides for the repetition of verse 1 as the conclusion of the hymn; which does something to correct the balance of the verses (pivoting, as they do, about the final line of verse 4). Notations in hymnals about how individual lines should be sung are rightly out of fashion; my own choice would be for verse 1, if repeated as verse 7, to signal a change of mood from the triumphalism of verses 5 & 6 to the realities of present temptation, by being sung softly and prayerfully.

JESUS IS THE LORD OF LIVING   87 87 87

Theme	the Lord Jesus Christ
Written	at Ruan Minor, August 1974
Suggested tune	THE LANCASHIRE COTTON WEAVER (traditional) or DISMISSAL by W. L. Viner or GRAFTON (French traditional)

Published in

Songs of Worship, 1980 to COTTON WEAVER
arranged by Robin Sheldon
Hymns for Today's Church, 1982 to (1) COTTON
WEAVER (2) REGENT SQUARE by Henry Smart

This hymn owes its origin to a children's TV programme in a series on the BBC entitled 'Bagpuss', about 'a saggy old cloth cat'. I was watching this one day with my young family in the Spring of 1974, when we were living at Postwick, near Norwich. The programme contained a theme-tune, charmingly played and sung, which took my fancy as a possible tune for a hymn. I wrote to the creator of the programme, Oliver Postgate, who told me that the tune was an arrangement of a traditional folk song, 'the Lancashire Cotton Weaver' and sent me a tape of the programme. Working from this, the text was written that summer, primarily (but I hope not exclusively) with young people and the needs of schools in mind.

See Appendix 5, pp. 286ff.

JESUS MY BREATH, MY LIFE, MY LORD   88 88 6

Theme   Christ in experience
Written   at Ruan Minor, August 1979
Suggested tune   MANOR PARK by Derek Kidner, specially written for
                    this text
Published in   The Hymn (Hymn Society of America), April 1981
                    (words only)

David Winter asked me once in a radio interview if I was aware how often references to God and to heaven as 'high' appeared in my hymns; and whether this indicated a preoccupation with the transcendence of God, rather than with his immanence—his indwelling, his prèsence among us. Both aspects of God have been celebrated continually by hymn-writers; and this text speaks perhaps more intimately than most in this collection of the sense of God's presence in and near us.

'Breath' is used in Scripture (for example in Genesis 2.7, Job 33.4, Exekiel 37.9, and John 20.22) as the sign of life imparted by God into both body and spirit.

These notes have recorded already the debts I owe to Derek Kidner; among them that on reading this text in MS he wrote a tune for it, entitled MANOR PARK, a phrase from the postal address of his home near Cambridge.

JESUS, PRINCE AND SAVIOUR   65 65 triple

Theme   Eastertide
Written   at Ruan Minor, August 1974
Suggested tune   ST GERTRUDE by Arthur Sullivan

Published in	*News Extra*, March 1975 (words only)
	Songs of Worship, 1980 to ST GERTRUDE
	Declare His Glory, 1981 to ST GERTRUDE
	A Supplement to Congregational Praise, 1982 (words only)
	Making Melody, 1983 to ST GERTRUDE

This Easter text was written from the conviction that Easter is the most suitable time for Christian triumph; and that in Sir Arthur Sullivan's ST GERTRUDE we have a tune of stirring power, wedded to words by Sabine Baring-Gould whose 'militarism' no longer makes them suitable for every occasion of rejoicing. Both tune and words have stern critics as well as stalwart advocates.

Onward, Christian Soldiers, written in 1864, was first sung to a tune by Haydn from his 'Imperial' Symphony. ST GERTRUDE was published in 1871, named after the hostess (Mrs Gertrude Clay-Ker-Seymer) in whose house Sullivan was staying at the time he wrote it. Tunes and words, therefore, were not always as inseparably linked as they appear today.

The phrase 'Prince and Saviour' comes from Acts 5.31 when Peter and the apostles are bearing witness to the high priest about the resurrection and exaltation of Christ.

Lines 3 and 4 of the last verse embody the ancient Easter greeting of the Church. I have sometimes thought how effectively they might be sung by giving line 3 to be sung by, say, choir only; with line 4 as a congregational response.

LET HEARTS AND VOICES BLEND   66 66

Theme	the Lord Jesus Christ
Written	at Ruan Minor, August 1975
Suggested tune	ST CECILIA by L. G. Hayne
Published in	*Book of Worship*, Church of St Luke, St Paul, Minnesota, 1979 to STARLIGHT by Anthony Hedges

It will be clear at a glance that this text is an experiment using a device familiar in hymnody (the repetition of the final line of one verse as the opening line of the next) but using it consistently in every verse. It derives from the practice of repeated lines in the French form called 'the villanelle', of which perhaps the best-known modern example is Dylan Thomas's 'Do not go gentle into that good night'. Something of the same can be seen in Richard Wilbur's Christmas hymn 'A stable-lamp is lighted'. Such a pattern requires lines of identical metrical length (in this case 66.66), and rhymes made up of trios rather than pairs.

Based on	a prayer from St Augustine
Theme	Christ in experience
Written	at Ruan Minor, August 1976
Suggested tune	MOVILLE (Irish traditional)
Published in	*Songs of Worship*, 1980 to WOLVERCOTE by W. H. Ferguson
	A Supplement to Congregational Praise, 1982 (words only)
	Hymns for Today's Church, 1982 to KING'S LYNN (English traditional) arranged by R. Vaughan Williams

This text was written to the tune MOVILLE, which I had by me on a cassette recorder; and takes its theme from a passage in the *Meditations* of St Augustine, frequently adapted as a traditional and beautiful prayer. It is an example of how much more easily hymns can be addressed to God using 'Thee and Thou' language: 'Light of the minds that know thee' would be an excellent opening line, whereas '. . . that know you' I find unacceptable. The hymn is therefore cast in its present less directly personal form.

I have been taken to task for presuming that the reference to the Emmaus road will be self-evident to modern worshippers. I feel strongly that while convoluted imagery from the typology of the Old Testament may be questioned for modern hymns, a familiarity with the Gospels is a reasonable expectation. Proper names can be powerful in their associations; but require careful handling. Harold Nicholson in his book *Tennyson* (Constable, London 1923) refers to 'this device, so popular with English poets from Milton to Flecker, of enlivening the gray colours of our native speech by the introduction of resonant and flamboyant foreign names'.

The reference in verse 4 to heaven is based on some words from the Sarum Antiphoner, dating back certainly to the fourteenth century. I used to see them when, as a member of the General Synod of the Church of England, I spent long days in the debating chamber at Church House, London. It is a fine circular hall, and around the base of the dome are inscribed these words:

> Holy is the true light and passing wonderful, lending radiance to them that endured in the heat of the conflict; from Christ they inherit a home of unfading splendour, wherein they rejoice with gladness evermore.

LIGHTEN OUR DARKNESS 11 11 11 5

Based on	the Collect for aid against all perils
Theme	evening
Written	at Ruan Minor, August 1977
Suggested tune	CHRISTE SANCTORUM (French traditional)

Published in   *Anglican Hymn Book Supplement*, 1978 (words only)
Hymns for Today's Church, 1982 to CHRISTE SANCTORUM arranged by David Iliff

The prayer on which this hymn is based—the third collect at Evening Prayer in the Book of Common Prayer—goes back in its original form for well over a thousand years, and perhaps as far back as the sixth or seventh century. Verse 2 of my text carries echoes of Romans 13.12, the passage which St Augustine found himself reading when he heard in the garden the voice chanting 'Take up and read' (*Confessions* 8.22); and to Psalm 130.6.

As originally written the hymn contained a middle verse:

Power of all power, upholding nature's forces,
King of all kings, in ordered splendour reigning;
stars in their stations, planets in their courses,
all things sustaining.

This departs however from the simpler concept of the original prayer; and probably owes its origin to line 3 above which I had long been wanting to set in a hymn when the opportunity came.

LIVING LORD, OUR PRAISE WE RENDER   87 87

Based on	Romans 6.5–11
Theme	new life in Christ; Eastertide
Written	at Sevenoaks, February 1972
Suggested tune	by Michael A. Baughen, arranged by Norman Warren (see below) or ALL FOR JESUS by John Stainer or ADORATION by J. E. Hunt
Published in	*Psalm Praise*, 1973 to a tune specially composed by Michael A. Baughen, arranged by Norman Warren *Keswick Praise*, 1975 to ST OSWALD by J. B. Dykes

This text was written as a 'New Testament Psalm' or canticle for *Psalm Praise*. 'Splendour' in verse 1, line 3, is the New English Bible version of the AV's 'by the glory of the Father'. It is the NEB also which by its rendering 'in union with Christ Jesus' paves the way for 'One with Christ' at the start of verse 3. Verse 10 of this passage provides the title and the six-times-repeated refrain for one of Dylan Thomas's best known lyrical poems 'And death shall have no dominion'.

See Appendix 5, pp. 286ff.

LONG BEFORE THE WORLD IS WAKING   87 87 77

Based on	John 21
Theme	Eastertide; the lakeside

Written	at Poldhu Cove and Ruan Minor, August 1981
Suggested tune	ALL SAINTS (German traditional)
Published in	*Symphony*, Spring/Summer 1983 (words only)

Jesus' resurrection appearance to the disciples at the lakeside, on the shore of the Sea of Galilee, occupies the whole of the final chapter of St John's Gospel. It is a story of which Professor Tasker has written 'Few passages in the New Testament have a more numinous quality, or are so haunting in their beauty; and there can be few readers who remain insensitive to the awe and mystery which pervade it'. It is a passage to which I return year by year in the days after Easter; and one on which I had wanted to write a hymn for some years before completing this text. 'John 21' was in the list of possible themes which went on holiday with me for several summers—and will do so again, since I by no means believe this to be the only (or indeed, the best) text that I have it in me to write upon this theme.

The hymn is narrative in form for the first three verses; and in the last two it relates the experience of the disciples to our own experience of Christ's presence today—finding in him forgiveness for the past (surely the fire on the beach must have reminded Peter of the fire in the High Priest's courtyard), bread for the new day, a renewed call to work for him, and the assurance of his continuing friendship. Indeed, I recall the pleasure with which I found a final couplet to conclude the hymn and to sum up the meaning of this story of dawn on the beach, with its message of resurrection life. For me, this chapter fitly concludes John's Gospel by opening a door between his day and our own.

LOOK, LORD, IN MERCY AS WE PRAY   86 86 D (DCM)

Theme	unity
Written	at Ruan Minor and Poldhu Cove, August 1980
Suggested tune	LADYWELL by W. H. Ferguson or ST MATTHEW by William Croft
Published in	*Church of England Newspaper*, 2 January 1981 (words only) *Hymns for Today's Church*, 1982 set to CHRISTMAS CAROL by H. Walford Davies

I believe that the prayer of this text is one which more people find in their hearts today than in most previous generations. It is still true of us and our churches, in the telling phrase, 'that our scandalous divisions are by no means always the most scandalous thing about us'; but there is an unwillingness to settle merely for Christian co-operation; and a sense that to maintain unity (Ephesians 4.3) means to maintain it visibly. In that context, this hymn offers a prayer for motivation (fire us anew'); and a reminder (as indeed a number of hymns have done) of the things we hold in common, on the common foundation of Scripture. Such a foundation seems to me essential: in the words of Cranmer's prayer for the church militant, our prayer is still that 'they that do confess thy holy Name may agree in the truth of thy holy Word, and live in unity . . .'

Moreover (verse 2, lines 7,8) unity is for mission.

In the light of the above, it is no surprise to see from my MS book that the reference to Scripture in verse 2 was drafted and redrafted in successive versions:

> One in the faith of Christ, made known
> in Scripture's living page;
> the Word of God revealed and shown
> as truth for every age.

or:

> One in the faith of Christ, received
> in Scripture's sacred page;
> one living word of truth believed
> as truth for every age.

or:

> by saints in every age.

The text was originally planned as six verses of four lines each, 86 86; and could, I suppose, still be sung that way; though verse 2 would then be left with no main verb.

LORD, AS THE DAY BEGINS   66 66 88

Theme	morning
Written	at Ruan Minor, August 1980
Suggested tune	LITTLE CORNARD by Martin Shaw, to which the words were written
Published in	*Hymns for Today's Church*, 1982 set to SAMUEL by A. Sullivan
	The Hymn (Hymn Society of America), January 1983 (words only)

This text arose from the combination of tune (a desire to try my hand at a text to LITTLE CORNARD) and theme (I had already three texts on the theme of *evening*; nothing on *morning*.)

LITTLE CORNARD was written originally for Charles Oakley's 'Hills of the North rejoice'; and apart from the change of rhythm in the final lines of each verse, it is unusual in the stress that falls on the opening word in each of the first four lines. Few texts in the metre of 66 66 88 are suitable therefore—as can be seen by trying, for example, to fit the words of Isaac Watts' 'Join all the glorious names' to this tune.

Verse 1 asks for a heart turned towards God from the beginning, knowing his forgiveness, protection and guidance, so as to live to his glory. Verse 2 thinks of daily work and life in community, and the inter-dependence of the human family; our days filled with the fruit of the Spirit (Colossians 3.2; Galatians 5.22). Verse 3 asks for strength, direction, safety and sustenance; and for continual thankfulness (Ephesians 5.20). The change in line 2 between verse 1 and verse 4, though appearing at a late stage in revision, provides the keynote of the text.

Theme   anniversary; thanksgiving; dedication
Written   in February 1967
Suggested tune   LORD OF THE YEARS by Michael A. Baughen and
                       David G. Wilson or
                   ST OSYTH by Thomas Wood or
                   HIGHWOOD by Richard Terry
Published in   *Youth Praise 2*, 1969 to LORD OF THE YEARS
                   Family Worship, 1971 (words only)
                   Thirty Hymns, CPAS 1972 (words only)
                   Keswick Praise, 1975 to LORD OF THE YEARS
                   UTC Hymnbook, Bangalore, 1975 (words only)
                   Anglican Hymn Book Supplement, 1978 (words
                       only)
                   Partners in Praise, 1979 to LORD OF THE YEARS
                       adapted by T. Brian Coleman
                   Songs of Worship, 1980 to LORD OF THE YEARS
                   A Supplement to Congregational Praise, 1982
                       (words only)
                   Hymns for Today's Church, 1982 to LORD OF
                       THE YEARS arranged by David Iliff
                   A Service for Remembrance Sunday, 1982 (words
                       only)
                   Making Melody, 1983 to LORD OF THE YEARS
                   Mission England Praise, 1983 to LORD OF THE YEARS
Recorded on   *Here is Youth Praise*, Reflection RL 308, 1975 to
                       LORD OF THE YEARS
                   Tell the World, Word SAC 5096, 1980 to LORD OF
                       THE YEARS: words on sleeve only

In 1867 a remarkable organization called 'the Children's Special Service
Mission' was founded, following the visit to England of an American,
Payson Hammond, who conducted a number of children's missions.
Twelve years later a children's 'Scripture Union' was begun under the same
auspices. Today the name 'Scripture Union' is the one commonly used, but
the organization continues, grows and flourishes, undertaking a huge
variety of Christian work among young people. In 1967 I was asked to try
my hand at a hymn for the centenary service, which would be held at St
Paul's Cathedral. As I recall, the tune FINLANDIA was suggested because it
was available with orchestral parts.

Owing much to the Scripture Union in my own spiritual pilgrimage, I
agreed to try; and I recall writing this text on a train, travelling home from
Nottingham to London in the early evening. It was sung at the Service,
included in *Youth Praise 2* a couple of years later, and found a place as a
young people's hymn of consecration in a number of books. It is also sung
surprisingly often at weddings.

Verse 3 is often omitted (at the time it was written the CSSM and
Scripture Union was less seen as an international movement than would be
the case today) perhaps because the word 'commonwealth' implies to many

not simply the community in their common life and interests, but has undertones of Empire! I have sometimes had comments that the trilogy 'pleasure, wealth and care' is true to experience—a fact which should not surprise us, as it is drawn directly from Luke 8.14.

The tune written for this text, LORD OF THE YEARS, is so called because in *Youth Praise* titles were often given to texts, other than the opening words of the first line. The text therefore appeared under this title. I have discontinued this practice in the case of my own texts, as it leads to confusion—but I am pleased that the phrase, which was in my mind when writing the text and is found in the last line of verse 1, remains current in the title of Michael Baughen's and David Wilson's tune.

See Appendix 5, pp. 286ff.

LORD, GIVE US EYES TO SEE   66 86 (SM)

Based on	Matthew 9.37,38
Theme	Embertide; the ordained ministry
Written	at Sevenoaks, May 1966
Suggested tune	DOMINICA by H. S. Oakeley

This text was written following the suggestion made to me by the then Recruitment Secretary of the Advisory Council for the Church's Ministry that there was a lack of hymns about vocation, especially to the priesthood. It is for this reason that (for churches like my own which do not at present ordain women priests) I have not felt it right or necessary to change the final line to be more inclusive. The hymn has only appeared in print in the private *Supplementary Hymnbook*, published in 1980, of All Souls' Church, Langham Place, London. 'Ember Days' traditionally date back at least to A.D. 250. They were originally associated with the crops and the seasons (which makes the harvest imagery appropriate) and only more recently with the ordination of the church's ministers.

See Appendix 5, pp. 286ff.

LORD OF THE CHURCH, WE PRAY FOR OUR RENEWING
11 10 11 10 D

Theme	the church; renewal
Written	at Ruan Minor, August 1976
Suggested tune	LONDONDERRY AIR (Irish traditional)
Published in	*Songs of Worship*, 1980 to LONDONDERRY AIR arranged by Robin Sheldon
	Hymns for Today's Church, 1982 to LONDONDERRY AIR arranged by John Barnard
	Making Melody, 1983 to LONDONDERRY AIR arranged by Robin Sheldon

'Christ over all' was the fine watchword of the National Evangelical Anglican Congress held at Keele University in 1967; and though this hymn was not written until nine years later, that was the source of the phrase which both starts and ends the text. The expression 'to turn to Christ' has found a new currency in the Church of England with its inclusion as the first of the promises at Baptism and Confirmation in the new Alternative Services; even though in Scripture the phrase is usually in the form 'turn to God' (Acts 26.20) or 'turn to the Lord' (Acts 9.35).

Any text in this metre will always carry echoes of F. W. H. Myers' famous poem *St Paul* published in 1867; and must be careful lest it too slip into the echoing cadences of rhetoric in verse, where the sound takes over from the meaning: as in the anonymous parody of Myers:

> I who am I, and no one shall deny it—
> I who am I, and none shall say me Nay—
> Lo, from the housetops to the hills I cry it:
> I have forgotten what I meant to say!

LORD, WHO LEFT THE HIGHEST HEAVEN   87 87 87

Theme	home; social concern
Written	at Sevenoaks, February 1962
Suggested tune	ALL SAINTS (German traditional) or HIGHEST HEAVEN by Michael A. Baughen
Published in	*Anglican Hymn Book*, 1965 to ALL SAINTS
	Youth Praise 1, 1966 to HIGHEST HEAVEN
	Family Worship, 1971 (words only)
	Thirty Hymns, CPAS 1972 (words only)
	UTC Hymnbook (Bangalore), 1975 (words only)
	Hymns for Today's Church, 1982 to HIGHEST HEAVEN arranged by Norman L. Warren

This is one of my first texts, written at the request of the editors of the *Anglican Hymn Book*, then in preparation, for something on the theme of 'home'. I was once told that a number of hymns are written by people ill in bed; and this is one of them. At that stage I was so inexperienced that it did not occur to me to see whether each verse would fit a single tune (in fact adjustments have to be made); and I had not quite settled on the use of 'You language' rather than 'Thees and Thous'. Hence it became one of only two texts using those forms; the other being *Faithful vigil ended* which follows the usage at that point of the New English Bible. As I have described in the *notes* to that text, I eventually decided to revise both in order to provide versions in 'you form'; and I took that opportunity to eliminate one or two weaknesses and infelicities in this text which had become more obvious with the passing of time. The original version can still be found in the hymnals marked in the list above with an asterisk, but this is now the standard text.

The original MS indicates a first attempt in eight line stanzas, 87 87D; the final four lines of each verse being a variation on:

Hear us now who sing before thee.
Give us hearts to praise and pray
For our homes and for our children
And the lives we build today

but by the time I came to tackle verse 4, this was seen to be unsatisfactory and the 87 87 87 form develops. Verse 2, rather to my regret, is sometimes omitted.

MERCY, BLESSING, FAVOUR GRACE   77 77

Based on	Psalm 67, Deus Misereatur
Theme	the blessing of God; harvest
Written	at Sevenoaks, July 1971
Suggested tune	by David G. Wilson (see below) or HARTS by Benjamin Milgrove; or PSALM 67 by Alan Davies
Published in	*Psalm Praise*, 1973 to (1) a tune specially composed by David G. Wilson (2) PSALM 67
	Grace Hymns, 1975 to (1) PSALM 67 (2) ST BENEDICT by John Stainer
	Hymns II (USA), 1976 to the tune by David G. Wilson

Psalm 67, of which this is a metrical version, is one of the canticles set for the Service of Evening Prayer in the Book of Common Prayer. It is of course well served by the metrical version 'God of mercy, God of grace' by H. F. Lyte; though Professor Barkley in his *Handbook to the Church Hymnary* (Oxford 1979) rightly calls that 'not really a paraphrase of the psalm but a hymn based upon it.' I would not wish to claim more for this text.

I remember working on this text in the grounds of St Julian's, a country club near Sevenoaks where we then lived, using a number of modern translations; and indeed 'saving power' is clearly derived from them (e.g. Knox, RSV, NEB). I cannot trace the source of the word 'favour' and I am not now taken with the opening couplet of the hymn. It is perhaps an example of a text which found its way too early into print; and was thereby placed beyond the reach of substantial revision. In the light of its inclusion in three current hymnals, I have not withdrawn it; but I hope one day to attempt a better version.

NAME OF ALL MAJESTY   66 55 666 4

Theme	the Lord Jesus Christ
Written	at Ruan Minor, August 1979
Suggested tune	ALL MAJESTY by Norman L. Warren MAJESTAS by Michael Baughen

Published in	*Hymns for Today's Church*, 1982 to (1) ALL MAJESTY (2) MAJESTAS arranged by Noël Tredinnick *Ten New Hymns in Praise of God*, 1982 to CONSERVATION (adapted) by Michael Dawney *The Wider Look*, October/December 1983 (words only)
Recorded on	*Hymns for Today's Church*, Word WST 9623, 1982 to MAJESTAS by the choir, orchestra and congregation of All Souls Church, Langham Place, London

In the early months of 1979 I was enjoying the *Collected Poems* of Walter de la Mare, having only read him previously in anthologies. A page in my MS book at that time shows three extracts from his poems copied out for the sake of their metrical form. It is upon one of these that this text came to be loosely based; but I am reluctant to identify it further, since I fear most of the de la Mare magic is missing, simply in terms of rhythm (let alone language or meaning), in the text herewith.

When originally published in my privately issued *Collection* it carried the note that it was 'awaiting a composer' since I knew of no existing tune to fit these words. Since then two tunes have been supplied by the editorial team of *Hymns for Today's Church*, including orchestral parts. The MS reveals few changes, apart from the transposition of certain lines, a lot of attention to punctuation, and the substitution of the present third line of verse 1 in place of the original 'only-begotten'.

The final affirmation of each verse 'Jesus is Lord' is the primitive creed of Christianity. Archbishop Michael Ramsey has commented on the phrase:

> '*Jesus*: the word told of an historical person about whose life, words, and actions, much was known, and known not only in terms of the vehicle of a message, but in terms of a human figure whose example was to be imitated by Christian people . . .
>
> *Is*: the word told of one who belongs not only to the past, but to the contemporary because he had been raised from the dead . . .
>
> *Lord*: the word told of more than the Resurrection; it told of the sovereignty. Without becoming polytheists or idolaters the first Christians were led to be worshippers of Jesus, giving to him the kind of homage due from creatures to a creator.'
>
> (Quoted by Margaret Duggan in her *Through the year with Michael Ramsey*, Hodder & Stoughton, 1975; entry for 6 December.)

NO TEMPLE NOW, NO GIFT OF PRICE   886 D

Based on	Hebrews 10.1–25
Theme	grace; redemption; discipleship
Written	at Ruan Minor, August 1983
Suggested tune	CORNWALL by S. S. Wesley or INNSBRUCK NEW based on Heinrich Isaac

Hebrews 10 is a chapter that features in the Index of Scripture References (where one is provided) of many hymnals; but on examination, the texts referred to are often based on a single verse (verse 12 is particularly popular); and perhaps only Isaac Watts' hymn 'Not all the blood of beasts/On Jewish altars slain' explicitly sets out to celebrate the main theme of the chapter with its contrast between the law and the gospel.

I hope it is not fanciful to see the 'way into the holiest' of Hebrews 10.20 (cf. verse 3 of this text) as linked with 'the pilgrim path of faith' hinted at in verses 23–25. They are, in my mind, different stages on the journey but the same road, the road of John 14.6, which is Christ himself.

'Imperishable' (verse 3) is open to the comment that it is more commonly used of what is abstract or impersonal. However the Oxford Dictionary gives 'immortal' as a synonym; and in the RSV, I Corinthians 15.52 has '. . . the dead will be raised imperishable . . .' It serves, I hope, to point the contrast with the Old Testament priesthood, in accordance with the theme of Hebrews 10.

NO TRAMP OF SOLDIERS' MARCHING FEET   86 86 D (DCM)

Based on	Luke 19.35–40
Theme	Palm Sunday; the triumphal entry
Written	at Ruan Minor, August 1979
Suggested tune	LADYWELL by W. H. Ferguson

Christ's 'triumphal entry' into Jerusalem is recorded by all four evangelists; and is a fulfilment of Zechariah's prophecy in Zechariah 9.9. The militaristic expectations of verse 1 of this text are an echo of the disciples' bewilderment, as indicated in John 12.16: 'His disciples did not understand this at first; but when Jesus was glorified, then they remembered that this has been written of him and had been done to him'. The phrase 'King of glory' in this context (line 4 of each verse) is a reference to Psalm 24.9: 'Lift up your heads, O gates! and be lifted up, O ancient doors! that the King of glory may come in. Who is this King of glory? The Lord of hosts, he is the King of glory!' The other repeated line, 'Behold, your King', refers again to Zechariah 9.9, quoted by both Matthew and John ('Behold, thy King cometh unto thee . . .') and also, in verse 3 of this text, to John 19.5, the 'Ecce Homo' of much religious painting. Pilate there presents Jesus to the crowd beaten and bleeding and wearing a crown of thorns, in mockery of his kingship, with the words 'Behold, the man!'

Line 3 of verse 4 is a direct reference to Philippians 2.7, and the 'Hosanna' of line 5 to the greetings of the crowd in Matthew 21.9.

NO WEIGHT OF GOLD OR SILVER   76 76 D

Based on	1 Peter 1.18,19: Isaiah 53.3–6: 2 Corinthians 5.17,18
Theme	new life in Christ

Written	at Ruan Minor, August 1972
Suggested tune	ARGENT by Noël Tredinnick or
	MORDEN PARK by Norman Warren or
	CRÜGER by Johannes Crüger or
	LLANGLOFFAN (Welsh traditional)
Published in	*Psalm Praise*, 1973 to (1) ARGENT
	(2) MORDEN PARK (3) as an alternative suggestion,
	to CRÜGER
	Hymns for Today's Church, 1982 to
	(1) ARGENT (2) MORDEN PARK
Recorded on	*Here is Psalm Praise*, Reflection RL 311, 1975 to
	ARGENT

Written originally for *Psalm Praise* as 'a Passiontide Psalm', this text draws heavily on the three passages of Scripture indicated. I cannot claim that the rhyme in lines 7 & 8 of verse 1 is original; indeed, it is probably more common in hymnody than I know. It is however used with great effectiveness in one of the closing sequences of John Masefield's poem 'The Everlasting Mercy':

> '. . . The corn that makes the holy bread
> By which the soul of man is fed,
> The holy bread, the food unpriced,
> Thy everlasting mercy, Christ.'

The lines in question can be found set as a hymn for congregational use in *Songs of Praise*.

The repeated phrase 'Lamb of God' occurs first in scripture in John 1.29, coined, it seems, by John the Baptist as a description of Jesus in the new Covenant prefigured by the Passover. In Isaiah 53.7 the Servant of the Lord is 'led as a lamb to the slaughter'; while in the 2 Corinthians passage there is the fathomless reference to Christ's atoning death, that 'For our sake he made him to be sin who knew no sin, so that in him we might become the righteousness of God' (2 Corinthians 5.21).

See Appendix 5, pp. 286ff.

NOT IN LORDLY STATE AND SPLENDOUR   87 87 87

Theme	Christmas
Written	at Bramerton, January 1977
Suggested tune	PICARDY (French traditional)
Published in	*Carols* (USA), 1978 to PICARDY
	The Hymn (Hymn Society of America), January
	1980 to PICARDY
	Eternity magazine (USA), December 1981 to
	PICARDY
	A Song was heard at Christmas (USA), 1983 to
	PICARDY

This text appeared on our family Christmas card in 1977, eleven months after it was written. PICARDY, originally a French carol tune of the 17th century and described in Percy Dearmer's *Songs of Praise Discussed* (Oxford 1933) as 'dignified and ceremonious', well matches the mood of the words. In my own mind I see a break between the note of glory and triumph which concludes verse 3, and the repetition of verse 1 (slightly changed) to close the carol by a return to the stable at Bethlehem.

'Storied' is used here in more than one sense, to convey sumptuousness, grandeur and dignity. Technically it has at least three meanings: divided into stories (as in a great house), ornamented with scenes from history or legend (paintings, tapestries, etc), and celebrated or recorded in history or legend.

'Panoplied', literally 'clad in complete armour', is a transliteration of the Greek word in Ephesian 6.11, superbly used by Charles Wesley in his lines from 'Soldiers of Christ, arise':

> 'and take to arm you for the fight
> the panoply of God'.

'Sceptred sway' is a direct borrowing from Portia's famous speech beginning 'The quality of mercy . . .' in Shakespeare's *Merchant of Venice*. It has remained with me since I played the part in a school production at the age of twelve!

NOT TO US BE GLORY GIVEN   87 87 D

Based on	Psalm 115
Theme	the living God
Written	at Sevenoaks, April 1970
Suggested tune	by John Wycliffe-Jones (see below) or LUX EOI by Arthur Sullivan
Published in	*Psalm Praise*, 1973 to (1) a tune specially written by John Wycliffe-Jones (2) LUX EOI *Grace Hymns*, 1975 to BETHANY by Henry Smart *A Panorama of Christian Hymnody*, 1979 (words only)

Written for *Psalm Praise*, this text is now associated in my mind with Erik Routley's choice of it for his *Panorama of Christian Hymnody* and for his over-generous reference to it in *The Hymn* of October 1982 as 'a model of how a modern metrical psalm should look'. I had earlier pointed out to him one or two of its manifest weaknesses . . . but I could only be delighted that it took his fancy.

Among the difficulties that beset the writing of it, the second half of verse 3 proved the least tractable. At a late stage it stood as

> In His fear and love abiding
> as to Israel once He came
> so, their trust in Him confiding,
> God remembers them by name.

The text is concerned to make three parallel contrasts: that it is not to us, but to God that glory belongs; not in idols but in the living God that hope of blessing rests; and not the dead 'but we the living' who can sing his praise in the here and now of life on earth. As Derek Kidner writes, putting himself into the shoes of the psalmist: 'The alien realm of death and silence is no business of ours, only a fresh stimulus to give God the glory which the dead cannot offer' (*Psalms 73–150*, IVP London, 1975).

See Appendix 5, pp. 286ff.

NOW TO THE LORD WE BRING THE CHILD HE GAVE US
11 10 11 10

Theme	baptism
Written	at Ruan Minor, August 1976
Suggested tune	O PERFECT LOVE by Joseph Barnby

This is a text I should like to have sung at the baptism of one of my own children—but it was written ten years too late. It has been sung at baptisms; and I sometimes inscribe it on the fly leaf of a book given to a child at baptism. I think however that the metre does not make it easy to choose for singing at what is always a unique occasion.

Among biblical echoes might be the presentation of Samuel in the temple (which can stand as a type of other presentations, including that of our Lord)—see 1 Samuel 1.28. The Name, the word and the water come from Matthew 28.19, the 'sifting' from Luke 22.31. 'Covenant' refers to the theological basis of infant baptism as I understand it—the successor to the 'covenant of circumcision' (Acts 7.8), the sign of the 'new covenant' (Hebrews 8.10) which would be, not of the flesh, but of the mind and heart. 'Believe and trust' is an echo of the new Baptism Service of the Church of England, as is the word 'turn'; while 'Christ's faithful soldier' echoes the traditional words of baptism in the Book of Common Prayer. Verse 4 speaks of three of the consequences of baptism: membership, discipleship, companionship.

The hymn took its origin from a Saturday morning walk on the beach at Poldhu Cove.

O CHANGELESS CHRIST, FOR EVER NEW
86 86 (CM)

Theme	the Lord Jesus Christ; Christ in experience; Holy Communion
Written	at Ruan Minor and St Julian's, Coolham; August and October 1981
Suggested tune	BALLERMA by François H. Barthélémon or ST BOTOLPH by Gordon Slater
Published in	*Hymns for Today's Church*, 1982 to BALLERMA

An account of the writing of this text appears earlier in this book (pp. 31ff.).
The opening epithet is derived from Hebrews 13.8

Theme	Christmas; the Lord Jesus Christ
Written	at St Anthony-in-Meneage and Ruan Minor, August 1981
Suggested tune	FOREST GREEN (English traditional) or KINGSFOLD (English traditional)

This text, which appeared on our family Christmas card in 1982, was begun, for want of anything else to write on, in the blank pages of a small account book which lives in the pocket of my car. We were on a family picnic at St Anthony, a natural tidal harbour in South Cornwall, when the text began to take shape. Line 3 of verse 1, obvious enough in itself, was nevertheless the nucleus about which the rest began to grow. I had in my mind the picture of the child Jesus growing up in a foreign country, and hearing from his mother, even before he was old enough to understand, the songs of home.

Originally the text was conceived in three verses, looking in turn at the Son of Mary (humanity), the Son of Man (suffering) and the Son of God (triumph). All that remains of this pattern is the final couplet of verse 3. 'The shadow of a sword' is a reference to the Song of Simeon in Luke 2.35; while in the final lines the sword is seen as a symbol of victory and conquest.

Those who know the poems of Sir John Betjeman will recollect his use of the epithet 'resin-scented' from which mine must have been unconsciously (or at most half-consciously) derived. I read his *Collected Poems* (a number of them Cornish in theme and setting) every summer holiday; and the word comes there at least twice: 'Resin-scented rain' is from *Love in a Valley* and 'resin-scented air' in *The Town Clerk's Views*. Robert Frost has pointed out that in general the intention (which was not mine here) to make use of a special word borrowed from another poet is fraught with danger:

'Words that are the product of another poet's imagination cannot be passed off again. They have done their work. One of my abominations is the word 'immemorial', which every poet for years has pulled in whenever he has need of a long word. They can't get away with it. One poet has made an effort to use in his poetry Shakespeare's word 'incarnadine'. And again no one has been able, although many have tried, to employ with success Keats' 'alien' in the beautiful line, 'She stood in tears amid the alien corn'. All this use of poetic diction is wrong. I use only the words I find in conversation, making them poetic as best I can with what power I can command.'

(*Interviews with Robert Frost*, edited by E. C. Latham, Jonathan Cape, London 1967, page 26).

Frost's thought here is not unlike the warning of John Wesley's famous *Preface* quoted already in these pages:

'By labour a man may become a tolerable imitator of Spenser, Shakspeare, or Milton; and may heap together pretty compound epithets, as "pale-eyed", "meek-eyed", and the like; but unless he be *born* a poet he will never attain the genuine spirit of poetry.'

But I am unrepentant, and indeed pleased with the word in this context, where I believe it is at home.

O CHRIST THE SAME   11 10 11 10 D

Theme	anniversary, thanksgiving
Written	at Sevenoaks, September 1971
Suggested tune	SALVATOR MUNDI by K. W. Coates or LONDONDERRY AIR (Irish traditional—see below)
Published in	*Hymns for Today's Church*, 1982 to SALVATOR MUNDI

This hymn was written on request, to be sung at the Service to mark the opening of the new premises of the Cambridge University Mission in Bermondsey, in November 1972. The Mission had been my home, in a tiny flat at the top of three old terrace houses, during the two years I spent as Head of the Mission from 1953–55.

The starting point of the text is Hebrews 13.8, 'Jesus Christ the same, yesterday, today and for ever'; and this is worked out in the three verses with their emphasis on thanksgiving for past, present and future.

The titles given to Christ in this hymn are drawn directly, or by implication, from Scripture as follows: eternal Lord, from Deuteronomy 33.27 (eternal God) and 1 Timothy 1.17 (King eternal); King of ages (cf. Ephesians 3.21 & Psalm 145.13); living Word (John 1.14); friend of sinners (Matthew 11.19); Son of Man (e.g. Matthew 8.20 and throughout the four gospels); Prince of life (Acts 3.15); Lord of love (cf. Ephesians 5.2).

The words 'to you' ('We bring our thanks *to you* . . .') can be added to the final line of each verse to make it possible to sing this hymn to the LONDONDERRY AIR.

See Appendix 5, pp. 286ff.

O CHRIST, WHO TAUGHT ON EARTH OF OLD   88 88 88

Theme	the Lord Jesus Christ—his parables; Scripture; harvest
Written	at Bramerton, February 1982
Suggested tune	ST MATTHIAS by W. H. Monk

'The Parables' is one of the Sunday themes in the *Alternative Service Book, 1980* of the Church of England; and this text is one of a pair, written on consecutive days, and (unusually) written in winter and at home, rather than when away on holiday in August. The text tries, as far as possible to allude to certain main groupings of parables rather than to mention them at random; verse 2, for example, could be taken as referring to a wide range of the 'nature' and 'harvest' parables. In verse 3, some of the key words are applicable to more than one of our Lord's parables, and verse 4 takes three of its four allusions from the major parables found only in St Luke—the rich man and Lazarus (Luke 16.19–31); the good Samaritan (Luke 10.25–37) and the prodigal son (Luke 15.11–32). Those who feel that the words of a hymn should be self-evident to worshippers with little or no Christian background will find this an impossible text, clearly written for 'insiders' and making few concessions. I would like to think, however, that with a minimum of explanation (that the hymn alludes to a number of Jesus's best-known stories) it would be singable as sense, rather than nonsense, by almost anyone; and might provoke sufficient curiosity to awake interest in finding the parables themselves. What more could one wish!

Line 3 of verse 3 was originally written (with some changes in the punctuation of the verse) as

> when sparrows fall and lilies blow

but the reference to vineyards seems to me happier, and of wider application (cf. for example, Matthew 20, 1–16; Matthew 21, 33–42; Luke 13, 6–9).

O LORD, YOURSELF DECLARE   66 86 (SM)

Theme   Prayer
Written   at Ruan Minor, August 1981
Suggested tune   ST GEORGE by H. J. Gauntlett

'Prayer' was one of the themes I was given by the editor of a new collection, after surveying the gaps in his material. My first plan was to adopt the metre 55 88 55 (as in 'Round me falls the night') thus:

> Lord, yourself declare
> to our souls in prayer;
> not in lightnings, storms and thunders,
> not in nature's signs and wonders.
> In your still, small voice
> let our hearts rejoice.

But after two verses (this is the first) it became clear that I was barking up the wrong tree. I then tried 66 66, and again wrote two verses, not unlike verses 1 and 3 of this text, complete in themselves. But, apart from anything else, they were altogether too reminiscent of Bishop Wordsworth's 'Lord, be thy Word my rule', a hymn with a special place in my affections as it was sung at my wedding. Finally I settled on three verses in SM; the first with echoes of Hebrews 10.20 and Luke 11.1, and the second drawing on the mnemonic ACTS. This stands for a framework of prayer consisting of Adoration, Confession, Thanksgiving and Supplication; in this text the order of the final two is reversed.

For verse 3, with its reference to God's purposes and promises, and to faith in Christ's Name, see for example Ephesians 3.11, Hebrews 10.23, 1 John 2.25, John 14.14 and Acts 3.16.

Theme	Christmas; peace
Written	at Bramerton, December 1978
Suggested tune	RECTORY MEADOW by Erik Routley specially written for this text
Published in	*The Hymn* (Hymn Society of America), July 1980 (words only)
	Word and Music, October/December 1982, to RECTORY MEADOW
	Hymns for Today's Church, 1982 to RECTORY MEADOW
	A Song was heard at Christmas (USA), 1983 to RECTORY MEADOW
	Eternity magazine (USA), December 1983 to RECTORY MEADOW

'Prince of peace' and 'Prince of life' are both biblical titles, the one of the Messiah who was to come, in Isaiah 9.6; the other of the Lord Jesus Christ who came and died and rose, in Peter's sermon in Acts 3.15. This text employs the word 'Peace' as a salutation, indeed as a prayer, fifteen times from start to finish, and perhaps it is worth quoting the following passage from R. C. Trench's *The Study of Words* (London 1851) to set this in context:

'The innermost distinctions between the Greek mind and the Hebrew reveal themselves in the several salutations of each, in the "Rejoice" of the first, as contrasted with the "Peace" of the second. The clear, cheerful, world-enjoying temper of the Greek embodies itself in the first; he could desire nothing better or higher for himself, nor wish it for his friend, than to have *joy* in his life. But the Hebrew had a deeper longing within him and one which finds utterance in his "Peace". It is not hard to perceive why this latter people should have been chosen as the first bearers of that truth which indeed enables truly to *rejoice*, but only through first bringing *peace*; nor why from them the word of life should first go forth.'

The text was half-written before the device which gives it its special character, the cumulative lines before the final line, began to appear; and when it was printed in *The Hymn* for July 1980 there was still no tune to which it could possibly be sung. Erik Routley, with characteristic generosity, sent me a tune in MS which he had himself composed, and it is to this that the text is set in *Hymns for Today's Church*. There you may see that the tune is called, as its author called it on his original MS, RECTORY MEADOW: the name of my home in Bramerton, near Norwich, where Erik Routley was once, for a single evening, our guest. The house is indeed a former Rectory, and we coined the name *Rectory Meadow* because of the glebe field in front of it. The text appeared on our family Christmas card for 1980, with a reference to Erik Routley's tune.

O SAVIOUR CHRIST, BEYOND ALL PRICE 86 86 D (DCM)

Theme	commitment to Christ
Written	at Bramerton, April 1978
Suggested tune	FOREST GREEN (English traditional)

This is a text with a strong repetitive structure, as can be seen from
the collect-like opening, with the vocative 'O Christ' (and 'O Saviour
Christ . . .', 'O sovereign Christ . . .') followed by a descriptive reference
to the Lord; and then in the second half of each verse the shift from the
Lord to the worshipper in the repeated 'I come . . .', to plead and to bring,
to follow and to find.

　　Line 3 of verse 1 is a conscious echo of the Communion Service in
the Book of Common Prayer with its '. . . full, perfect, and sufficient
sacrifice . . .'. In verse 3, line 4 refers to John 15.15; while 'companion' in
line 1 is barely used in the New Testament, however much the thought is
present. As applied, however, to the Christian disciple with his Lord, the
true meaning of the word is full of symbolism. Archbishop Trench in his
Study of Words already quoted reminds us that 'a companion is one with
whom we share our bread'. Line 4 of verse 4 refers to Colossians 1.16,
where these spiritual beings are shown as owing their existence to the
creative power of the eternal Word, existing with a view to his glory, and
serving his purposes.

　　The text is dated April 1978; when passiontide and Easter would have
been fresh in my mind.

OUR SAVIOUR CHRIST ONCE KNELT IN PRAYER 88 88 88

Based on	Mark 9.2–10
Theme	the transfiguration
Written	at Bramerton, March 1978
Suggested tune	SURREY by Henry Carey
Published in	*Hymns for Today's Church*, 1982 to (1) DAS NEUGEBORNE KINDELEIN (from a medieval melody by M. Vulpius) (2) SURREY

The transfiguration of Christ is described in all three of the synoptic
Gospels; and finds a place within the calendar both of the Book of
Common Prayer and of the *Alternative Service Book, 1980* of the Church
of England. Few hymns, however, seem to have taken this as their theme.

　　I have followed the traditional view that the scene may have been Mount
Hermon, within easy reach of Caesarea Philippi (in which case the hills of
Galilee—line 6 of verse 1—would be in the far distance); and have left open
the possibility, often accepted, that the transfiguration occurred at night. It
seems reasonable, if that were so, that the journey up the mountain would
have been made by daylight, with darkness falling during their time of
prayer.

　　In verse 3, the final lines refer of course to the representative character of

Elijah and Moses, whose presence is understood to typify the Prophets and the Law, which together stand for the Old Testament revelation. Line 6 of verse 4 is an allusion, following Mark and Matthew, to our Lord's immediate reference to his coming suffering and death, about which he spoke with these disciples 'as they came down from the mountain' (Matthew 17.9; Mark 9.9).

'Narration' is one of the classifications of hymnody allowed by Robert Bridges in his *A practical discourse on some principles of hymn-singing* (Blackwell, Oxford 1901), and he calls it 'a very proper and effective form for general praise'. Eighty years on from that judgment, most worshippers would look, I think, for some link to be suggested between the narration of the historic events, and our life as Christians today. This need I have tried to meet in the final verse, which moves from a rehearsal of past events to a prayer for ourselves arising out of them.

OUT OF DARKNESS LET LIGHT SHINE   77 77

Based on	2 Corinthians 4.6 (NEB)
Theme	the gospel; new life in Christ
Written	at Ruan Minor, August 1978
Suggested tune	NORTHAMPTON by C. J. King or
	HARTS by Benjamin Milgrove
Published in	*Hymns for Today's Church*, 1982 to HARTS

In 2 Corinthians 4.6 St Paul draws a deliberate parallel, which forms the theme of this text, between God's creative 'Let there be light' of Genesis 1.3 and the light of the gospel (verse 4) shining in the heart of the believer who is 'turned from darkness to light, and from the power of Satan to God' (Acts 26.18). Verse 1 of this text, therefore, is rooted in the creation story of Genesis 1, with the word of the Lord bringing order to an earth 'without form, and void' and without light (Genesis 1.2).

It is this parallel that explains the phrase 'dawn of dawn' in verse 3; meaning the very first sunrise of the very first morning. My notes show some hesitation between a number of alternatives, including as the most likely 'as the new-made dawn on earth'; but 'dawn of dawn', once considered, is to me more expressive of my meaning.

The final line is justified in terms of John 1.9.

See Appendix 5, pp. 286ff.

PRAISE BE TO CHRIST   88 88 D (DLM)

Based on	Colossians 1.15–20
Theme	praise; the Lord Jesus Christ
Written	at Bramerton, March 1980
Suggested tune	LONDON by John Sheeles

Published in   *On the Move* (Australia), October 1981 (words only)
Symphony, Autumn/Winter 1982/3 (words only)
Hymns for Today's Church, 1982 to YE BANKS AND
BRAES (Scottish traditional) arranged by Norman
L. Warren.

This text, unusual for me in its rhyming structure (a,b,b,a; c,d,c,d), arose directly out of a reading of Colossians as expounded by R. C. Lucas in his book *Fulness and Freedom* (IVP, London 1980). He notes there

'that within three decades of the crucifixion, language like this was in normal circulation among the churches to describe Jesus of Nazareth. What such testimony shows is that there never was a time, from the beginning of the church's life, when the highest honours of the Godhead were not given to his name' (p. 45).

The same chapter goes on to work out the thought of the passage in terms of the connections between the supremacy and sufficiency of Christ; between Christ as Creator and redeemer; and between Christ before time, on earth and over all. Traces of these differing emphases can be discerned clearly in my text, which is at the same time very directly drawn from the language of a number of modern translations.

Robert Frost says of writing poetry that 'There are the days you can and the days you can't and both are training towards the future days you can' (*Interviews with Robert Frost*, ed. E. C. Latham, Jonathan Cape, London 1967). This text, over which I made various attempts which came to nothing, is to me a case in point. One afternoon, off work unwell, I wrote verse 1 before tea, verse 2 afterwards, and verse 3 in bed between 10.00 and 11.30 the same evening.

PRAISE THE GOD OF OUR SALVATION   87 87

Based on	Psalm 146
Theme	praise & worship; thanksgiving; redemption
Written	at Ruan Minor, August 1982
Suggested tune	SHIPSTON (English traditional) or
	ANIMAE HOMINUM by Alfred Blanchet

This is one of a small number of metrical psalms written in the summer of 1982 at the request of David G. Preston, the compiler of a projected collection. The verse proved very intractable, as may indeed be evident from the result, and the work was done in several attempts and with much discarded material. The original draft was 'Praise the Lord while life remains'; and 'down the years' remained as the start of the second line until the final revision, when it was replaced by the present version as truer to the original. Verse 4 presented particular difficulties; and a reference to Isaac Watts' 'I'll praise my Maker' (in spite of masterly lines and phrases) suggests that I am not alone in finding this.

Based on	Psalm 148
Theme	praise and worship
Written	at Sevenoaks, January 1972
Suggested tune	PRAISE THE LORD OF HEAVEN by Norman Warren or CUDDESDON by W. H. Ferguson or EVELYNS by W. H. Monk
Published in	*Psalm Praise*, 1973 to PRAISE THE LORD OF HEAVEN *Anthem* to music by Hal H. Hopson, Hope Publishing Co., (USA), 1982 *Hymns and Psalms*, 1983 to PRAISE THE LORD OF HEAVEN

Originally written for *Psalm Praise*, it was some time after publication that I became aware of the similarities between this version and that of T. B. Browne, No. 381 in *Hymns Ancient and Modern Revised*. Samuel Johnson complained of Isaac Watts' devotional poetry that 'the paucity of its topicks enforces perpetual repetition'; and it is perhaps not surprising that two versifiers at work not only on the same 'topick' but on the same psalm should find their work to have much in common. Certainly Browne's first line is identical with my first two lines, and his second line very similar to my third and fourth. I considered, when I discovered this unconscious plagiarism, whether I should withdraw the text. In the event I decided not to do so, since Browne's original was published over 100 years ago in 1862; and because the similarities can be traced directly to the common source in the Coverdale version of the psalm.

The first draft of the text shows, as lines 5 & 6 of verse 3:

> Saints and sinners praise Him,
> all his power proclaim . . .

but I find the revision not only more satisfying, as moving towards a conclusion; but also closer to the thought of the psalmist.

REMEMBER, LORD, THE WORLD YOU MADE 86 86 (CM)

Theme	the world's need
Written	at Ruan Minor, August 1978
Suggested tune	ST BOTOLPH by Gordon Slater
Published in	*The Hymn* (Hymn Society of America), April 1981 (words only) *Hymns for Today's Church*, 1982 to LONDON NEW (Scottish Psalter 1615)

Among the themes listed on the front page of my MS book, dated 11 August 1978, is 'social conscience'; and this text, written during the last weekend of our summer holiday, is the fruit of that intention. I have been asked about the use of 'Remember . . .' and questioned as to whether the twice-repeated 'seem' of verse 5 is strong enough. As to the first, I use the word in the sense of 'to bear in mind', with the implication of 'remember *for good*' as in the concluding words of the book of Nehemiah, or the prayer of the penitent thief (Luke 23.42). As for the second, I choose this form of expression in recognition that a hymn belongs to a whole congregation, none of whom know for a certainty the circumstances of the rest. It is not always those who *appear* the most generous by their response to some need or appeal who necessarily are so. God looks on the heart, we look on the 'outward appearance' (1 Samuel 16.7); and it is therefore right that we should talk in terms of what *seems* rather than what *is*. There is a further reason; in that like the church at Laodicea (Revelation 3.17) we who seem (to ourselves as well as others) to be rich may in reality be poor indeed. Some third-world Christians, I believe, would dispute whether we are always right to think of ourselves as 'rich' when it is true of so many of us western Christians only in a materialistic sense.

Verse 2, line 3, contains an echo from the Burial Service of the Book of Common Prayer, derived from material at least a thousand years old in Christian worship. Verse 2, line 4 is a reminder of the Lord's special care for orphans, the 'fatherless' of much Old Testament scripture (e.g. Psalm 68.5; see also James 1.27).

See Appendix 5, pp. 286ff.

SAFE IN THE SHADOW OF THE LORD   86 86 (CM)

Based on	Psalm 91
Theme	confidence in God
Written	at Sevenoaks, January 1970
Suggested tune	by Christopher Seaman (see below) or CREATOR GOD by Norman Warren or NUN DANKET ALL by Johannes Crüger
Published in	*Psalm Praise*, 1973 to (1) a tune specially written by Christopher Seaman (2) CREATOR GOD
	Hymns II (USA), 1976 to CREATOR GOD
	Book of Worship, Church of St Luke, St Paul, Minnesota, 1979 to HEAVENLY DOVE (Sacred Harp, 1855)
	Hymns for Today's Church, 1982 to (1) CREATOR GOD (2) STANTON by John Barnard.
Recorded on	*Psalm Praise: Sing a new song*, Word WST 9586, 1978 to CREATOR GOD

Written for *Psalm Praise*, the repeated phrase which forms the third and fourth line of every verse is intended as an affirmation of confidence, the keynote of the text as it is of the psalm. In verse 5, line 2, a variant reading 'Kept by the Father's care' has sometimes crept in when the text has circulated in manuscript; but it is correct in almost all the published versions listed above.

Theme	the Lord Jesus Christ
Written	at Ruan Minor, August 1978
Suggested tune	SAVIOUR CHRIST by Norman L. Warren
Published in	*Hymns for Today's Church*, 1982 to SAVIOUR CHRIST

The theme of this short hymn is the fulness, perfection and completeness of Christ in his Person and Work; and the key can be found in the word *all*, repeated in every verse. The metre is singularly terse, so much so that a tune had to be written specially, before the text could be included in *Hymns for Today's Church*. The structure, however, is regular from verse to verse, with the exception of the last. Line 1 of each verse takes a title of Christ, line 2 follows on from the title given, line 3 carries the reference to 'all', and line 4 consists of a verb or participle followed by a colon. The whole is therefore governed by the final verse, which adds 'rejoicing' and 'adoring' to the 'praise' of verse 1.

SEE, TO US A CHILD IS BORN   7 7 or 77 77 or 77 77 77 77

Based on	Isaiah 9.6,7
Theme	Christmas
Written	at Ruan Minor, August 1982
Suggested tune	INNOCENTS (77 77) by W. H. Monk
Published in	*A Song was heard at Christmas* (USA), 1983 to INNOCENTS
	On the Move (Australia), July 1983 (words only)

The plan to try a hymn-text based on Isaiah 9 came to me at Christmas 1981; and I entered into my MS book translations of Isaiah 9.6,7 from the RSV, Knox, the Jerusalem Bible, the Good News Bible, and the RV. RSV was there to indicate the variants of the other versions; AV and NEB would be available to me when I came to write.

Originally planned as a hymn upon the titles of the Messiah in that passage, the text as written took shape quickly, and assumed 'antiphonal' form almost of its own accord. The first draft was written at the end of a wet morning and only two minor revisions followed: 'Every creature' for 'Hear the angels' in v.6; and 'He' for 'Peace' in v.8. Looking back through rough notes in my MS book I find the couplet

> 'Hear the bells of Christmas say
> Christ was born on Christmas Day'

jotted down fully a year before. No doubt the theme and metre had been running in my head, almost unknown to me.

Because the text is in eight couplets, there is a wide variety in the way they can be combined to make verses of 2,4 or 8 lines each. It is not of course necessary to sing the lines antiphonally, though some sense of the complementarity of odd and even lines should be conveyed.

Based on	Psalm 113
Theme	praise & worship; grace; the living God
Written	at Ruan Minor, August 1983
Suggested tune	WELLS by D. Bortnianski

This is one of a group of six psalms which were sung by custom before the Passover meal; and as such, probably the last psalms sung by Jesus immediately before Gethsemane.

Two conscious quotations need to be identified: the repeated 'All who stand before his face' comes from the reference to 'all who stand before you in earth and heaven' in (for example) the first eucharistic prayer from Rite A Holy Communion in the Church of England *Alternative Service Book, 1980*; and the line 'hears from heaven his dwelling-place' is taken from Solomon's prayer of dedication in, for example, 1 Kings 8. 30, 39, 43, 49.

Verse 2, line 3, originally written as 'Utmost east to utmost west' was changed in the process of revision both because in this metre it is not easy to sing; and also because that has strong associations with Prebendary A. C. Ainger's 'God is working his purpose out'.

The four verses are intended to point to the Lord of heaven, the Lord of time and space, the Lord of creation, and the Lord who is Father and Redeemer of his children.

SET YOUR TROUBLED HEARTS AT REST   77 77

Based on	John 14.1 (NEB)
Theme	peace and confidence
Written	at Ruan Minor, August 1979
Suggested tune	HARROWBY by James Gillespie or HARTS by Benjamin Milgrove or VIENNA by Justin H. Knecht
Published in	*On the Move* (Australia), April 1980 (words only)

The repetition of a single line in each verse of a text requires that the line in question is strong enough to stand repetition; and also a pattern which allows each line to be metrically identical. The repeated line here is from the New English Bible translation of John 14.1, the words of the Lord to the disciples following the departure of Judas from the Last Supper, and the foretelling of how short a time Jesus would be with them.

Though begun in the garden at Ruan Minor, much of this text was written on a cliff overlooking Poldhu Cove. The hymn is addressed to ourselves, fellow-members of a congregation, in exhortation; of which the key is in the repeated 'hear again' of verses 1 and 4. Within that context, we urge each other (and our own hearts) to be set at rest, to be at peace, to rejoice, to trust, to find and to experience.

Based on	Psalm 98, Cantate Domino
Theme	praise and worship
Written	at Ruan Minor, September 1971.
Suggested tune	ONSLOW SQUARE by David G. Wilson
Published in	*Psalm Praise*, 1973 to (1) ONSLOW SQUARE (2) a tune specially written by A. H. Davies
	Sound of living waters, 1974 to ONSLOW SQUARE
	Worship II (USA), 1975 to ONSLOW SQUARE
	Hymns II (USA), 1976 to ONSLOW SQUARE
	Sing to the Lord (USA), 1978 (words only)
	Partners in Praise, 1979 to ONSLOW SQUARE
	New Harvest (New Zealand), 1979 (words only)
	Methodist Church Overseas Division Calendar, 1980 (words only)
	Hymns Plus (USA), 1980 to ONSLOW SQUARE
	Their words, my thoughts, 1981 to ONSLOW SQUARE
	Anthem to music by John F. Wilson, Hope Publishing Co., (USA), 1982
	Jesus Praise, 1982 to ONSLOW SQUARE
	Hymns for Today's Church, 1982 to ONSLOW SQUARE
	Gather to Remember (USA), 1982 to ONSLOW SQUARE (here called CANTATE DOMINO)
	Hymns and Psalms, 1983 to (1) ONSLOW SQUARE (2) BARNARDO by Alan Gulliver
	Mission England Praise, 1983, to ONSLOW SQUARE
Recorded on	*Psalm Praise: Sing a new song*, Word 9586, 1978 to ONSLOW SQUARE

Much of the popularity of this hymn derives from David Wilson's attractive tune, written (like the words) for *Psalm Praise* in 1971, and taking the name ONSLOW SQUARE with its inclusion in *Partners in Praise* in 1979. Psalm 98 is set in the Book of Common Prayer of the Church of England as an alternative canticle to the Magnificat in the Order for Evening Prayer.

The first drafts of a metrical attempt for this psalm show a verse framed to the metre 11.10.11.10:

> Sing a new song to the Lord and acclaim him
> He to whom wonders and worship belong;
> Mighty in power and in victory name him,
> Come now before him and sing a new song.

Line 3 of verse 3 gave some trouble. The 'shawms' of the Prayer Book version (verse 6 of the Psalm) are given as 'cornets' in the AV and RV, but as 'horns' in more recent translations; the 'voices in chorus' of that line was originally 'music and melody' which proved difficult to sing, and from the consideration of four alternatives came the version now in use.

SPIRIT OF GOD WITHIN ME

76 86 86 86

Theme	the Holy Spirit; Whitsuntide; Pentecost
Written	at Sevenoaks, June 1968
Suggested tune	RUACH by Michael A. Baughen, arranged by David G. Wilson or LIVING FLAME by Norman L. Warren
Published in	*Youth Praise 2*, 1969 to RUACH *Keswick Praise*, 1975 to RUACH *Preist Ihn* (Germany), 1978 (translation by Brigitte Mayer) to RUACH *Hymns for Today's Church*, 1982 to LIVING FLAME *Hymns and Psalms*, 1983 to RUACH

This hymn to the Holy Spirit was written for *Youth Praise 2*. My original notes show that the titles included in the text (Spirit of God, truth, love, life and Christ) were chosen from a much wider circle of possibilities (e.g. of faith, wisdom, grace). Verses 1 and 4 of course, make reference to the Spirit seen in wind and flame at Pentecost; verse 2 to 2 Corinthians 4.4 and John 8.32,36; verse 3 to 1 Corinthians 13.7; verse 4 to 2 Corinthians 5.1, echoing (perhaps) Job 4.19. Exception has been taken to verse 1, line 5; and it should be noted first that 'Strive' is still addressed to the Holy Spirit (cf. Genesis 6.3); and that the word 'lost' need not be pressed to mean more than 'lost in its perfection'. Charles Hodge in his *Systematic Theology* distinguished two main reformed views of the effect of the fall upon the image of God in man. He quotes the Lutheran view that 'The image of God ... was that which was lost by the fall, and is restored by redemption' (Vol II, p. 97 of the 1875 edition), and it is in that general sense that the words here may be understood. 'New minted' (verse 1, line 6) is an epithet drawn from coinage, as in Matthew 22.20; with an echo of A. E. Housman's line (*A Shropshire Lad*, No XXIII)

'They carry back bright to the coiner the mintage of man'

—a line that takes account of creation in God's image, but not of our fallen nature.

See Appendix 5, pp. 286ff.

STARS OF HEAVEN, CLEAR AND BRIGHT

77 77 D

Theme	Christmas
Written	at Ruan Minor, August 1983
Suggested tune	MAIDSTONE by W. B. Gilbert

Written for our family Christmas card, 1983, the key to this text is in the repeated final line of each verse. It is this thought of the contrast between earth and heaven, a gulf nevertheless bridged by the nativity, which unites the whole. In verse 1, it is introduced in terms of the comparison between the stars, which seem to us so unchanging and are yet temporal, and the permanent realities of the eternal world; and also between Bethlehem's stable and the courts of heaven. Verse 2 takes up the same contrast in each of the three couplets. In verse 3 it is seen in the first couplet ('shepherds . . . angels') and the third ('immortal . . . earthly'); while in verse 4 the paradox is contained in individual single lines.

Readers of the essay on 'Hymns and Poetry' earlier in this volume may be struck with the liberty I have allowed myself in certain rhymes. This is deliberate, as a means of introducing and emphasising an evocative multi-syllable within the basically simple word-style of each verse. Verse 5 uses instead 'come/home' (about which that essay adds a comment) and verse 2 coins 'aureoled'—though not as part of the rhyme-structure—to serve something of the same purpose.

In the light of the pre-occupation of this text with earth and heaven, I add the derivations of these words from R. C. Trench's *The Study of Words* (London, 1861, p. 233):

'"Heaven" is only the perfect of "to heave" and is so called because it is "heaved" or "heaven" up, being properly the sky as it is raised aloft; while the "earth" is that which is "eared" or ploughed.'

I think myself that the attempt to de-mythologise religious language (of a kind, for example, which looks 'up' to heaven), whatever logic it may have on its side, is dealing with matters that are more deep-seated in human tradition (and in the human heart, even?) than we care to recognize: and can succeed only at the expense of destroying our appreciation of those essential truths which such language manages mysteriously to preserve.

'Enmities' in verse 5 looks to, e.g. Romans 5.10 or Colossians 1.21.

TELL HIS PRAISE IN SONG AND STORY   87 87 D

Based on	Psalm 34
Theme	praise and testimony
Written	at Ruan Minor, August 1976
Suggested tune	PLEADING SAVIOUR (USA traditional); or OPUS 2, AVE VERUM, by Edward Elgar
Published in	*Hymns for Today's Church*, 1982 to WEALDSTONE by John Barnard

Written too late for inclusion in *Psalm Praise*, this text takes a favourite psalm for its basis—one which lies behind the familiar 'Through all the changing scenes of life' adapted from Tate and Brady's *New Version of the Psalms of David*, 1696.

Verse 1, line 3, uses an expression from Psalm 62.7; while line 7 has a direct borrowing from Bunyan's 'Who would true valour see' in part II of the Pilgrim's Progress (1684 edition).

There is an intentional reference to the Gospels in verse 4, line 4; where the Lord's words, 'It is I', addressed to the terrified and troubled disciples alone on the lake (Matthew 14.27) provide a New Testament fulfilment of the psalmist's confidence in God.

See Appendix 5, pp. 286ff.

TELL OUT, MY SOUL   10 10 10 10

Based on   Luke 1.46–55, the Magnificat (NEB translation)
Theme   praise; the song of Mary
Written   at 84a, Vanbrugh Park, Blackheath, the first home of
                    our married life, in May 1961.

Suggested tune   WOODLANDS by Walter Greatorex or
                    TELL OUT MY SOUL by Michael A. Baughen

Published in   *Anglican Hymn Book*, 1965 to TIDINGS by William
                        Llewellyn
                    Youth Praise 1, 1966 to TELL OUT MY SOUL
                    100 Hymns for Today, 1969 to WOODLANDS
                    Thirteen Psalms, CPAS 1970 (words only)
                    Sing Praise to God, 1971 (Roman Catholic) to
                        WOODLANDS
                    Family Worship, 1971 (words only)
                    The Hymn Book (of the Anglican and United Church
                        of Canada), 1971 to ELING by Geoffrey Ridout
                    Catholic Book of Worship (Canada), 1972 to
                        WOODLANDS
                    The Book of Praise (of the Presbyterian Church in
                        Canada), 1972 to WOODLANDS
                    Psalm Praise, 1973 to (1) TELL OUT MY SOUL
                        (2) WOODLANDS
                    *Giver of bread and justice: acts of worship for
                        Christian Aid Week*, 1973 (words only)
                    Church Hymnary (Oxford, third edition), 1973 to
                        MAPPERLEY by Frank Spedding
                    The Hymnal (of the Baptist Federation of Canada),
                        1973 to WOODLANDS
                    The Hymnal of the United Church of Christ (USA),
                        1974 to WOODLANDS
                    Praise for Today, 1974 to MORESTEAD by Sydney
                        Watson
                    Baptist Assembly Hymns (Canada), 1974 (words
                        only)
                    Music for Courses Book 4, (RSCM) 1974 to
                        WOODLANDS
                    Keswick Praise, 1975 to TELL OUT MY SOUL
                    New Church Praise, 1975 to WINTON by George
                        Dyson
                    Sing a Celebration (Australia), 1975 to TELL OUT MY
                        SOUL
                    Grace Hymns, 1975 to WOODLANDS

— 258 —

English Praise, 1975 to WOODLANDS
Christian Worship, 1976 to WOODLANDS
Cliff Hymns, 1976 to WOODLANDS
Hymns II (USA), 1976 to WOODLANDS
Westminster Praise (USA), 1976 to CALDERON by
  Martin Shaw
Sixty Hymns from Songs of Zion (USA), 1977 to
  BENNETT by Keith Landis
The Australian Hymnbook, 1977 to WOODLANDS
Christian Hymns (Wales), 1977 to WOODLANDS
Partners in Praise, 1979 to WOODLANDS
With One Voice, 1979 to WOODLANDS
Hymns III (Church Hymnal Series, USA) 1979 to
  BIRMINGHAM from Francis Cunningham's *A
  Selection of Psalm Tunes* (1834)
Cantate Domino (USA), 1979 to WOODLANDS
Pilgrim's Manual (Walsingham), 1979 (words only)
Exploring the Bible (United Methodist, USA), 1979
  to WOODLANDS
A Panorama of Christian Hymnody, 1979 (words
  only)
Pocket Praise, 1979 (words only)
Songs of Worship, 1980 to (1) TELL OUT MY SOUL
  (2) WOODLANDS
Cry Hosanna, 1980 to WOODLANDS
Walsingham Devotions (Roman Catholic), 1980
  (words only)
Lion Book of Favourite Hymns, 1980 (words only)
*Fulness of Life: an Order of Service for Christian Aid
  Week*, 1981 (words only)
Declare His Glory, 1981 to WOODLANDS
Broadcast Praise, 1981 to MORESTEAD
A Supplement to Congregational Praise, 1982
  (words only)
Hymn of the Month, set 5, (USA), 1982 to
  WOODLANDS
Hymns for Today's Church, 1982 to
  (1) WOODLANDS   (2) GO FORTH (the name given in
  Hymns for Today's Church to the tune called TELL
  OUT MY SOUL by Michael A. Baughen) arranged by
  Noël Tredinnick
More Songs of the Spirit, 1982 to WOODLANDS
Parish Sunday Vespers, 1982 to WOODLANDS
Sing Praise, 1982 to WOODLANDS
Covenant Songs (Australia), 1982 to TELL OUT MY
  SOUL
Hymns Ancient & Modern New Standard, 1983 to
  WOODLANDS
Hymns for Today, 1983 to WOODLANDS
Hymns and Psalms, 1983 to WOODLANDS
Choral Descants (Volume 5) by Randall DeBruyn,
  1983 to WOODLANDS

Mission England Praise, 1983 to (1) TELL OUT MY
SOUL   (2) WOODLANDS
New Creation Song Book, Australia, 1983 (words
only)

Recorded on   *Hymns from the new Anglican Hymn Book*, Herald
LLR 533, 1965 to TIDINGS
Here is Psalm Praise, Reflection RL 311, 1975 to
TELL OUT MY SOUL
All Souls Celebrates, Word WST 9539, 1975 to
WOODLANDS
Liverpool Cathedral Festival of Praise, Abbey MVP
774, 1976 to WOODLANDS
Lydia Servant Songs, Anchor Recordings AR 12
(cassette only), 1982 to WOODLANDS

Among the first texts I wrote (and not written as a hymn—see above, pp. 7,
12) this must be the best known and most widely sung of my texts. Hardly
a week goes by without a request for its use at a special Service (often a
wedding) or in a local-church Supplement. Sir John Betjeman spoke of it in
a broadcast in 1976 as 'one of the very few new hymns really to establish
themselves in recent years'. Readers of the *Church Times* (16 November
1979) named it as their first choice of new favourite hymns. It has been
used increasingly on great occasions in Cathedrals and elsewhere; and
Christian Aid have included it in their Orders of Service for Christian Aid
week in 1973 and again in 1981.

The use of the hymn has been greatly encouraged by setting it to Walter
Greatorex's tune WOODLANDS, a choice which I owe primarily to the
editors of *100 Hymns for Today*. The combination is an interesting one in
that both he and I (though we never met, and belong to different
generations) were at school in Derbyshire and later associated with
Norfolk. Greatorex was music master at Gresham's School, Holt, from
1911 (he died in 1949); while I came to Norfolk as Archdeacon of
Norwich in 1973. 'Woodlands' is the name of one of the houses at
Gresham's.

THANKFUL OF HEART   88 88 D (DLM)

Theme   thankfulness; faith; joy; hope
Written   at Ruan Minor, August 1979
Suggested tune   JERUSALEM by C. H. H. Parry has been suggested
(repeating verse 1 of the music for each verse of
this text)

The three verses of this text point to past, present and future with
thanksgiving, joy and hope. 'Inward eye' in verse 1, although an expression
used also by others (for example, by William Blake), is most familiar from
William Wordsworth's poem 'I wandered lonely as a cloud'. 'Tale' (line 4)
carries with it the sense not only of story, but of reckoning. The 'sunlit
hours' of line 6 have an echo of the sundial, whose boast it is that it only
tells the sunny hours. Verse 2, line 5 is a reference to our Lord's words in

Matthew 19.6f. 'Hope', of course, in the final line of the text is used in the fully biblical sense of an assurance for the future founded in faith in God, buttressed by recollection of the past and experience of the present, in which the believer will never be disappointed (Romans 5.5).

The text owes its origin to the simple concept of a hymn in which each verse would begin with the same word. As with 'All shall be well' (but three years later) much of it was sketched out walking from St Anthony beside Carne Creek near Manaccan in Cornwall.

THE DARKNESS TURNS TO DAWN   66 86 (SM)

Based on	selected verses of Scripture, mainly from Isaiah, Luke, John, Philippians and Hebrews
Theme	Christmas
Written	at Sevenoaks, May 1970
Suggested tune	SAIGON by Norman Warren or CARLISLE by Charles Lockhart or GAIRLOCHSIDE by K. G. Finlay or SANDYS (English traditional)
Published in	*Crusade* magazine, December 1971 (words only) *Psalm Praise*, 1973 to SAIGON *Hymns II* (USA), 1976 to SAIGON *Carols* (USA), 1978 to SAIGON *Hymns for Today's Church*, 1982 to SAIGON *A Song was heard at Christmas* (USA), 1983 to SAIGON

This text was deliberately written for *Psalm Praise* as a 'Christmas Canticle' to echo familiar (and less familiar) words and phrases from a number of New Testament passages describing the incarnation.

In manuscript form, it carried one or more bible references in the margin beside almost every line as follows:

verse 1: *line 1*, Isaiah 9.2; *line 2*, Luke 1.78; *lines 3 & 4*, Isaiah 9.6
verse 2: *line 1*, Luke 1.32; *line 2*, Proverbs 8.22; *line 3*, Isaiah 7.14; *line 4*, Luke 19.10
verse 3: *lines 1 & 2*, John 1.11; *line 3*, Hebrews 1.3; *line 4*, Isaiah 7.14
verse 4: *lines 1 & 2*, 2 Corinthians 8.9; *line 3*, Philippians 2.7; *line 4*, John 1.4
verse 5: *lines 1 & 2*, Philippians 2.7; *lines 3 & 4*, 1 Peter 2.24
verse 6: *lines 1 & 2*, Philippians 2.8; *lines 3 & 4*, Hebrews 1.3
verse 7: *line 1*, Romans 5.5; *line 2*, 1 John 4.10; *line 3*, Luke 2.11; *line 4*, Luke 1.33

'Dayspring' in line 2 is now admittedly archaic (we should say daybreak) but familiar in the AV and Prayer Book translation of Luke 1, sung regularly in the Service of Morning Prayer from the Book of Common Prayer as one of the canticles.

The text first appeared on our family Christmas card in December 1970.

THE HEAVENS ARE SINGING
12 11 12 11 (12 11 12 11 6 6 11 in the alternative version)

Based on	echoes of Isaiah 44 & 45
Theme	praise; redemption; rejoicing
Written	at St Julian's, Coolham, October 1981
Suggested tune	WAS LEBET, WAS SCHWEBET by Johann Heinrich Reinhardt (12 11 12 11)

This hymn, written during a period of reading and writing at the Retreat House of St Julian's in Sussex, appears in two versions. In my private *Collection* only the shorter version appeared, as it is the only one for which a tune is available. The text was written, however, in its longer form; and I include that here in case it appeals to a composer ready to tackle an unusual metre. The longer metre brings out more clearly one of the characteristics of the text, namely its use of repetition; which appears centrally in line 1, and at the end of line 3, as well as in lines 5 & 6, of each verse. Repetition is also a characteristic of these two chapters of Isaiah—as can be seen, for example, in verses 22, 23 and 24 of chapter 44 (redemption); or in verses 5, 6, 14, 18, 21, 22 of chapter 45 (cf. verse 4, line 4 of my text).

The phrase in verse 2, line 2, 'the stars in their courses' (which is drawn from Judges 5.20 in the AV) is one I had carried for some time in my MS book, waiting for a chance to incorporate it into a hymn text.

THE LORD IN WISDOM MADE THE EARTH   86 86 88

Based on	Proverbs 8.22f; 1 Corinthians 1.24
Theme	the Wisdom of God; creation
Written	at Rectory Meadow, February 1982; revised at Ruan Minor, August 1982; further revised at Rectory Meadow, September 1982
Suggested tune	PEMBROKE by John Foster or PALMYRA by Joseph Summers

'The Wisdom of God' is one of the Sunday themes of the *Alternative Service Book, 1980* of the Church of England (for the fifth Sunday after the Epiphany); and though there are a number of hymns with references to the divine Wisdom, there are few substantially on that theme. In writing my first draft, I followed the Old Testament in personifying Wisdom with a feminine gender; but I was advised by Derek Kidner, when submitting the draft for criticism, that since the personification of Wisdom in the New Testament is Christ Himself, the feminine form is found only in the Old Testament and the Apocrypha. Hence the further revision on my return from holiday.

The first line as written in February was originally 'O God who gave the stars their birth' (or 'Our Father gave . . .') but this was changed in a re-casting of the opening during the August revision.

Theme	the fall of man
Written	at Ruan Minor, August 1977
Suggested tune	BIRLING (traditional) or
	O AMOR QUAM ECSTATICUS (French traditional) or
	GONFALON ROYAL by P. C. Buck
Published in	*Songs of Worship*, 1980 to BIRLING adapted by
	Geoffrey Shaw
	Hymns for Today's Church, 1982 to (1) THE HOLY
	SON by Peter Hurford (2) BIRLING
	Making Melody, 1983 to BIRLING

In the mid-1970s one or two writers were commenting on the lack of
hymns taking the fall of the human race as a major theme. The *Alternative
Service Book, 1980* of the Church of England makes this subject one of its
suggested Sunday themes (for the 8th Sunday before Christmas) and
suitable hymns were few in number. Hence this text.

The references to Adam must be understood, not only in terms of the
creation story in Genesis, but also of Paul's argument in 1 Corinthians 15.
'Innocence' in verse 3 should be taken with some of the force of its original
derivation of 'doing no hurt'.

The text is included in Appendix 5 as one in which I do not find it
possible to make the changes required if the language is to be fully inclusive
since (apart from the problems of verse 2 which, though requiring a change
of rhyme, are not insoluble) the opening line would be affected, and the
hymn therefore known by alternative titles.

An earlier draft of a few verses, in common metre (8 6 8 6) contains the
lines:

> No other Name beneath the skies
> new life from death can give.
> A fallen race in Adam dies
> and yet in Christ may live.

See Appendix 5, pp. 286ff.

THE SHINING STARS UNNUMBERED   76 76 887 87

Theme	Christmas
Written	at Ruan Minor, August 1976
Suggested tune	SONG OF THE HOLY SPIRIT (Dutch traditional)
Published in	*A Song was heard at Christmas* (USA), 1983 to
	SONG OF THE HOLY SPIRIT harmonized by Arthur
	Hutchings

This text owes its origin to the attractions of the metre, which I met first in
G. B. Timms' hymn 'Upon that Whitsun morning' published in *English*

Praise in 1975. This text appeared on our family Christmas card in December 1978.

See Appendix 5, pp. 286ff.

THE STARS DECLARE HIS GLORY 76 86 86

Based on	Psalm 19
Theme	creation; God's providential order; praise and worship
Written	at Sevenoaks, April 1970
Suggested tune	by Michael A. Baughen and Elisabeth Crocker, arranged by Norman Warren (see below)
Published in	*Psalm Praise*, 1973 to a tune specially written by Michael A. Baughen and Elisabeth Crocker arranged by Norman Warren
	Anthem with organ accompaniment by Hal H. Hopson, H. W. Gray Publications (USA), 1981

This text was written for *Psalm Praise*; and if an author is allowed favourites among his texts, this is one of mine. In re-reading it (I seldom hear it sung) I recall the solution of a number of technical problems in a manner more satisfying than one can often hope for. The psalm itself combines the two themes of 'the eloquence of nature and the clarity of Scripture' (Derek Kidner, *Psalms 1–72*, IVP 1973, p. 97f) and is the basis of Addison's famous hymn 'The spacious firmament on high'. The thought of 'order' in the final verse may be going beyond the immediate meaning of the psalmist; but it is not, I think, inconsistent to ask that he who orders the heavens and gives the stars their laws will also direct and order (within the bounds of their own freedom) the lives of his children, according to the laws he makes for them.

THE WILL OF GOD TO MARK MY WAY 86 86 (CM)

Based on	selected verses from Psalm 119
Theme	God's will and word
Written	at Sevenoaks, September 1970.
Suggested tune	by Norman Warren (see below) or GERONTIUS by J. B. Dykes or BALLERMA by François H. Barthélémon
Published in	*Psalm Praise*, 1973 to (1) a tune specially written by Norman Warren (2) GERONTIUS
	Keswick Praise, 1975 to CONTEMPLATION by F. A. G. Ouseley

Written for *Psalm Praise*, the text is drawn from the later part of the psalm, verses 129–144; and is not intended to do more than echo certain dominant themes.

See Appendix 5, pp. 286ff.

THIS CHILD FROM GOD ABOVE 66 86 (SM)

Theme	baptism
Written	at Ruan Minor, April 1974
Suggested tune	SANDYS (English traditional)
Published in	*Partners in Praise*, 1979 to EGHAM attributed to W. Turner
	Book of Worship, Church of St Luke, St Paul, Minnesota, 1979 to JAMES HARRIS (American traditional)
	Baptism Eucharist and Ministry, British Council of Churches, 1983 (words only)
	Hymns and Psalms, 1983 to WINDERMERE by Arthur Somervell

This text reflects the view that (as with circumcision, the sign of the old covenant) baptism with water in the threefold Name is the appointed means whereby a child of believing parents receives the sign of the new convenant, including the name of Christ and the sign of his cross, carrying with it obligations to discipleship, obedience, witness and membership of Christ's church. It includes the expectation that the repentance and faith expressed on behalf of the child will be personally appropriated and renewed in future years. The word 'divine' in verse 1 is not to be taken as implying anything divine in human nature; but in the quality of the giving; a royal gift, for example, is one we receive at royal hands, or which reflects the royal nature of the giver. Verse 3 refers to Mark 8.34 and to Philippians 2.8.

THIS DAY ABOVE ALL DAYS 66 86 66

Theme	Eastertide; Sunday
Written	at Ruan Minor, August 1977
Suggested tune	SOUND OF WIND by Robin Sheldon or VINEYARD HAVEN by Richard Dirksen
Published in	*Songs of Worship*, 1980 to SOUND OF WIND
	Hymns for Today's Church, 1982 to CARDINGTON by Paul C. Edwards

In June 1977, on the one occasion that Erik Routley stayed at our home, he addressed a small number of invited friends on his impressions of hymnody in America; and introduced us to Richard Dirksen's tune, VINEYARD HAVEN, of which he had a number of copies with him. I felt at the time that Dean Plumptre's accompanying words 'Rejoice, ye pure in heart' (written for a cathedral festival over a century before) had 'dated'; and perhaps because of this I wrote two texts later that summer with this metre in mind (the other is 'When God the Spirit came'). As can be seen, in both of them I incorporated what Plumptre uses as a chorus into the body of the text, retaining only an identical fifth line to link the verses together.

'Prince of life' (verse 3) is a title given to Jesus in Peter's sermon at Solomon's porch (Acts 3.15).

'Death's dominion' (verse 2) is a reference to Romans 6.9; 'Christ being raised from the dead dieth nor more; death hath no more dominion over him'.

The text is intended, not just for the Easter season, but for any Sunday, being 'the first day of the week' on which Christians celebrate anew Christ's resurrection.

TIMELESS LOVE! WE SING THE STORY   87 87 77

Based on	Psalm 89.1–18
Theme	the Love of God; praise and worship
Written	at Sevenoaks, April 1970
Suggested tune	TIMELESS LOVE by Norman Warren or ALL SAINTS (German traditional)
Published in	*Psalm Praise*, 1973 to (1) TIMELESS LOVE (2) ALL SAINTS *Hymns for Today's Church*, 1982 to (1) PATRIXBOURNE by John Barnard (2) TIMELESS LOVE *Hymns and Psalms*, 1983 to (1) TIMELESS LOVE (2) ALL SAINTS *Mission England Praise*, 1983 to TIMELESS LOVE
Recorded on	*Here is Psalm Praise*, Reflection RL 311, 1975 to TIMELESS LOVE

Among the earlier texts written for *Psalm Praise*, this hymn looks only at a small part of one of the longer psalms; and the description 'based on' is not meant to claim any very close correspondence with the text. 'Timeless' in the first line is an echo of the repeated 'for ever', 'to all generations', of the opening verses of the psalm. 'North and South' I take to be symbolic of the universal sway of God (as one might say 'from East to West') as indicated even more widely in verse 11 of the psalm, with its reference to the heavens and the earth. In the final couplet, 'Shield' is drawn directly from verse 18 of the psalm; 'Sun and Shield' as a pair are drawn from Psalm 84.11 (but note the reference here in verse 15 to 'the light of thy countenance'); and 'Shield and Reward' as a pair from Genesis 15.1, where the Lord so describes himself to Abram in a vision.

TO CHRIST OUR KING IN SONGS OF PRAISE
86 86 (CM)

Theme	the Lord Jesus Christ; discipleship
Written	at Bramerton, October 1976
Suggested tune	BISHOPTHORPE by Jeremiah Clarke

'Light', 'Life' and 'King' are the key words of this text, found in the opening and final verses in conjunction; and used in turn for the invocation of Christ in each of the other verses. As originally written the text included a sixth verse; and although it now seems very obvious, it was only after considerable reflection that it came to me that this verse was intruding both into the order of thought (light out of darkness, life out of death, leading to commitment, witness and praise) and the symmetry of the structure.

TO HEATHEN DREAMS OF HUMAN PRIDE
86 86 88

Based on	Psalm 2
Theme	the rule of God
Written	at Bramerton, July 1982
Suggested tune	PEMBROKE by John Foster or PALMYRA by Joseph Summers

This is one of a small number of metrical psalms written in the summer of 1982. Having no Hebrew, I tend to work from a variety of English translations; and usually with Derek Kidner's *Commentary* (IVP 1973) at my side. In this instance, the text has a number of echoes from the New English Bible, while the thought of 'dreamers' comes from the *Liturgical Psalter* (Collins, 1977) which has as its first verse:

> 'Why are the nations in tumult:
> and why do the peoples cherish a vain dream?'

Indeed, my original opening line was

> 'To what vain dream of human pride'

later changed to read 'To what fond dreams . . .'. But the traditional 'Why do the heathen rage?' of both AV and the Coverdale version persuaded me to retain 'heathen' in the opening line.

WE COME AS GUESTS INVITED
76 76 D

Theme	Holy Communion
Written	at Ruan Minor, August 1975

Suggested tune	AURELIA by S. S. Wesley
Published in	*Songs of Worship*, 1980 to PASSION CHORALE by Hans Hassler & J. S. Bach
	A Supplement to Congregational Praise, 1982 (words only)
	Making Melody, 1983 to PASSION CHORALE
Recorded on	*Songs of Worship*, Word WST 9590, 1980 set to PASSION CHORALE

The phrase 'guests invited' is a reference to the recorded words of Jesus as they came to us in St Luke; 'Do this in remembrance of me' (Luke 22.19). In verse 2, lines 3 & 4 incorporate the final words of the administration from the Book of Common Prayer: 'Feed on him in your hearts by faith with thanksgiving.' The three verses move from the recital of what is taking place, into our own participation and experience of Christ, and so to the united family receiving together the gifts of love.

The text was originally written in five verses of four lines each; and completed by the addition of what is now the second half of verse 2, to make three eight-line verses. As much as any text that I remember, this is to me an example of a familiar experience: the struggling fruitlessly (it always seems) with a text, in this case over a period of three days; finally to have it 'come together' so that even the additional four lines referred to above came spontaneously and without difficulty.

WE SING THE LORD OUR LIGHT   66 66 88

Based on	Psalm 27
Theme	God our strength; the love of God
Written	at Ruan Minor, August 1982
Suggested tune	DARWALL'S 148TH by J. Darwall

This is one of a small number of metrical psalms written in the summer of 1982 for a projected collection. In this instance I cast about probably more than usual before settling on a metre and a tune. Verse 3 of an early attempt is in the metre of 'The Church's one foundation' and with strong overtones of that text:

> Though trial and tribulation
> unsheathe their sharpest sword,
> my light and my salvation
> are in the living Lord.
> Though doubt and fear oppress me,
> though long and dark the night,
> the Lord is near to bless me
> and be himself my light.

An earlier opening verse was an attempt to write for the tune LEONI (of 'The God of Abraham praise'):

> We sing the Lord our light,
> our strength who walk his way;
> though dark and full of fears the night
> and long the day.
> His loving mercy kind
> his children freely claim,
> and all their souls' salvation find
> in his great Name.

This is getting warmer; and paves the way for the text as it now stands. 'Father and mother' of verse 12 presented a metrical problem; 'parents' besides being (to my ear) indefinably unsuitable was little better. 'Kith and kin', with a respectable Old English etymology, was a resolution of the problem which I was glad to grasp.

WE TURN TO CHRIST ANEW   66 84 D

Based on	parts of the Confirmation Service of the *Alternative Service Book, 1980* of the Church of England
Theme	confirmation; adult baptism; discipleship; dedication and renewal.
Written	at Ruan Minor, August 1982
Suggested tune	LEONI (adapted from a Synagogue melody)

For some years I have wanted to write a confirmation hymn; and the fact that more recently as a bishop I find myself conducting many Confirmation Services has strengthened this desire. I had hoped to write an alternative to 'O Jesus, I have promised'; and while I do not think this text serves just that purpose, I see it none the less as particularly but not exclusively suitable for use at confirmation. The three 'T's of the opening lines (echoed in the final lines) of the three verses refer to different parts of the Service: the renewal of baptismal vows, the first of which is 'I turn to Christ'; the affirmations of faith, with the thrice-repeated 'Do you believe and trust . . .'; and the traditional confirmation prayer that those confirmed 'may continue yours for ever.'

Though closely built around that particular Service, I feel the hymn is not tied to it. Turning to Christ, trusting him, and living true to him, are basic parts of Christian experience in any church. Moreover, the word 'anew' in the first line indicates that though a 'turning to Christ' may be a once-for-all never-to-be-repeated moment of conversion, nevertheless in another sense all discipleship is a daily 'turning to him anew' in obedience, loyalty and service.

WHEN GOD THE SPIRIT CAME 66 86 66

Based on   Acts 2
Theme   Pentecost; Whitsuntide; the Holy Spirit
Written   at Ruan Minor, August 1977
Suggested tune   SOUND OF WIND by Robin Sheldon or
                    VINEYARD HAVEN by Richard Dirksen
Published in   *Anglican Hymn Book Supplement*, 1978 (words
                    only)
                    Songs of Worship, 1980 to SOUND OF WIND
                    Making Melody, 1983 to SOUND OF WIND

See the notes on 'This day above all days' for an account of how the text came to be written to this metre, and in this form.

Almost all that is referred to in this text is drawn directly from Acts 2, including the final verses describing the life of the Christian community; with the exception of the final line of verse 3, which draws on Galatians 5.22.

See Appendix 5, pp. 286ff.

WHEN HE COMES 3 3 11 8 8 11 and chorus 11 11 8 8 11

Based on   1 Thessalonians 4.14–17
Theme   Advent; the return of Christ
Written   on a journey, June 1967
Suggested tune   by J. D. Thornton (see below)
Published in   *Youth Praise 2*, 1969 to a tune specially written by
                    J. D. Thornton
                    Sing to God, 1971 to the tune by J. D. Thornton
                    Keswick Praise, 1975 to the tune by J. D. Thornton
                    Preist Ihn (Germany), 1978 (translation by Brigitte
                    Mayer) to the tune by J. D. Thornton
                    Jesus Praise, 1982 to a traditional tune arranged by
                    Norman Warren (using as a first line the third line
                    of each verse; and so indexed as 'We shall see the
                    Lord in glory'.)
Recorded on   *Tell the World*, Word SAC 5096, 1980 to the tune by
                    J. D. Thornton; words on sleeve only

This text, which began as something I sang to myself on a car-journey, found a place in *Youth Praise 2*; and in a number of song-books or collections for young people since then. Paul's phrase in 1 Thessalonians 4.17 is 'Then we which are alive and remain shall be caught up . . .' and I take this as justification for a text written from the viewpoint of those who are alive when the Lord returns at his second Advent. I admit that the 'alleluias' are an inference of my own; but Paul says that we are to 'encourage one another' with what he here tells us; and 'Alleluia' seems to me a fitting accompaniment to this encouragement!

WHEN JESUS LIVED AMONG US 76 76 triple

Theme	the Lord Jesus Christ, his life and work; Holy Communion
Written	at Ruan Minor and St Anthony-in-Meneage, August 1980
Suggested tune	THAXTED by Gustav Holst, to which the words were written

This text on the earthly life of Jesus was written to the tune THAXTED at the suggestion of (I think) an editor who felt that there were none too many hymns on this subject, and that the tune could bear more use than it receives with Cecil Spring-Rice's text 'I vow to thee, my country'.

'Likeness' in line 2 is an echo of Philippians 2.7; and the final line of verse 1 refers to St. Luke's words in Luke 2.52. I take my use of the verb 'grow' to include a reference to the 'increased in stature' of that verse. Other phrases are designed to bring to mind the biblical narrative; for example, from verse 2, 'friend of sinners' (Luke 7.34); 'the gospel of his kingdom' (Mark 1.14); 'signs and wonders' (John 4.48).

Verse 3 begins with the Lord's own words from Mark 8.31; 'sacrifice for sins', is from Hebrews 10.12; 'our risen life', while not a quotation in that form, is a reference to, e.g. Colossians 2.12. The final line of verse 3 is based on John 1.12.

See Appendix 5, pp. 286ff.

WHEN JOHN BAPTISED BY JORDAN'S RIVER 98 98 D

Based on	the accounts of the baptism in Matthew 3, Mark 1, and Luke 3
Theme	the Lord Jesus Christ—his baptism; baptism and confirmation
Written	at Ruan Minor, August 1979 and 1982
Suggested tune	RENDEZ À DIEU by Louis Bourgeois

In December 1978 I received a letter from the Reverend Dirk van Dissel, of Keith in South Australia, asking if I had written a hymn upon the Baptism of Christ. He pointed out that there is not much on this subject in the older hymnals, and that 'recent Supplements have done little to supply the dearth'; while adding that all the revised Calendars and Liturgies include the Baptism of Christ as a feast on the First Sunday after Epiphany. This is the case, for example, in the 'Sunday themes' of the Church of England *Alternative Service Book, 1980*. I see from Fred Pratt Green's *Hymns and Ballads* (p. 34) that his hymn on the same theme 'When Jesus came to Jordan' also sprang from a similar correspondence.

Accordingly, I tried my hand in the summer of 1979; and achieved two versions of an opening verse. One is clearly the first draft for verse 1 of this text, while the second was in the metre 76 76 D beginning 'To John by Jordan's river'. I returned to the text in 1981, making no further progress; but in 1982 things 'came together' based on the abortive efforts of previous years, and incorporating as the final quatrain a fragment intended for a hymn upon the theme of confirmation. Once the mental block that had held me up for two years was broken, the text took shape in a single day, partly on the beach at Poldhu. I should like to think that its usefulness is not confined to Services which have the Baptism of Christ as their theme, but that it could be sung at Services of Baptism, and indeed of confirmation. The final prayer of verse 3 would be specially appropriate here, echoing as it does the traditional confirmation prayer of the Church of England.

WHEN THE LORD IN GLORY COMES   77 77 77 D

Theme	Advent; the return of Christ
Written	at Sevenoaks, January 1967
Suggested tune	GLORIOUS COMING by Michael A. Baughen arranged by David G. Wilson
Published in	*Youth Praise 2*, 1969 to GLORIOUS COMING
	Family Worship, 1971 (words only)
	Renewal Songbook, 1971 (words only)
	Thirty Hymns, CPAS 1972 (words only)
	Keswick Praise, 1975 to GLORIOUS COMING
	Anglican Hymn Book Supplement, 1978 (words only)
	Preist Ihn (Germany), 1978 (translation by Brigitte Mayer) to GLORIOUS COMING
	Partners in Praise, 1979 to GLORIOUS COMING
	Hymns for Today's Church, 1982 to GLORIOUS COMING
Recorded on	*A Tribute to Youth Praise*, Key KL 003, 1969 to GLORIOUS COMING

When *Youth Praise 2* was in preparation, and we were seeking more material in a 'youth idiom', I happened to hear on television one evening a song with a very pronounced beat, an emphatic rhythm which stayed in my head. Taking a late-night stroll round the streets near my home, I found the beginning of this text coming into my mind as I walked. I sent the words to Michael Baughen in Manchester, who asked me if I had any *tune* in mind. I had to explain that the tune I had heard on television was unknown to me, and probably unsuitable. I did attempt to give some indication of the beat that had been running in my head—but I think entirely unsuccessfully! Michael Baughen, however, produced the tune which was included in *Youth Praise 2*; and which later became known as GLORIOUS COMING.

See Appendix 5, pp. 286ff.

WHEN TO OUR WORLD   88 88 (LM)

Theme   medical missions; the ministry of healing

Written   at Bramerton, December 1977

Suggested tune   by Michael A. Baughen, arranged by Noël
                       Tredinnick (see below); or
                    EISENACH by J. H. Schein or
                    ST LAWRENCE by L. G. Hayne

Published in   *Anglican Hymn Book Supplement*, 1978 (words
                       only)
                    Medical Missionary Association Centenary Leaflet,
                       1978 to a tune specially written by Michael A.
                       Baughen, arranged by Noël Tredinnick
                    Songs of Worship, 1980 to CHURCH TRIUMPHANT by
                       James W. Elliott
                    Making Melody, 1983 to CHURCH TRIUMPHANT

In December 1977 I was asked by the Secretary of the Medical Missionary
Association if I would write a hymn for their centenary the following year.
I was particularly glad to attempt this, since I had lived for four or five
years before my marriage in their hostel in Bedford Place, London, a
minister among medical students, while working for the Evangelical
Alliance whose offices were adjacent. This hymn, to Michael Baughen's
specially-commissioned tune, was first sung at the Centenary Service of the
Association.

See Appendix 5, pp. 286ff.

WHO IS JESUS   87 87 87

Theme   the Lord Jesus Christ

Written   at Bramerton, May 1975

Suggested tune   GRAFTON (French traditional)

Published in   *Songs of Worship*, 1980 to GRAFTON harmonized by
                       Sidney Nicholson

The theme of this text is the life, death and resurrection to glory of the Lord
Jesus Christ. His humanity and divinity are proclaimed in verse 1. Verse 2
includes references to four major themes: The Man of sorrows or Suffering
Servant of Isaiah 53; the Prince of life of Peter's sermon in Acts 3; the
Lamb of God of John 1 (and pre-eminently also of the Book of Revelation);
and (in line 2) the 'emptying of himself' of Philippians 2. In verse 3, 'first
born' is taken from Romans 8.29, seen in the light of the two Colossians
references, 1.15 and 1.18.

In verse 3, the epithet in the final line was first written as 'everlasting' (cf.
1 Timothy 6.16). However the line 'Christ, the everlasting Lord' is
inseparable from Wesley's use of it in 'Hark the herald angels sing'; and
'ever-living' is perhaps, on its own merits, a better description in the
context of the resurrection (cf. Hebrews 7.25).

See Appendix 5, pp. 286ff.

WHO IS THERE ON THIS EASTER MORNING 98 98 98

Based on	John 20.1–18
Theme	Easter
Written	at Ruan Minor, August 1980
Suggested tune	FRAGRANCE (French traditional)
	Betty Pulkingham has written a new tune, EASTER MORNING, to these words.
Published in	*On the Move* (Australia), October 1981 (words only)

At a Carol Service in Norwich Cathedral at Christmastime, 1979, it occurred to me that the tune FRAGRANCE would lend itself to a carol rooted more strongly in the doctrine of the incarnation than is the traditional text, 'Whence is that goodly fragrance flowing'. When I examined this thought again, I realized that this is what Frank Houghton had done with his carol 'Thou who wast rich beyond all splendour'. Unwilling to leave the tune, I turned instead to the theme of Easter, and especially to John 20.1–18 and (in verse 3) the evocative phrase from John 21.4 (NEB): 'Morning came, and there stood Jesus.'

The hymn was first sung in May 1983, in Westminster Abbey, during one of their regular lunch-hour Services entitled 'Come and Sing'.

WITHIN A CRIB MY SAVIOUR LAY 888 7

Theme	the Lord Jesus Christ
Written	on Arnside Knott, August 1968
Suggested tune	LORD OF LOVE by Norman L. Warren or EWHURST by C. J. Allen
Published in	*Youth Praise 2*, 1969 to LORD OF LOVE
	Hymns for Today's Church, 1982 to LORD OF LOVE

Arnside Knott is one of my special places. It is a celebrated tree-crowned hillside overlooking the estuary of the river Kent, with fine views of the hills of the Lake District on the distant skyline. I was walking there when *Youth Praise 2* was in preparation, turning over in my mind a number of ideas for hymn texts, including the well-known trio of the crib, the cross and the crown. This simple text was the result.

By a happy accident my prayer for this *Collection* is found in the line that concludes each verse of this final text:

ALL GLORY BE TO JESUS

Part Five

APPENDICES & INDICES

Appendix 1: Hymnals

*Details of hymnals referred to in the Notes,
in order of date of publication*

Anglican Hymn Book, Church Book Room Press, London 1965

Youth Praise 1, Falcon Books, London 1966

Youth Praise 2, Falcon Books, London 1969

100 Hymns for Today (a supplement to Hymns Ancient and Modern), London 1969

Thirteen Psalms, Church Pastoral-Aid Society, London 1970

Sing Praise to God (Roman Catholic), Bradford 1971

Sing to God, Scripture Union, London 1971

Renewal Songbook, Fountain Trust, London 1971

Family Worship, Falcon Books, London 1971

The Hymn Book (of the Anglican and United Church of Canada), Canada 1971

Catholic Book of Worship (Roman Catholic), Gordon V. Thompson Ltd., Ontario 1972

The Book of Praise (Presbyterian Church in Canada), Ontario 1972

Thirty Hymns, Church Pastoral-Aid Society, London 1972

Psalm Praise, Falcon Books, London 1973

Church Hymnary, third edition, Oxford University Press, London 1973

The Hymnal (Baptist Federation of Canada), Canada 1973

Baptist Assembly Hymns (Baptist Federation of Canada), Canada 1974

Sound of Living Waters, Hodder & Stoughton, London 1974

The Hymnal of the United Church of Christ, United Church Press, Philadelphia, USA 1974

Praise for Today (a supplement to the Baptist Hymn Book), Psalms and Hymns Trust, London 1974

Music for Courses, Book 4 (Easter), Royal School of Church Music, Croydon 1974

Worship II (Roman Catholic), GIA Publications Inc., Chicago, USA 1975

United Theological College Hymn Book, Bangalore 1975

Living Songs (sung on the Continent of Africa), Africa Christian Press, Zambia 1975

Hear the Bells of Christmas (A Christmas Cantata), OMF Publishers, Manila 1975

Keswick Praise, Trustees of the Keswick Convention, London 1975

New Church Praise (United Reformed Church: Supplement to Revised Church Hymnary; Church Hymnary; Congregational Praise) St Andrew's Press, Edinburgh 1975

Sing a Celebration, Anglican Church in Western Australia, Perth 1975

Grace Hymns (Association of Strict Baptist Churches), Grace Publications Trust, London 1975 (Music edition 1976)

English Praise (a Supplement to the English Hymnal), Oxford University Press, London 1975

Christian Worship, Paternoster Press, Exeter 1976

Cliff Hymns, Cliff College, Derbyshire 1976

Hymns II, Inter-Varsity Press, Illinois, USA 1976

The Australian Hymn Book, Collins, Sydney 1977

Sixty Hymns from Songs of Zion (a hymnal supplement), Praise Publications, Inc.; Whittier, California, USA 1977

Christian Hymns, Evangelical Movement of Wales; Byntirion, Bridgend 1977

Preist Ihn, STIWA Drück und Verlag; Urbach, Germany 1978

Sing to the Lord, Literature Crusades, Illinois, USA 1978

Carols, Inter-Varsity Press, Illinois, USA 1978

Come and Praise (BBC Radio for Schools), British Broadcasting Corporation, London 1978

Anglican Hymn Book Supplement, Vine Books, London 1978

Christmas Carols, Vine Books, London 1978

Merrily to Bethlehem, A & C Black, London 1978

With One Voice (first published as *The Australian Hymn Book*) Collins, London 1979

Hymns III, The Church Hymnal Corporation, New York, USA 1979

Cantate Domino (a supplement to The Hymnal 1940), Episcopal Diocese of Chicago, GIA Publications Inc., Chicago, USA 1979

Pilgrim's Manual, Walsingham, Norfolk 1979

Partners in Praise (Methodist Church Division of Education and Youth), Stainer and Bell, London 1979

Book of Worship, Church of St Luke, St Paul, Minnesota, USA 1979

New Harvest, St Paul's Outreach Trust, Auckland, New Zealand 1979

A Panorama of Christian Hymnody by Erik Routley, the Liturgical Press, Collegeville, Minnesota, USA 1979

Pocket Praise, Stainer & Bell Ltd (for the Youth Unit of the British Council of Churches), London 1980

Songs of Worship, Scripture Union, London 1980

Cry Hosanna, Hodder & Stoughton, London 1980

More Hymns for Today (a second Supplement to Hymns Ancient and Modern), Colchester 1980

Walsingham Devotions (Roman Catholic) Mayhew-McCrimmon Ltd., Great Wakering 1980

Lion Book of Favourite Hymns, Lion Publishing, Tring 1980

Hymns Plus, selected and arranged by Helen Kemp, Hinshaw Music, Chapel Hill, North Carolina, USA 1980

Their words, my thoughts (The Leicestershire Hymn Book), Oxford 1981

Declare His Glory, Universities and Colleges Christian Fellowship, Leicester 1981

Broadcast Praise (a supplement to the BBC hymnbook), London & Oxford 1981

Lutheran Worship (the Commission on worship of the Lutheran Church—Missouri Synod), Concordia Publishing House, St Louis, USA 1982

Jesus Praise, Scripture Union, London 1982

A Purple Robe (five choral settings in Chinese, compiled and arranged by S. Y. Suen), China Alliance Press, Hong Kong, 1982

A Supplement to Congregational Praise, The Congregational Federation, Nottingham, 1982

Hymn of the Month, Set 5, Christian Schools International, Michigan, USA 1982

Hymns for Today's Church, Hodder and Stoughton, London 1982

More Songs of the Spirit, Kevin Mayhew, Leigh-on-Sea, 1982

Gather to Remember, edited by Michael A. Cymbala, GIA Publications Inc., Chicago, USA 1982

Ten New Hymns in Praise of God, privately published by Michael Dawney, composer of the music; 5 Queen's Road, Parkstone, Poole, Dorset, BH14 9HF, 1982

Parish Sunday Vespers, ed. by Michael Beattie SJ, Collins, London 1982

Sing Praise (a loose-leaf hymnal), Kevin Mayhew Ltd., Leigh-on-Sea 1982

Covenant Songs, Covenant Music, Victoria, Australia 1982

Christian Hymns Observed, by Erik Routley; Prestige Publications Inc., Princeton, New Jersey, USA 1982

Hymns for Today (combined edition of *100 Hymns for Today* and *More Hymns for Today*), Norwich 1983

Hymns Ancient and Modern New Standard Edition, Norwich 1983

Son of the Highest, a choral presentation for Christmas, Lillenas Publishing Co., Kansas City, USA 1983

Making Melody Hymn Book, Assemblies of God Publishing House, Nottingham 1983

A Song was heard at Christmas, Hope Publishing Co., Illinois, USA 1983

Hymns and Psalms, Methodist Publishing House, London 1983

Choral Descants (Volume 5) by Randall DeBruyn, Oregon Catholic Press, Oregon, USA 1983

Mission England Praise, Marshal Morgan & Scott, Basingstoke 1983

New Creation Song Book, New Creation Teaching Ministry, Blackwood, South Australia 1983

Unless otherwise stated, Great Britain is the country of publication

Appendix 2: Sheet Music

Special settings of individual hymns, published as sheet music,
in order of date of publication

Christ be my leader

set to SLANE harmonized by Henry V. Gerike for S.A.T.B., Oboe (Flute), and Organ;
Concordia Choral Series, Concordia Publishing House, St Louis, Missouri 63118,
USA 1978 (Ref. 98–2378)

When to our world

set to a tune by Michael A. Baughen, arranged by Noël Tredinnick, published by the
Medical Missionary Association, 6 Canonbury Place, London 1978

Glory to God in the highest

set to RUSSWIN by Richard Proulx, for Unison Voices and Organ with S.A.T.B. and
Descants; in 'Two new hymn tunes by Richard Proulx', GIA Publications, Inc.,
Chicago, Illinois 60638, USA 1980 (Ref. G-2310)

The stars declare his glory

set as an anthem for S.A.T.B. with organ accompaniment; by Hal H. Hopson,
published by H. W. Gray Publications, Melville, New York 11747, USA 1981 (Ref:
GCMR 3450)

As water to the thirsty

set as an anthem for S.A.T.B. a cappella; by Hal H. Hopson, published by Agape (a
division of Hope Publishing Company) Carol Stream, Illinois 60188, USA, 1981
(Ref: JM 4079)

Chill of the nightfall

set as a carol for S.A.B. voices, accompanied; by Hal H. Hopson, published by
Agape (see above) 1982 (Ref: HH 3919)

Sing a new song to the Lord

set as an anthem for S.A.T.B. a cappella; by John F. Wilson, for the 75th anniversary
of the Chicago Sunday Evening Club, published by Hope Publishing Company (see
above) 1982 (Ref: A538)

Chill of the nightfall

set as an anthem for S.A.T.B; by Robert Kircher, arranged by Dick Bolks, published
by Beacon Hill Music (Lillenas Publishing Co.), Kansas City, Missouri 64141, USA
1982 (Ref: AN-3900)

Praise the Lord of heaven

set as an athem for S.A.T.B. with accompaniment for Organ and optional Brass
Quartet and optional Handbells; by Hal H. Hopson, published by H. W. Gray
Publications (see above) 1982 (Ref. GCMR 3462)

A purple robe

five choral settings in Chinese (translated and arranged by S. Y. Suen), to A PURPLE
ROBE by David G. Wilson, published by China Alliance Press, Hong Kong 1982

Chill of the nightfall

set as an anthem for Unison/2 Part with Handbells (or Harp and Piano) Organ and optional Strings; by Richard E. Frey, distributed by the Lorenz Corporation, Dayton, Ohio 45401, USA 1983, for the Choristers Guild, Garland, Texas 75041 (Ref: CGA-292)

Unless otherwise stated, Great Britain is the country of publication.

Appendix 3: Sound recordings

*Details of sound recordings referred to in the Notes,
in order of date of issue*

Hymns from the new Anglican Hymn Book: Herald LLR 533, 1965
presented by the London Recital Group, conducted by Richard Sinton,
organist Robin Sheldon
    'Tell out, my soul' to TIDINGS

A Tribute to Youth Praise: Key KL 003, 1969
sung by the Crusader Youth Singers, Elim Church, Portsmouth,
led by Dave Smith
    'When the Lord in glory comes' to GLORIOUS COMING

Here is Youth Praise: Reflection RL 308, 1975
sung by Charisma, and the congregation of All Souls Church, Langham Place,
London
    'Lord, for the years' to LORD OF THE YEARS
    'A purple robe' to A PURPLE ROBE

Here is Psalm Praise: Reflection RL 311, 1975
with the choir, orchestra and friends of All Souls Church, Langham Place, London
    'Timeless Love!' to TIMELESS LOVE
    'No weight of gold or silver' to ARGENT
        'I lift my eyes' to the tune by Michael A. Baughen and Elisabeth Crocker
        (later known as UPLIFTED EYES)
    'Tell out, my soul' to TELL OUT MY SOUL
    'He walks among the golden lamps' to REVELATION

All Souls Celebrates: Word WST 9539, 1975
with the choir, orchestra and congregation of All Souls Church, Langham Place,
London, conducted by Noël Tredinnick
    'Tell out, my soul' to WOODLANDS

Christmas Music: Philips 6833 157, 1975
sung by the choir of St. Paul's Cathedral, London, directed by Christopher Dearnley,
organist Christopher Herrick
    'Child of the stable's secret birth' to MORWENSTOW

Christmas Praise: Fountain FTN 2501, 1976
with the Croft children's choir under the direction of Joyce Farrington; and Kerry
Eighteen, soloist
    'Holy child' to HOLY CHILD

I lift my eyes to the quiet hills: IVR TM, USA 1976
sung by a choir, with musical ensemble, directed by Hughes Huffman, Director of
Music, Christ Church of Oak Brook, Illinois USA
    'I lift my eyes' to LIFT MY EYES

Liverpool Cathedral Festival of Praise: Abbey MVP 774, 1976
with the Cathedral Choir, Diocesan Church choirs, and the Merseyside Police Band
(Brass section), directed by Ronald Woan, organist Noel Rawsthorne
    'Tell out, my soul' to WOODLANDS

Psalm Praise—Sing a new song: Word WST 9586, 1978
with the choir, orchestra and congregation of All Souls Church, Langham Place,
London under the direction of Noël Tredinnick

'Sing a new song to the Lord' to ONSLOW SQUARE
'Safe in the shadow of the Lord' to CREATOR GOD
'God of gods, we sound his praises' to GOD OF GODS

Songs of Worship: Word WST 9590, 1980
with the All Souls Singers conducted by Noël Tredinnick, from All Souls Church,
Langham Place, London
'We come as guests invited' to PASSION CHORALE

Tell the World: Word SAC 5096, 1980
with Evelyn McNichol at the piano of All Souls Church, Langham Place, London.
Words appear on the record-sleeve only.
'Lord, for the years' to LORD OF THE YEARS
'When he comes' to music by J. D. Thornton

Lydia Servant Songs: Anchor AR 12 (cassette only), 1982
choir and instrumentalists, with solo voices
'Tell out, my soul' to WOODLANDS

Hymns for Today's Church: Word WST 9623, 1983
with the choir, orchestra and congregation of All Souls Church, Langham Place,
London conducted by Noël Tredinnick
'As water to the thirsty' to OASIS
'A purple robe' to A PURPLE ROBE
'Name of all majesty' to MAJESTAS

'Son of the Highest'—a presentation for Christmas: Lillenas L-9044, USA 1983
arranged and conducted by Dick Bolks, drama by Paul M. Miller, produced by Paul
Stilwell
'Chill of the nightfall' to the tune by Robert Kircher arranged by Dick Bolks.

Unless otherwise stated, Great Britain is the country of issue

Appendix 4: Biblical references & other sources

Some biblical passages on which texts have been based.
Please see the Foreword for further details.

Genesis	1.3	Out of darkness let light shine
Psalm	2	To heathen dreams of human pride
	19	The stars declare his glory
	25	All my soul to God I raise
	27	We sing the Lord our light
	34	Tell his praise in song and story
	56	Merciful and gracious be
	63	God is my great desire
	65	Every heart its tribute pays
	67	Mercy, blessing, favour, grace
	89	Timeless love!
	91	Safe in the shadow of the Lord
	93	God is King! The Lord is reigning
	95	Come, let us praise the Lord
	98	Sing a new song to the Lord
	113	Servants of the living Lord
	115	Not to us be glory given
	119	The will of God to mark my way
	121	I lift my eyes to the quiet hills
	134	Bless the Lord as day departs
	146	Praise the God of our salvation
	147	Fill your hearts with joy and gladness
	148	Praise the Lord of heaven
Isaiah	6.6–8	'How shall they hear'
	9.6,7	See, to us a child is born
	44 & 45	The heavens are singing
	53.3–6	No weight of gold or silver
Daniel	2.20–23	Beyond all mortal praise
Matthew	6.9–13	Father who formed the family of man
	9.37,38	Lord, give us eyes to see
	28.20	'How shall they hear'
Mark	9.2–10	Our Saviour Christ once knelt in prayer
Luke	1.46–55	Tell out, my soul
	2.29–32	Faithful vigil ended
	19.35–40	No tramp of soldiers' marching feet
	24.13f	At Cana's wedding, long ago
John	2.1–11	At Cana's wedding, long ago
	14.1	Set your troubled hearts at rest
	14.6	Christ be my leader
	20.1–18	Who is there on this Easter morning?
	21	Long before the world is waking
Acts	2	When God the Spirit came

Romans	6.5-11	Living Lord, our praise we render
	8	Born by the Holy Spirit's breath
	10.14	'How shall they hear?'
2 Corinthians	4.6	Out of darkness let light shine
	5.17,18	No weight of gold or silver
Galatians	5.22,23	Fruitful trees, the Spirit's sowing
Ephesians	6.10–18	Be strong in the Lord
Colossians	1.15–20	Praise be to Christ
1 Thessalonians	4.14f	When he comes
Hebrews	10.1–25	No temple now, no gift of price
James	1.17	Father of lights
1 Peter	1.18,19	No weight of gold or silver
Revelation	1.12–18	He walks among the golden lamps
	4 & 5	Heavenly hosts in ceaseless worship

See also *Index of subjects* (Church's Year) for texts on the Christmas and Easter story

Other Canticles and Prayers
see above for: Cantate Domino (Psalm 98)
　　　　　　　Deus Misereatur (Psalm 67)
　　　　　　　Magnificat (Luke 1.46–55)
　　　　　　　Nunc Dimittis (Luke 2.29–32)
　　　　　　　Venite (Psalm 95)

Te Deum God of gods, we sound his praises

Gloria in Excelsis   All glory be to God on high
　　　　　　　　　　　Glory to God in the highest

The Evening Collect Lighten our darkness

A Prayer from St Augustine Light of the minds that know him

Appendix 5: Inclusive Language

As the *Foreword* makes plain, I have taken the opportunity afforded by this *Collection* to look at the problem of 'inclusive language' in texts written over a period of years, some of them dating back to a time when this was not an issue of which writers or editors in my own country were particularly aware.

I am not here concerned with the larger question of whether it is right to use the masculine gender when talking to, and of, the Deity. This is a theological issue; and for me at least it is settled by the usage found in Scripture. I am however anxious to smooth the path of those (whether or not I happen to agree with them) who are offended by the continuous use of 'Sons' to mean 'Children' or 'Mankind' to mean 'All men and women'. I have therefore tried to make, or authorise, certain alterations which will go some way towards easing this difficulty.

The problem of such textual alterations is here approached in three distinct ways. First, in some nine or ten instances, the necessary change is minor enough to constitute 'invisible mending'; and has been adopted as the definitive text, and so included in the texts earlier in this volume. I hope this will not cause trouble or inconvenience to those who have used the texts in their unemended form. For the most part these changes are small enough to escape largely unnoticed. They are listed as Group A in the table that follows.

Secondly, I have to accept, and ask others to accept, that there are certain texts where the use of the generic 'man' is so closely woven into the fabric, either of sound or sense (or perhaps both) that to alter it is to mutilate the text in an unacceptable way. This seems to me to apply to eight or nine texts; where an editor will have to choose either to print them as they are, or to omit them. They include:

Father who formed the family of man

Jesus is the Lord of living

Lord, give us eyes to see

Out of darkness let light shine

Remember, Lord, the world you made

The Lord made man

When Jesus lived among us

When to our world the Saviour came

Lastly, I list a group of fourteen texts where I am ready to authorize an optional alternative reading for those who wish to avoid any generic use of the masculine; and these permitted variations will be found set out below as Group B. They do not necessarily propose any alterations where the use of 'man' is specific rather than generic—as applied, for example, to the Lord Jesus Christ himself: nor where the text is directly following Scripture (for example, Luke 2.14 or 29).

Group A: Changes in the definitive text

The line quoted below is the form in which it was originally written (and, in many cases, published), now overtaken by the form in which it appears in this present book.

As for our world (verse 3, line 7)
   With burdens more than man was meant to bear

Dear Lord, who bore our weight of woe (verse 3, lines 3 & 4)
   Of all man's sin, the final sum
     for love of man he paid

High peaks and sunlit prairies (verse 3, line 2)
   has Man no news to hark?

Not to us be glory given (verse 2, line 5)
   lifeless gods, men yet adore them,

O Christ the same (verse 1, line 7)
   O Christ the same, who wrought man's whole salvation

Tell his praise in song and story (verse 2, line 2)
   poor men cry in their distress

The shining stars unnumbered (verse 2, line 7)
   a sign for all men's seeing

The will of God to mark my way (verse 3, line 2)
   from man's oppression freed,

When God the Spirit came (verse 2, line 3)
   to men of every tribe and race

When the Lord in glory comes (verse 3, line 5)
   not the man by men denied

Group B: Permitted variations

The line quoted below may be substituted for the corresponding line in the text at the editor's discretion. In two instances the best solution seems to be the omission of a particular verse.

A purple robe
   omit verse 3

A song was heard at Christmas (verse 2, line 3)
   that all might know the way to go
and (verse 4, line 4)
   the son of God made man.

All shall be well
   omit verse 4

As water to the thirsty (verse 3, line 6)
   and all we long to see,

Born by the Holy Spirit's breath (verse 3, line 1)
   Children and heirs of God most high,

Child of the stable's secret birth (verse 2, line 4)
   the world he made, through the eyes of man:

Donkey plod and Mary ride (verse 1, line 3)
   theirs the way that all must come,
and (verse 5, line 4)
   light to lighten humankind.

Every heart its tribute pays (verse 1, line 5)
   there by grace may humankind

Holy child (verse 5, line 2)
   all the lost to seek and save,

Living Lord, our praise we render (verse 3, line 4)
   life is ours through Jesus' Name.

Lord, for the years (verse 4, line 1)
   Lord, for our world; when we disown and doubt him,

No weight of gold or silver (verse 1, line 5)
no sinners find their freedom

Spirit of God within me (verse 2, line 7)
the truth made known to all in Christ

Who is Jesus? (verse 1, line 6)
Son of Man, to seek and save.

Appendix 6: Discontinued texts

The following texts which have appeared in the collections shown no longer seem to me satisfactory, and I do not want to encourage their further use. It seems right, however, since they have appeared in print, to list them here for the sake of completeness.

Father, we bring you   55 54 D
written on request for a Bible Society leaflet published in connection with the Queen's Jubilee, 1976

Merciful and gracious be   77 77 77
based on Psalm 56 and written for *Psalm Praise*, 1973. It was reprinted in *Songs of Worship*, 1980

O God, our Father and our King   86 86 (CM)
written on request for the Church of England Board of Education, and published in *Our Mum: five themes for Family Services*, 1975

O thank the Lord for he is good   88 7
based on Psalm 136 and written for *Psalm Praise*, 1973

Our God has turned to his people   88 88 D
based on Luke 1.68–79 (the Benedictus), and written for *Psalm Praise*, 1973

Metrical index

3 3 11 8 8 11 and chorus 11 11 8 8 11
When he comes

3 5 3 3
Saviour Christ, in praise we name him

4 5 8 4 5 7
I lift my eyes

4 6 4 6
All shall be well
  (also under 10 10)

5 5 4 6 5 5 5 5
Had he not loved us
  (also under 10 10 10 10)

5 5 5 4 D
Chill of the nightfall

5 5 5 5 6 5 6 5
Be strong in the Lord

5 5 6 5 D
Hush you, my baby

6 5 6 5
Faithful vigil ended
Father, now behold us

6 5 6 5 D
Praise the Lord of heaven

6 5 6 5 triple
Jesus, Prince and Saviour

6 6 5 5 6 6 6 4
Name of all majesty

6 6 6 6
Let hearts and voices blend

6 6 6 6 8 8
Beyond all mortal praise
Come, let us praise the Lord
Lord, as the day begins
We sing the Lord our light

6 6 8 4 D
God is my great desire
We turn to Christ anew

6 6 8 6 (Short metre: SM)
God of eternal grace
Lord, give us eyes to see
O Lord, yourself declare

The darkness turns to dawn
This child from God above

6 6 8 6 6 6
This day above all days
When God the Spirit came

7 6 7 6 D
High peaks and sunlit prairies
In endless exultation
Light of the minds that know him
No weight of gold or silver
We come as guests invited

7 6 7 6 triple
When Jesus lived among us

7 6 7 6 6 6 4 4 6
As water to the thirsty

7 6 7 6 8 8 7 8 7
The shining stars unnumbered

7 6 8 6 D
A song was heard at Christmas

7 6 8 6 8 6
The stars declare his glory

7 6 8 6 8 6 8 6
Spirit of God within me

7 7
See, to us a child is born

7 7 7 7
Holy child
In my hour of grief or need
Mercy, blessing, favour, grace
Out of darkness let light shine
See, to us a child is born
Set your troubled hearts at rest

7 7 7 7 D
Every heart its tribute pays
See, to us a child is born
Stars of heaven, clear and bright

7 7 7 7 7 7
All my soul to God I raise
Christ from heaven's glory come
Donkey plod and Mary ride
Here within this house of prayer
Servants of the living Lord

77 77 77 D
When the Lord in glory comes

77 11 8
Sing a new song to the Lord

78 78
Bless the Lord as day departs

86 86 (Common Metre: CM)
A purple robe
All flowers of garden, field and hill
Behold, as love made manifest
Dear Lord, who bore our weight of woe
How faint the stable-lantern's light
O changeless Christ, for ever new
Remember, Lord, the world you made
Safe in the shadow of the Lord
The will of God to mark my way
To Christ our King in songs of praise

86 86 D (Double Common Metre: DCM)
Look, Lord, in mercy as we pray
No tramp of soldiers' marching feet
O Child of Mary, hark to her
O Saviour Christ, beyond all price

86 86 88
The Lord in wisdom made the earth
To heathen dreams of human pride

86 88 6
All glory be to God on high
By loving hands
Christ be the Lord of all our days
He comes to us as one unknown

86 88 86
He walks among the golden lamps

87 87
Fruitful trees, the Spirit's sowing
Living Lord, our praise we render
Praise the God of our salvation

87 87 D
Heavenly hosts in ceaseless worship
Not to us be glory given
Tell his praise in song and story

87 87 77
Long before the world is waking
Timeless love!

87 87 87
Fill your hearts with joy and gladness
God of old, whom saints and sages

Jesus is the Lord of living
Lord, who left the highest heaven
Not in lordly state and splendour
Who is Jesus?

87 87 88 87
God of gods, we sound his praises

87 88 87 77
God is King! The Lord is reigning

88 5 D
From afar a cock is crowing

88 6 D
No temple now, no gift of price

88 87
Within a crib my Saviour lay

88 88 (Long Metre: LM)
Born by the Holy Spirit's breath
Father of lights, who brought to birth
'How shall they hear,' who have not
    heard
The Lord made man, the Scriptures tell
When to our world the Saviour came

88 88 D (Double Long Metre: DLM)
Praise be to Christ
Thankful of heart for days gone by

88 88 6
Jesus my breath, my life, my Lord

88 88 88
And sleeps my Lord in silence yet
At Cana's wedding, long ago
Father on high to whom we pray
Glory to God in the highest (*Dactylic*)
O Christ, who taught on earth of old
Our Saviour Christ once knelt in prayer

89 99 98
Child of the stable's secret birth

98 98 98
Who is there on this Easter morning?

98 98 D
When John baptised by Jordan's river

10 10
All shall be well (also under 4 6 4 6)

10 10 4 10 10 4 10 10
As for our world we lift our hearts in
    praise

10 10 10 6
Father who formed the family of man

10 10 10 10
Christ be my leader
Had he not loved us (also under 5 5 4 6
   5 5 5 5)
Tell out, my soul

10 10 11 11
Be strong in the Lord

11 10 11 10
Lord, for the years
Now to the Lord we bring the child he
   gave us

11 10 11 10 D
Lord of the church
O Christ the same

11 10 11 10 11 10
Come now with awe

11 11 11 5
Christ high-ascended (see Note on
   p. 209)
Lighten our darkness

11 11 11 6
Christ high-ascended

12 11 12 11
The heavens are singing

12 11 12 11 6 6 11
The heavens are singing (alternative
   version)

Irregular
O Prince of peace

Index of tunes

as published; or suggested in the Notes

ABBOT'S LEIGH
Heavenly hosts in ceaseless worship

ADORATION
Living Lord, our praise we render

ALFORD
A song was heard at Christmas

ALL FOR JESUS
Fruitful trees, the Spirit's sowing
Living Lord, our praise we render

ALL MAJESTY
Name of all majesty

ALL SAINTS
Long before the world is waking
Lord, who left the highest heaven
To Christ our King in songs of praise

ANIMAE HOMINUM
Praise be to Christ

ARFON
Donkey plod and Mary ride

ARGENT
No weight of gold or silver

ASHBURTON
Here within this house of prayer

AUDEN
He walks among the golden lamps

AURELIA
We come as guests invited

AVE VERUM
Tell his praise in song and story

BALLERMA
Behold, as love made manifest
How faint the stable-lantern's light
O changeless Christ
The will of God to mark my way

BANGOR
Dear Lord, who bore our weight of woe

BARNARDO
Sing a new song to the Lord

BEACH SPRING
Fill your hearts with joy and gladness

BENNETT
Tell out, my soul

BETHANY
Not to us be glory given

BIRLING
Born by the Holy Spirit's breath
The Lord made man

BIRMINGHAM
Tell out, my soul

BISHOPTHORPE
To Christ our King in songs of praise

BLAENWERN
Heavenly hosts in ceaseless worship

BODMIN
Father of lights
'How shall they hear'

BRESLAU
Born by the Holy Spirit's breath

BUNESSAN
Chill of the nightfall

CALDERSON
Tell out, my soul

CANTATE DOMINO
Sing a new song to the Lord

CARDINGTON
This day above all days

CARLISLE
The darkness turns to dawn

CHERRY TREE CAROL
A song was heard at Christmas

CHRISTE SANCTORUM
Christ high-ascended (see Note on
  p. 209)
Lighten our darkness

CHRISTMAS CAROL
Look, Lord, in mercy as we pray

CHURCH TRIUMPHANT
Born by the Holy Spirit's breath
When to our world the Saviour came

CONSERVATION
Name of all majesty

CONSOLATION
I lift my eyes

CONTEMPLATION
The will of God to mark my way

CORNWALL
No temple now, no gift of price

COTTON WEAVER
see: Lancashire Cotton Weaver, The

CREATOR GOD
Safe in the shadow of the Lord

CRÜGER
High peaks and sunlit prairies
In endless exultation
No weight of gold or silver

CUDDESDON
Praise the Lord of heaven

DARWALL'S 148TH
Beyond all mortal praise
Come, let us praise the Lord
We sing the Lord our light

DAS NEUGEBORNE KINDELEIN
Our Saviour Christ once knelt in prayer

DISMISSAL
Jesus is the Lord of living

DIX
Christ from heaven's glory come
Here within this house of prayer

DOMINICA
God of eternal grace
Lord, give us eyes to see

EASTER SKIES
All shall be well

EGHAM
This child from God above

EISENACH
And sleeps my Lord in silence yet
Born by the Holy Spirit's breath
When to our world the Saviour came

ELING
Tell out, my soul

ELLERS
Had he not loved us

ENGLAND'S LANE
Christ from heaven's glory come
Donkey plod and Mary ride

EVANGELISTS
From afar a cock is crowing (see Note
on p. 216)

EVELYNS
Praise the Lord of heaven

EWHURST
Within a crib my Saviour lay

FAIRMILE
Holy child

FAITHFUL VIGIL
Faithful vigil ended

FARLEY CASTLE
Had he not loved us

FAWLEY LODGE
Faithful vigil ended

FINLANDIA
Come now with awe

FOREST GREEN
O Child of Mary, hark to her
O Saviour Christ, beyond all price

FRAGRANCE
Who is there on this Easter morning

FULDA
Born by the Holy Spirit's breath

GAELIC MELODY
Christ be my leader

GAIRLOCHSIDE
The darkness turns to dawn

GATESCARTH
Christ be the Lord of all our days

GERONTIUS
The will of God to mark my way

GLENFINLAS
Faithful vigil ended

GLORIOUS COMING
When the Lord in glory comes

GOD OF GODS
God of gods, we sound his praises

GOLDEN LAMPS
He walks among the golden lamps

GONFALON ROYAL
The Lord made man

GRAFTON
Who is Jesus?

HARROWBY
Set your troubled hearts at rest

HARTS
Mercy, blessing, favour, grace
Out of darkness let light shine
Set your troubled hearts at rest

HEAVENLY DOVE
Safe in the shadow of the Lord

HEAVENLY HOSTS
Heavenly hosts in ceaseless worship

HEINLEIN
In my hour of grief or need

HIGHEST HEAVEN
Lord, who left the highest heaven

HIGHWOOD
Lord, for the years

HOLY APOSTLES
A song was heard at Christmas

HOLY CHILD
Holy child

HOLY FAITH
Father on high to whom we pray

HOLY SON, THE
The Lord made man

HYFRYDOL
Heavenly hosts in ceaseless worship

INNOCENTS
See, to us a child is born

INNSBRUCK NEW
No temple now, no gift of price

JAMES HARRIS
This child from God above

JERUSALEM
Thankful of heart for days gone by

JULIUS
Had he not loved us

KINDELEIN
Our Saviour Christ once knelt in prayer

KINGSFOLD
O Child of Mary, hark to her

KING'S LYNN
Light of the minds that know him

LADYWELL
Look, Lord, in mercy as we pray
No tramp of soldiers' marching feet

LANCASHIRE COTTON WEAVER, THE
Jesus is the Lord of living

LAUS ET HONOR
Fill your hearts with joy and gladness

LEONI
God is my great desire
We turn to Christ anew

LIFT MY EYES
I lift my eyes

LITTLE CORNARD
Lord, as the day begins

LIVING FLAME
Sing a new song to the Lord

LONDON
Praise be to Christ

LONDON NEW
Remember, Lord, the world you made

LONDONDERRY AIR
Lord of the church, we pray for our
   renewing
O Christ the same

LORD OF LOVE
Within a crib my Saviour lay

LORD OF THE YEARS
Lord, for the years

LUX EOI
Not to us be glory given

MAESYNEAUDD
Heavenly hosts in ceaseless worship

MAIDSTONE
Every heart its tribute pays
Stars of heaven, clear and bright

MAJESTAS
Name of all majesty

MANOR PARK
Jesus my breath, my life, my Lord

MAPPERLEY
Tell out, my soul

MORDEN PARK
No weight of gold or silver

MORESTEAD
Tell out, my soul

MORWENSTOW
Child of the stable's secret birth

MOVILLE
Light of the minds that know him

MUNDAYS
Father who formed the family of man

NORTH COATES
Father, now behold us

NORTHAMPTON
Out of darkness let light shine

NUN DANKET ALL
Safe in the shadow of the Lord

O AMOR QUAM ECSTATICUS
The Lord made man

O PERFECT LOVE
Now to the Lord we bring the child he
    gave us

OASIS
As water to the thirsty

OLD 104TH
Be strong in the Lord

OMBERSLEY
'How shall they hear'

ONSLOW SQUARE
Sing a new song to the Lord

OPUS 2, AVE VERUM
Tell his praise in song and story

PALMYRA
The Lord in wisdom made the earth
To heathen dreams of human pride

PASSION CHORALE
We come as guests invited

PASTOR PASTORUM
Faithful vigil ended
Father, now behold us

PATRIXBOURNE
To Christ our King in songs of praise

PEMBROKE
The Lord in wisdom made the earth
To heathen dreams of human pride

PICARDY
Not in lordly state and splendour

PLEADING SAVIOUR
Tell his praise in song and story

PRAISE THE LORD OF HEAVEN
Praise the Lord of heaven

PSALM 47
Mercy, blessing, favour, grace

PURPLE ROBE, A
A purple robe

RECTORY MEADOW
O Prince of peace

REGENT SQUARE
Fill your hearts with joy and gladness
Jesus is the Lord of living

RENDEZ À DIEU
When John baptised by Jordan's river

REPTON
All glory be to God on high
By loving hands the Lord is laid
Christ be the Lord of all our days
He comes to us as one unknown

REVELATION
He walks among the golden lamps

RHUDDLAN
God of old, whom saints and sages

RUACH
Spirit of God within me

RUSSWIN
Fruitful trees, the Spirit's sowing

SAIGON
The darkness turns to dawn

ST BENEDICT
Mercy, blessing, favour, grace

ST BOTOLPH
How faint the stable-lantern's light
Remember, Lord, the world you made

ST CECILIA
Let hearts and voices blend

ST GEORGE
O Lord, yourself declare

ST GERTRUDE
Jesus, Prince and Saviour

ST LAWRENCE
When to our world the Saviour came

ST MATTHEW
Look, Lord, in mercy as we pray

ST MATTHIAS
Father on high to whom we pray
O Christ, who taught on earth of old

ST OSWALD
Living Lord, our praise we render

ST OSYTH
Lord, for the years

SALVATOR MUNDI
O Christ the same

SAMUEL
Lord, as the day begins

SANDYS
The darkness turns to dawn
This child from God above

SAVIOUR CHRIST
Saviour Christ, in praise we name him

SECRET BIRTH
Child of the stable's secret birth

SHIPSTON
Praise the God of our salvation

SLANE
Christ be my leader

SONG 46
All shall be well

SONG OF THE HOLY SPIRIT
The shining stars unnumbered

SOUND OF WIND
This day above all days
When God the Spirit came

STANTON
Safe in the shadow of the Lord

STARLIGHT
Let hearts and voices blend

STELLA
Father on high to whom we pray

SURREY
Our Saviour Christ once knelt in prayer

SURSUM CORDA
Had he not loved us

TELL OUT MY SOUL
Tell out, my soul

THAXTED
When Jesus lived among us

THEODORA
In my hour of grief or need

THIS ENDRIS NYGHT
Dear Lord, who bore our weight of woe
How faint the stable-lantern's light

TIDINGS
Tell out, my soul

TIMELESS LOVE
Timeless love!

TRISAGION
Christ be my leader

UNIVERSITY
All flowers of garden, field and hill

UPLIFTED EYES
I lift my eyes

VIENNA
Set your troubled hearts at rest

VINEYARD HAVEN
This day above all days
When God the Spirit came

WAS LEBET, WAS SCHWEBET
The heavens are singing

WEALDSTONE
Tell his praise in song and story

WELLS (by D. Bortnianski)
Servants of the living Lord

WELLS (by Basil Johnson)
All my soul to God I raise

WHITSUN PSALM
Born by the Holy Spirit's breath

WINDERMERE
This child from God above

WINTON
Tell out, my soul

WOLVERCOTE
Light of the minds that know him

WOODLANDS
Tell out, my soul

WYCH CROSS
At Cana's wedding
Father on high to whom we pray

YE BANKS AND BRAES
Praise be to Christ

I maintain a file of MS music sent to me by composers who have written tunes to texts in this Collection, and will gladly send details to editors or others who may wish to consult it.

TDS

Index of subjects

Advent
See: Church's Year—Advent

Anniversary
(see also: Thanksgiving)
Here within this house of prayer
Lord, for the years
O Christ the same

Armour of God
Be strong in the Lord

Baptism
Father, now behold us
Now to the Lord we bring the child he
   gave us
This child from God above
We turn to Christ anew
When John baptised by Jordan's river

Bible
God of old, whom saints and sages
O Christ, who taught on earth of old
The will of God to mark my way

Christmas
See: Church's Year—Christmas &
   Epiphany

Christian experience and discipleship
(see also: The Lord Jesus Christ
               New life in Christ)
Christ be my leader
Christ be the Lord of all our days
Father of lights, who brought to birth
Father who formed the family of man
Jesus my breath, my life, my Lord
Light of the minds that know him
No temple now, no gift of price
O changeless Christ, for ever new
O Christ the same
To Christ our King
We turn to Christ anew

Church and Ministry
Here within this house of prayer
Lord, give us eyes to see
Lord of the church

Church's Year
Advent
   When he comes
   When the Lord in glory comes

Christmas and Epiphany
   A song was heard at Christmas
   Child of the stable's secret birth
   Chill of the nightfall
   Christ from heaven's glory come
   Come now with awe
   Donkey plod and Mary ride
   Had he not loved us
   High peaks and sunlit prairies
   Holy child
   How faint the stable-lantern's light
   Hush you, my baby
   Not in lordly state and splendour
   O Child of Mary
   O Prince of peace
   See, to us a child is born
   Stars of heaven, clear and bright
   The darkness turns to dawn
   The shining stars unnumbered
   Within a crib my Saviour lay
Palm Sunday
   No tramp of soldiers' marching feet
Passiontide
   A purple robe
   Behold, as love made manifest
   Dear Lord, who bore our weight of
      woe
   No weight of gold or silver
   O Saviour Christ, beyond all price
Eastertide
   All shall be well
   And sleeps my Lord in silence yet
   By loving hands
   From afar a cock is crowing
   Jesus, Prince and Saviour
   Living Lord, our praise we render
   Long before the world is waking
   This day above all days
   Who is there on this Easter morning
Ascension
   Christ high-ascended
   He walks among the golden lamps
   Name of all majesty
   Saviour Christ, in praise we name him
   Thankful of heart for days gone by
Whitsun
   Born by the Holy Spirit's breath
   Fruitful trees, the Spirit's sowing
   Spirit of God within me
   When God the Spirit came

Trinity
  All glory be to God on high
  Father on high to whom we pray
  God of gods, we sound his praises
  Here within this house of prayer
Transfiguration
  Our Saviour Christ once knelt in
    prayer
Embertide
  Lord, give us eyes to see

Confidence and peace
(see also: Trust in God)
All shall be well
I lift my eyes to the quiet hills
O Prince of peace
'Set your troubled hearts at rest'
The will of God to mark my way

Confirmation
(see also: Christian experience &
  Discipleship; Dedication and
  Renewal)
We turn to Christ anew
When John baptised by Jordan's river

Creation
(see also: Harvest)
In endless exultation
Praise be to Christ
The heavens are singing
The Lord in wisdom made the earth
The stars declare his glory

Cross of Christ
See: Church's Year—Passiontide

Death
(see also: Church's Year—Eastertide)
Christ be the Lord of all our days
Faithful vigil ended
Jesus my breath, my life, my Lord
Lighten our darkness
O Christ the same
'Set your troubled hearts at rest'

Dedication & Renewal
Look, Lord, in mercy as we pray
Lord, for the years
Lord of the church
O Saviour Christ, beyond all price
We turn to Christ anew

Deliverance
Faithful vigil ended
In my hour of grief or need
Living Lord, our praise we render
Lighten our darkness
Safe in the shadow of the Lord
Tell his praise in song and story

Discipleship
See: Christian experience &
  Discipleship

Eastertide
See: Church's Year—Eastertide

Embertide
See: Church & Ministry; Church's
  Year—Embertide

Epiphany
See: Church's Year—Christmas and
  Epiphany

Evangelism
See: Mission & Evangelism

Evening
Bless the Lord as day departs
Faithful vigil ended
Lighten our darkness

Faith
See: Trust in God

Fall of Man
The Lord made man

Family
See: Home & Family

Flower Festival
All flowers of garden, field and hill

Fruit of the Spirit
Fruitful trees, the Spirit's sowing

God our strength
(see also: Pilgrimage & Conflict; Praise
  & Worship)
God is my great desire
We sing the Lord our light

God the Father: the living God
Father of lights
Father who formed the family of man
God is King! The Lord is reigning
God of eternal grace
God of gods, we sound his praises
Not to us be glory given
Servants of the living Lord
Tell out, my soul
The heavens are singing
Timeless love!
To heathen dreams of human pride

Gospel
See: New life in Christ

Grace
Behold, as love made manifest

— 300 —

God of eternal grace
No temple now, no gift of price
Servants of the living Lord

Harvest
(see also: Thanksgiving)
All flowers of garden, field and hill
Every heart its tribute pays
Fill your hearts with joy and gladness
Mercy, blessing, favour, grace
O Christ, who taught on earth of old

Healing
When to our world the Saviour came

Holy Communion
O changeless Christ, for ever new
We come as guests invited
When Jesus lived among us

Holy Spirit
See: Church's Year—Whitsun

Holy Trinity
See: Church's Year—Trinity

Home & Family
Father on high
Lord, who left the highest heaven

Lord Jesus Christ
(see also: Church's Year; Parables;
    Praise and Worship; New life in
    Christ)
As water to the thirsty
Had he not loved us
He comes to us as one unknown
He walks among the golden lamps
Jesus is the Lord of living
Jesus my breath, my life, my Lord
Let hearts and voices blend
Light of the minds that know him
Name of all majesty
O Child of Mary
O changeless Christ, for ever new
O Saviour Christ, beyond all price
Praise be to Christ
Saviour Christ, in praise we name him
To Christ our King
When Jesus lived among us
When John baptised by Jordan's river
Who is Jesus?

Love for God
God is my great desire
Jesus my breath, my life, my Lord

Love of God
(see also: Church's Year—Passiontide)
Born by the Holy Spirit's breath

Had he not loved us
Timeless love!
We sing the Lord our light

Marriage
At Cana's wedding, long ago

Ministry
See: Church & Ministry

Mission & Evangelism
(see also: Social concern & the world's
    need; Witness)
Christ high-ascended
'How shall they hear,' who have not
    heard
Look, Lord, in mercy as we pray
Lord of the church
Tell out, my soul
When God the Spirit came
Who is Jesus?

Morning
Come, let us praise the Lord
Lord, as the day begins

National
(see also: Thanksgiving)
Lord, for the years

Nature
See: Creation

New life in Christ
(see also: Baptism, Dedication &
    Renewal)
Born by the Holy Spirit's breath
Living Lord, our praise we render
No weight of gold or silver
Out of darkness let light shine
The Lord made man
We turn to Christ anew

Ordination
See: Church & Ministry

Palm Sunday
See: Church's Year—Palm Sunday

Parables
O Christ, who taught on earth of old

Passiontide
See: Church's Year—Passiontide

Peace
(see also: Confidence & Peace)
O Prince of peace
'Set your troubled hearts at rest'
Stars of heaven, clear and bright

Penitence
Dear Lord, who bore our weight of woe
The Lord made man

Pentecost
See: Church's Year—Whitsun

Pilgrimage & Conflict
(see also: Armour of God)
Christ be my leader
In my hour of grief or need
O Saviour Christ, beyond all price
Tell his praise in song and story
The Lord made man

Praise & Worship
All glory be to God on high
Beyond all mortal praise
Come, let us praise the Lord
Every heart its tribute pays
Fill your hearts with joy and gladness
Glory to God in the highest
God is King! The Lord is reigning
God of eternal grace
Heavenly hosts in ceaseless worship
In endless exultation
Mercy, blessing, favour, grace
Praise be to Christ
Praise the God of our salvation
Praise the Lord of heaven
Servants of the living Lord
Sing a new song to the Lord
Tell his praise in song and story
Tell out, my soul
The heavens are singing
The stars declare his glory
Timeless love!

Prayer
As for our world
Father who formed the family of man
Light of the minds that know him
O Lord, yourself declare

Redemption
(see also: Church's Year—Christmas
   and Passiontide; Deliverance; the
   Lord Jesus Christ)
All glory be to God on high
Dear Lord, who bore our weight of woe
Glory to God in the highest
God of gods, we sound his praises
Let hearts and voices blend
Living Lord, our praise we render
No temple now, no gift of price
Praise the God of our salvation
The heavens are singing

Rejoicing
(see also: Thanksgiving)
Come, let us praise the Lord
Fill your hearts with joy and gladness
God of gods, we sound his praises
In endless exultation
Sing a new song to the Lord
The heavens are singing

Renewal
See: Dedication & Renewal

Resurrection
See: Church's Year—Eastertide; New
   life in Christ

Return of Christ
See: Church's Year—Advent

Scripture
See: Bible

Social concern & the world's need
As for our world
Christ from heaven's glory come
Lord, who left the highest heaven
Remember, Lord, the world you made
When to our world the Saviour came

Sunday
This day above all days

Thanksgiving
All glory be to God on high
Fill your hearts with joy and gladness
Here within this house of prayer
Lord, for the years
O Christ the same
Praise the God of our salvation
Thankful of heart

Transfiguration
Our Saviour Christ once knelt in prayer

Trinity
See: Church's Year—Trinity

Trust in God
(see also: Confidence & Peace; Faith)
All my soul to God I raise
Safe in the shadow of the Lord

Unity
Father on high to whom we pray
Look, Lord, in mercy as we pray
Lord of the church

Wisdom of God
Father of lights, who brought to birth
Praise be to Christ
The Lord in wisdom made the earth

Witness
(see also: Mission & Evangelism)
Christ high-ascended
Come, let us praise the Lord
Tell his praise in song and story

World's need
See: Mission and Evangelism; Social
concern

Worship
See: Praise & Worship

Youth
(see also: Confirmation)
Christ be my leader
Jesus is the Lord of living

Index of first lines

	Text	Notes
A purple robe, a crown of thorn	45	197
A song was heard at Christmas	46	197
All flowers of garden, field and hill	47	198
All glory be to God on high	48	198
All my soul to God I raise	49	199
All shall be well	50	199
And sleeps my Lord in silence yet	51	200
As for our world we lift our hearts in praise	52	200
As water to the thirsty	53	200
At Cana's wedding, long ago	54	201
Be strong in the Lord	55	202
Behold, as love made manifest	56	203
Beyond all mortal praise	57	203
Bless the Lord as day departs	58	204
Born by the Holy Spirit's breath	59	204
By loving hands the Lord is laid	60	205
Child of the stable's secret birth	61	205
Chill of the nightfall	62	206
Christ be my leader	63	207
Christ be the Lord of all our days	64	207
Christ from heaven's glory come	65	208
Christ high-ascended	66	208
Come, let us praise the Lord	67	209
Come now with awe	68	209
Dear Lord, who bore our weight of woe	69	210
Donkey plod and Mary ride	70	210
Every heart its tribute pays	71	211
Faithful vigil ended	72	211
Faithful vigil ended (alternative version)	73	211
Father, now behold us	74	212
Father of lights, who brought to birth	75	213
Father on high to whom we pray	76	213
Father who formed the family of man	77	214
Fill your hearts with joy and gladness	78	214
From afar a cock is crowing	79	215
Fruitful trees, the Spirit's sowing	80	216
Glory to God in the highest	81	217
God is King! The Lord is reigning	82	217
God is my great desire	83	218
God of eternal grace	84	218
God of gods, we sound his praises	85	219
God of old, whom saints and sages	86	219
Had he not loved us	87	220
He comes to us as one unknown	88	220
He walks among the golden lamps	89	221
Heavenly hosts in ceaseless worship	90	222

	Text	Notes
Here within this house of prayer	91	222
High peaks and sunlit prairies	92	223
Holy child, how still you lie!	93	223
How faint the stable-lantern's light	94	224
'How shall they hear,' who have not heard	95	225
Hush you, my baby	96	226
I lift my eyes	97	226
In endless exultation	98	227
In my hour of grief or need	99	228
Jesus is the Lord of living	100	228
Jesus my breath, my life, my Lord	101	229
Jesus, Prince and Saviour	102	229
Let hearts and voices blend	103	230
Light of the minds that know him	104	231
Lighten our darkness now the day is ended	105	231
Living Lord, our praise we render	106	232
Long before the world is waking	107	232
Look, Lord, in mercy as we pray	108	233
Lord, as the day begins	109	234
Lord, for the years your love has kept and guided	110	235
Lord, give us eyes to see	111	236
Lord of the church	112	236
Lord, who left the highest heaven	113	237
Mercy, blessing, favour, grace	114	238
Name of all majesty	115	238
No temple now, no gift of price	116	239
No tramp of soldiers' marching feet	117	240
No weight of gold or silver	118	240
Not in lordly state and splendour	119	241
Not to us be glory given	120	242
Now to the Lord we bring the child he gave us	121	243
O changeless Christ, for ever new	122	243
O Child of Mary	123	244
O Christ the same	124	245
O Christ, who taught on earth of old	125	245
O Lord, yourself declare	126	246
O Prince of peace	127	247
O Saviour Christ, beyond all price	128	248
Our Saviour Christ once knelt in prayer	129	248
Out of darkness let light shine	130	249
Praise be to Christ	131	249
Praise the God of our salvation	132	250
Praise the Lord of heaven	133	251
Remember, Lord, the world you made	134	251
Safe in the shadow of the Lord	135	252
Saviour Christ, in praise we name him	136	253
See, to us a child is born	137	253
Servants of the living Lord	138	254
'Set your troubled hearts at rest'	139	254
Sing a new song to the Lord	140	255
Spirit of God within me	141	256
Stars of heaven, clear and bright	142	256

	Text	Notes
Tell his praise in song and story	143	257
Tell out, my soul	144	258
Thankful of heart for days gone by	145	260
The darkness turns to dawn	146	261
The heavens are singing	147	262
The heavens are singing (alternative version)	148	262
The Lord in wisdom made the earth	149	262
The Lord made man, the Scriptures tell	150	263
The shining stars unnumbered	151	263
The stars declare his glory	152	264
The will of God to mark my way	153	264
This child from God above	154	265
This day above all days	155	265
Timeless love! We sing the story	156	266
To Christ our King in songs of praise	157	267
To heathen dreams of human pride	158	267
We come as guests invited	159	267
We sing the Lord our light	160	268
We turn to Christ anew	161	269
When God the Spirit came	162	270
When he comes	163	270
When Jesus lived among us	164	271
When John baptised by Jordan's river	165	271
When the Lord in glory comes	166	272
When to our world the Saviour came	167	273
Who is Jesus? Friend of sinners	168	273
Who is there on this Easter morning	169	274
Within a crib my Saviour lay	170	274